THE INVISIBLE CONSTITUTION

INALIENABLE RIGHTS SERIES

GEOFFREY STONE AND OXFORD UNIVERSITY PRESS GRATEFULLY ACKNOWLEDGE THE INTEREST AND
SUPPORT OF THE FOLLOWING ORGANIZATIONS IN THE INALIENABLE RIGHTS SERIES: THE AMERICAN
BAR ASSOCIATION; THE AMERICAN LIBRARY ASSOCIATION; THE CHICAGO HUMANITIES FESTIVAL;
MCCORMICK TRIBUNE FREEDOM MUSEUM; THE NATIONAL CONSTITUTION CENTER; THE NATIONAL
ARCHIVES AND RECORDS ADMINISTRATION.

The Invisible Constitution

Laurence H. Tribe

OXFORD
UNIVERSITY PRESS

2008

OXFORD
UNIVERSITY PRESS

Oxford University Press, Inc., publishes works that further
Oxford University's objective of excellence
in research, scholarship, and education.

Oxford   New York
Auckland   Cape Town   Dar es Salaam   Hong Kong   Karachi
Kuala Lumpur   Madrid   Melbourne   Mexico City   Nairobi
New Delhi   Shanghai   Taipei   Toronto

With offices in
Argentina   Austria   Brazil   Chile   Czech Republic   France   Greece
Guatemala   Hungary   Italy   Japan   Poland   Portugal   Singapore
South Korea   Switzerland   Thailand   Turkey   Ukraine   Vietnam

Published by Oxford University Press, Inc.
198 Madison Avenue, New York, New York 10016

www.oup.com

Oxford is a registered trademark of Oxford University Press

Library of Congress Cataloging-in-Publication Data
Tribe, Laurence H.
The invisible constitution / Laurence H. Tribe.
p.   cm. — (Inalienable rights series ; v. 6)
Includes bibliographical references and index.
ISBN 978-0-19-530425-1
1. Constitutional law—United States. I. Title.
KF4550.T7865 2008
342.7302—dc22   2008008662

The illustrations within this volume were created by the author.

For Mark, Kerry, Isabel, Eno, and Sadie

Contents

CONTENTS

CONTENTS

CONTENTS

CONTENTS

[xi]

Editor's Note

We hold these truths to be self-evident, that all men are created equal, that they are endowed by their Creator with certain
unalienable Rights. . . .

THE DECLARATION OF INDEPENDENCE

WHAT IS THE CONSTITUTION of the United States? Much of
the Constitution, of course, consists of the text of the document
itself, as amended over the course of the past two centuries.
But as Laurence Tribe demonstrates in this book, much of what
we mean by the Constitution cannot be found in the visible text.
Indeed, the text of the Constitution is silent on many of the most
fundamental questions of constitutional law. Nothing in the text of
the Constitution, for example, tells us how to give meaning to the
text itself. Who is to interpret the text, by what methods, and using
what sources of authority? These are questions that the text simply
does not address.

As Tribe notes, the visible Constitution "floats in a vast and deep—and, crucially, invisible—ocean of ideas, propositions, recovered memories, and imagined experiences." More than we often realize, it is in the depths of this "ocean" that our Constitution finds meaning. Indeed, in Tribe's view, the invisible Constitution is at the very "center of the Constitution's meaning and of its inestimable value." His goal in this book is to make visible our invisible Constitution.

Consider such fundamental precepts as "ours is a government of laws, not men," "we are committed to the rule of law," "Congress may not commandeer states as though they were agencies or departments of the Federal Government," and "no state may secede from the Union." Each of these precepts is central to the American Constitution, but none of these precepts is stated in the text or flows inexorably from it. Indeed, as Tribe demonstrates, many of our most fundamental constitutional principles are not only not stated in the text of the Constitution, but cannot even be inferred from the visible Constitution in any of the usual ways we interpret texts. Like the "dark matter" that holds our universe together, the invisible Constitution gives essential form, substance, and direction to what we can see.

Across a broad range of central constitutional issues—including judicial review, federalism, abortion, separation of powers, habeas corpus, reapportionment, torture, intimate association, and economic substantive due process—Tribe explores the meaning, content, and origins of the invisible Constitution. But Tribe goes beyond identifying and evaluating these phenomena. More fundamentally, he explores the processes by which we uncover the invisible Constitution. How, he asks, do you "visualize and articulate the rules, principles, and rights that are part of our Constitution, but are not discernible in or directly derivable from...its text"?

In an original and brilliant leap, Tribe identifies six "modes of construction of the invisible Constitution," which he alliteratively names the *geometric*, the *geodesic*, the *global*, the *geological*, the *gravitational*, and the *gyroscopic*. As Tribe demonstrates, these six modes of construction illuminate the range of methodologies we have used over the past 200 years to derive constitutional principles of a nontextual character. With the benefit of these insights, we are better able to understand both our constitutional history...and our constitutional future.

Geoffrey R. Stone

Preface

⌒

Shortly before I had finished writing this book, a young friend of mine named Jeremy—the bright, lively, 11-year-old son of a couple with whom I have had a close friendship for some 25 years—told me that his fifth-grade class at Mason-Rice Elementary School in Newton, Massachusetts, had been studying the Constitution. For the "show and tell" exercise in his class, Jeremy said he'd like to bring me as his "exhibit." It seems he'd told his teacher and his two dozen or so classmates that he knew a grown-up who spent all his time studying, writing, and teaching about the Constitution, helping other countries like Russia and South Africa write constitutions of their own, and occasionally arguing constitutional cases in the U.S. Supreme Court. And, to get to the nub of the matter, his classmates thought he was spinning a yarn. So he hoped I'd rescue his reputation with his classmates by visiting his class during "show and tell." I love kids, and Jeremy, a particularly charismatic kid, is among my favorites, so it was a no-brainer: I said sure.

When I showed up at Jeremy's class, considerably more dressed-up than I am when I teach my own Harvard Law School students, I evidently looked the part, because I was treated with something approaching reverence. I don't mind admitting that it made me uncomfortable at first. My goal was regression—to end up being treated more or less like another kid (even though I couldn't fit into the desks). I hoped in that way to achieve a kind of transference, with the awe redirected from me and the object I study (the U.S. Constitution) to the processes of inquiry, exploration, and discovery that I hoped to show 11-year-olds are no less relevant to the Constitution and constitutional law than they are to science, music, art—or baseball. To judge by the wonderful collection of handwritten letters (literally written by hand, not by email or on a word processor!) that I received from Jeremy and his classmates not long after the hour or so that I spent with them, I seem to have succeeded.

The class had been engaged in drafting a "constitution" for itself, including provisions about how the rules of in-class conduct were to be made and enforced, but the class hadn't quite finished the exercise before voting on, and approving, an initial set of rules dealing with how the students were to behave in class and during recess, what would happen to those who misbehaved, how homework assignments were to be handled, and so forth. So I began by posing such questions as how the rules the class had drafted and approved by majority vote could "count" if the group had yet to settle on the constitutional metarules—I didn't call them that, of course—for how such rules were to be enacted and how to tell which ones were valid and which ones weren't.

Over some visible consternation on the teacher's part, I led the class through a discussion of why its members might be free to ignore rules of behavior that the class had approved, even unanimously, before those more basic, "constitutional," ground rules had been settled. That conversation led the class gradually to such other topics as the relationship between the "constitution" it was drafting and the rules of the school—and between those rules and the rules of the City of Newton, the Commonwealth of Massachusetts, and, of course, the United States of America. As the conversation turned to the latter two constitutions and the relationship between them, some students expressed surprise at the thought that the former had antedated the latter even though the latter were supreme and wondered how that could be if I was right that the ground rules of the whole system had to be settled before one could enact binding rules for the individual parts. One student asked about amending the basic ground rules, and after some discussion of the amendment process and its deliberate difficulty I asked the students whether they knew just how many times the U.S. Constitution had been successfully amended in the 218 years the Constitution had been in effect. One student surmised that the answer must be in the hundreds because more than two centuries had elapsed, but another student triumphantly announced that the answer was "only 26" because her copy of the Constitution contained no amendments more recent than the Twenty-sixth, ratified in 1971 to ensure that kids could vote once they reached the age of 18, a guarantee that the class found reassuring. Less reassuring was the news that most people think there have been 27 amendments to the Constitution, the most recent one proposed all the way back in 1789 but not ratified until 1992.

Particularly fascinating to the class was the thought that there could be a persistent controversy over whether that most recent provision, which I described in general terms as dealing with changes in congressional compensation, was in fact a valid part of the U.S. Constitution. I led the class through a discussion of why such controversy endured—and of the absence of any language or mechanism in the Constitution through which the controversy could be decisively resolved and made to go away.

The idea that the Constitution's text—the "visible" Constitution—couldn't answer all the questions people might have about what the Constitution commands and what it forbids mesmerized the class. We talked about other illustrations of the necessary gap between what's in "the Constitution" and what the deliberately spare text of the Constitution expressly says, and I left the class with its members seeming hungry to continue the conversation. I had been worried that my digression about the Twenty-seventh Amendment, unlike my explanations of the First and Second and Fourth Amendments, would have seemed to the class to be dry, abstract, and hypertechnical. I assumed that it was more discussion about religious freedom and sex discrimination and personal privacy for which the class yearned. I needn't have been concerned: When I read the letters so painstakingly written by Jeremy and his classmates, I was struck by how many of them said that what they found most interesting and "cool" was the incompleteness of the Constitution's text and the way it necessarily left open such basic questions as the one about what the Constitution includes and what it excludes. Most of the children did make some reference to how interesting they found some of the unsettled issues about freedom of speech, the right to own a gun, or the power of the government to look at their private text messages, but nearly every child in the class made at least some mention of the much less sexy Twenty-seventh Amendment and marveled at the puzzle of whether that mundane provision, whose substance interested just about nobody in the class, was or wasn't really part of the United States Constitution. The teacher had asked everyone in the class to identify which of the issues I'd raised interested them most, and more than two-thirds of the class wrote that it was the existential status of the Twenty-seventh Amendment. And these were fifth graders!

I decided then and there that the questions I had chosen to raise in this book about the invisible Constitution—far from being too arcane to engage and fascinate lay readers—go to the very heart of the things that make constitutional inquiry so universally intriguing and endlessly beguiling. If fifth graders—admittedly smart fifth graders, but fifth graders all the same—were turned on by these questions, I shouldn't underestimate the ability of such questions to engage people of all ages and walks of life. It is to the prospect of such engagement that I dedicate this book.

Acknowledgments

I AM GRATEFUL to my current and former Harvard Law School students Jon Berkon, Michael Fawcett, Adam Gershenson, Emily Gumper, Janie Kucera, Warren Postman, and Adam Unikowski—all of them very talented—for their conscientious and resourceful research assistance; to Professors Patrick O. Gudridge, Frank I. Michelman, Martha Minow, and Geoffrey R. Stone for reading and commenting insightfully on earlier versions of the manuscript; to my indispensable faculty assistant, Kathy McGillicuddy, for her help and encouragement throughout the project; to Elena Kagan, Dean of Harvard Law School, for her patience and flexibility with my academic schedule (a diplomatic way of saying "for sparing me some committee assignments") and for creating the best environment imaginable in which to teach and to write; and to Christine Dahlin, David McBride, and Brendan O'Neill, all of Oxford University Press, for putting up with me and my drawings as they worked diligently to produce an aesthetically and intellectually pleasing product.

PART I

Beyond the Visible

Identifying "The Constitution"

YOU DON'T HAVE to be a constitutional lawyer, a government official, or even a U.S. citizen to know that the Constitution of the United States makes an enormous difference in the life of everyone in this country—and in the lives of people around the world.

Who can read emails between you and a friend in Europe or the Middle East, and for what purposes? How can they use what they discover?

Can you be forced to submit a current driver's license in order to register to vote?

Can the government prevent you from keeping a handgun at home for self-protection?

Can you lose your job with the city government for advocating the decriminalization of marijuana?

Can you be prosecuted for having oral sex at home with your girlfriend or boyfriend?

Will your elderly parents be allowed to die with dignity? Will you?

In our society, these are questions about what the Constitution has to say about government power and its limits. The questions aren't imaginary; they are predicated on actual cases—and they're just the tip of the constitutional iceberg. We all look to the Constitution for the answers to such questions, but the Constitution we can see—the *visible* Constitution—doesn't spell the answers out in its text. This book is about the *invisible* Constitution to which we must turn for answers. One thing everybody knows before reading any further is that the answers we actually get when we ask questions of this sort depend to some degree on who is answering them—including who is sitting on the Supreme Court at the time we ask.

Supreme Court Justice Robert H. Jackson once remarked, "We are not final because we are infallible; we are infallible because we are final." Well, after two centuries of controversy, it's still up for grabs just how "final" the answers given by the justices really are and ought to be. That said, this much seems certain: The Constitution itself, which we amend from time to time (though not very often), is about as final at any given point in our history as anything in our country ever gets. So everyone should be concerned not just with the latest judicial rulings *about* the Constitution's meaning but with the *Constitution itself*, the thing every public official takes an oath to preserve, protect, and defend. What is *in* the Constitution they're sworn to uphold? How can we (or they) tell? Would reading it carefully suffice to provide the answers? Would reading it suffice even to get much of a clue? This book should help with such questions.

For starters, everyone knows the United States of America has a *written* Constitution. If you doubt it, just look at the document reprinted at the end of this book. You'll notice it's incredibly brief. Something else you may notice if you read it through to the end (or if you cheat) is that the most recent amendment is the Twenty-seventh—which requires a congressional election to intervene before any law changing the salaries of senators and representatives may take effect.

Many copies of the Constitution that you're likely to come across don't include that provision; they end with the Twenty-sixth Amendment, which lowered the voting age to 18 in 1971. The Twenty-seventh Amendment was ratified 21 years later, in 1992. Some copies of the Constitution that exclude the Twenty-seventh Amendment do so for the simple reason that they were published before its ratification. Some exclude it because their publishers lazily *copied* the Constitution verbatim from something published years earlier. And some exclude it for a more complex and interesting reason: those are the publishers who don't regard the Twenty-seventh Amendment as ever having been validly ratified.

You see, the Twenty-seventh is an amendment that, remarkably, was proposed by the First Congress in 1789, together with the first ten amendments, popularly known as the Bill of Rights. But, unlike the first ten amendments, all of which were ratified in 1791, what ended up as the Twenty-seventh Amendment was less than an overnight sensation: it wasn't ratified by the requisite number of state legislatures (a number that rose to 38 when the number of states reached 50, given Article V's requirement of ratification by "the Legislatures of three fourths of the several States") until the Michigan legislature finally voted to ratify it more than two centuries later.

Much too late, some lawyers argued, taking the position that Congress's proposal of an amendment for states to ratify, by analogy to any other contractual offer, lapses upon the passage of a "reasonable" length of time—unless the proposal contains specific language to the contrary, as a few amendments (the Eighteenth, Twentieth, Twenty-first, and Twenty-second) have. You might think that someone like Supreme Court Justice Antonin Scalia, famously a "rules man," would find that too squishy and subjective a standard for dealing with amendments sent to the states without an explicit time limit. Yet, when I published an opinion piece in the *Wall Street Journal* taking the position that the Twenty-seventh Amendment became part of the Constitution as soon as Michigan ratified it, Justice Scalia—in a conversation the two of us had at Princeton University—said he was inclined to disagree.

Nothing in the text of the Constitution tells us which of our views is the correct one. Just check the back of this book if you doubt me on this. So the written Constitution, the one we can *see*, fails to tell us just what's *in* it and what's not. Think about it: That's no minor omission. With a translation of a play by Sophocles or with one of Tom Stoppard's drafts of *Arcadia* or one of Tolstoy's drafts of *War and Peace*, figuring out what the author meant the final version to include would be an interesting intellectual exercise. But nothing much in the real world would turn on how we came out. Not so with deciding what counts as the Constitution.

One can speculate about just how much difference it makes whether the Twenty-seventh Amendment is in or out. At one level, it's a narrowly technical provision that calls for a form of congressional restraint that political common sense would probably lead Congress to exercise even without the amendment—and one that might even look out of place in a bill of rights. At another level, having the Bill of Rights include a provision whose obvious concern is with political participation and with the electorate's role in government might have underscored this sometimes overlooked dimension of individual rights like free speech, whose role in self-realization is occasionally emphasized at the expense of the role they play in a well-functioning system of representative government. In any event, under our traditions, it is most likely Congress, not the courts, that would have the last word both on the question of whether the Twenty-seventh Amendment had been ratified in time to make it into the Constitution and on the question of whether it has been complied with and what to do if it has not. Under long-standing doctrine, citizen taxpayers, whose interests the amendment might well have been intended to protect, would not have "standing" to challenge salary expenditures in violation of the Twenty-seventh Amendment by invoking the jurisdiction of the federal courts. Indeed, it's not at all clear that *anyone* would have standing to bring the federal courts into the act, and, even if the courts stepped in, they might well decline to resolve the dispute.

This illustrates the sense in which this book is concerned less with how the *courts* are to discern and apply constitutional principles than with how *any of us* is to cope with such principles. And the question of whether a particular amendment has indeed been lawfully ratified, even if it might not matter very much with the Twenty-seventh, would matter mightily with amendments as consequential as the three passed in the wake of the Civil War—the Thirteenth (abolishing slavery), the Fourteenth (defining citizenship and guaranteeing certain basic human rights to all persons in their dealings even with their own states), and the Fifteenth (abolishing racial qualifications for voting)—whose ratification by the legislatures of the former Confederate states was not exactly voluntary. Their acquiescence was secured by force, having been made a condition of their reentry into the Union from which they had attempted to secede.

Some scholars use this history to make the point that the Constitution may be validly amended by processes that fall outside the ambit of Article V of the Constitution, which provides that constitutional amendments proposed either by Congress or by a new Constitutional Convention become "valid to all Intents and Purposes, as Part of this Constitution," only when ratified—voluntarily, one assumes—"by the Legislatures of three fourths of the several States, or by Conventions in three fourths thereof, as the one or the other Mode of Ratification may be proposed by the Congress."

A major difference between such scholars' approaches to this subject and mine is that they focus on the way crucial turning points in our constitutional history ("constitutional moments") depend for their legitimacy on sources of law outside the Constitution's text, whereas I focus on the way the Constitution *at every moment* depends on extratextual sources of meaning. However that may be, one unmistakable conclusion is that the Constitution's text does not tell us how to decide whether particular amendments are valid parts of the Constitution. Nor does the Constitution's text tell us how to determine the lawfulness of equally momentous changes in constitutional understanding that are not reflected in any corresponding changes in its words. The prime example of such a change is the transformation ushered in by the Supreme Court's dramatic 1937 turnaround on both congressional power over the economy and state and local power over private contractual relations, which some scholars argue amounted to an entirely legitimate, albeit unwritten, "amendment" to the Constitution.

Equally basic, nothing in the visible text can tell us that what we are reading really *is* the Constitution, rather than an incomplete or otherwise inaccurate facsimile, or even a complete hoax. And even if we accept the copy in this book as accurate and complete, *it* cannot tell us—authoritatively, anyway—that it truly is the legitimate, binding, fundamental law of the United States, trumping all other sources of law. Oh, it *says* it's the "supreme Law of the Land," all right—right there in its own Article VI—but the fact that a text proclaims its own supremacy, while displaying confidence on the part of its authors and ratifiers, can't in itself *establish* that text as legitimate, much less as "supreme."

Indeed, it's worth noting that the Constitution itself, proposed to the 13 original states by Congress in 1787, was not ratified in accord with the rules laid down in the Articles of Confederation, under which only unanimity (rather than ratification by nine states, as set forth in Article VII of the new Constitution) would suffice. If the Constitution copied at the end of this book is to count as the fundamental and supreme law of the land, then it must be something *outside* both the visible text of that Constitution and the text of its immediate predecessor, through whose framework it was launched, that makes it so: it must be some combination of how it was adopted in the first instance (not a very promising factor, given the extreme narrowness of the Constitution's original constituency of propertied white males); why and how and by whom it has come to be accepted over time (again something of a problem, given the absence of any formal process for such "acceptance"); the sheer *fact* of its widespread and enduring use as the controlling frame of reference and as a constant point of departure and source of orientation; and perhaps the moral force of the claims made in support of the view that, all things considered—and compared with the imaginable alternatives—it *deserves* to be accepted, either because of some higher, "natural" law it supposedly reflects or at least approximates, or on the basis of some other theory of political morality.

In at least these basic respects, it seems obvious that we must have an invisible Constitution as well as a visible one: it's the *invisible* Constitution that tells us what text to accept as the *visible* Constitution of the United States, as well as how much force to ascribe to that text. True, we can argue endlessly about just what the invisible Constitution *says*—but that doesn't distinguish it from the *visible* Constitution, whose meaning, and even whose contents, are often very much in contention. The visible Constitution most of us have come to accept or at least to work within certainly doesn't answer very many of the persistent questions about what it means in any particular case and at any particular time. Indeed, the Constitution even *tells* us that it doesn't tell us: The Ninth Amendment, about which this book will have more to say later, expressly says: "*The enumeration in the Constitution of certain rights*

shall not be construed to deny or disparage others retained by the people."
In plain English, there's more there than meets the eye.

Whether people trying to figure out what that instruction means, or what anything else in the Constitution means, are to consult what the words meant to those who wrote them, or to those who debated and ultimately ratified them, or to the ordinary person in the public to whom they were originally addressed, or to readers of the text at the time it is being interpreted and applied, are issues that the Constitution's own text can't hope to resolve. Pursuing each of these possible sources of meaning entails investigating matters of empirical fact. And making choices *among* those sources of meaning is a task on which the Constitution's text is silent. Thus, in resolving such matters, readers are compelled to look outside of and beyond the text—to various possible historical accounts, to political and moral philosophy, to theories of language and meaning (i.e., to hermeneutics), to functional and pragmatic considerations of how well various alternatives would work, to institutional factors (who's asking and why?), and to a host of other sources beyond the Constitution that we can all see and read. Indeed, one of the ways the Constitution *works* is that it puts us all to work, pushing us to look more deeply into our shared and separate histories and values, making us confront what we might otherwise not notice or might even positively avoid. In reading it, we discover matters beyond its horizons that we must take into account in deciding who we are to become, or avoid becoming.

Distinguishing "The Constitution" from "Constitutional Law"

So THE VISIBLE CONSTITUTION necessarily floats in a vast and deep—and, crucially, invisible—ocean of ideas, propositions, recovered memories, and imagined experiences that the Constitution as a whole puts us in a position to glimpse. And what we glimpse—what we come to comprehend and remake in our own time's image—nurtures the living body of governing law, something more vibrant than an inert blueprint for a possible system of government or a set of political exhortations about a conceivable structure for governance constrained by a potential set of rights and privileges.

That swirling sea of assumptions and experiences includes not only the array of "higher law" or "natural law" ideas that many of the Constitution's framers took for granted but also the lessons drawn from thinking about the Constitution and its presuppositions and from the history of struggle to make it real. Together this set of materials constitutes what many constitutional scholars, political and moral philosophers, and social and political historians have described over the generations as the "unwritten Constitution," the subject of a classic study by William Bennett Munro published in 1930 called "The Makers of the Unwritten Constitution," which built on a still earlier and highly influential 1890 work by Professor Christopher G. Tiedeman called "The Unwritten Constitution of the United States." The scholarly work that sought to systematize that unwritten body of law and lore lay largely forgotten until it was resurrected in the writing of contemporary scholars beginning in the 1970s. The focus of such writing has been on crafting responses to the supposedly problematic legitimacy of having unelected and politically unaccountable judges resort to the unenacted norms of this "unwritten Constitution" when holding duly promulgated laws and executive actions "unconstitutional."

This book's discussion of the "invisible Constitution" differs in at least two important respects from that body of "unwritten Constitution" literature. First, my concern is not with justifying a high-profile role for judges, including especially the Supreme Court, but with exploring the *substance* of the Constitution regardless of *who* is attempting to understand and apply it. And second, my interest is less in what's invisible "around" the Constitution than in what is invisible *within* it. In exploring that topic, I mean to set aside rather than investigate in any detail the complex superstructure of rules, doctrines, standards, legal tests, judicial precedents, legislative and executive practices, and cultural and social traditions that together constitute what people call "constitutional law."

That body of materials, unlike the Constitution itself, is massive and continuously growing in volume and changing in content. Many capable scholars have argued that this elaborate edifice is entitled to great respect as the "law" of our Constitution, "law" whose legitimacy ironically is in many ways easier to defend than is the legitimacy of the underlying text itself, and whose role in enabling the Constitution to carry out the important functions it has come to perform in our history is not difficult to demonstrate.

Yet controversy has long swirled around the question whether this corpus of law, the bulk of which consists of lines of Supreme Court precedent, deserves anything like the influence it has come to exert on our society. Some notable scholars and some especially significant jurists, including Supreme Court Justice Clarence Thomas (and, on a bold day, Supreme Court Justice Antonin Scalia), are among the skeptics in this regard. They readily concede that the edifice of judicial opinions construing the Constitution forms a kind of "common law" that makes the task of judges easier and facilitates predictions about what courts will do in particular cases. But they argue that the towers of law that have been constructed over the years in the Constitution's name should be knocked down whenever it becomes clear that what has been built up in fact rests on a mistaken view of what the Constitution meant when it was originally adopted. Of course, what it means for something to become "clear" in this realm is itself anything *but* clear. And believing that one is in possession of the wisdom needed to dismiss the teachings of the past as unworthy of any deference or even much attention may be more indicative of inflated self-regard than of genuine insight. In any event, purely as a descriptive matter, it cannot be denied that the "brooding omnipresence" of ordinary jurisprudence constitutes a significant superstructure of doctrine and tradition that shapes the evolving interpretation, implementation, and down-to-earth enforcement of the Constitution as law— all of it importantly embedded in what has aptly been called the "constitutional culture."

Although this book will attend from time to time to that extraconstitutional matrix and will at times navigate the ocean of ideas that surrounds the Constitution, my main focus is on the Constitution itself. The invisible, nontextual foundations and facets of that Constitution will be the target of this exploration. But my reference to an "invisible" Constitution should not be confused with the way some people are prepared to disregard all or part of the Constitution in times of crisis, real or manufactured. My interest in this book is in what a mere reading of the Constitution's words cannot hope to reveal. I'll leave for another day the views of some that—because the Constitution is not, as they remind us, a "suicide pact"—we should sometimes act *as though* parts of what it says have conveniently *become* "invisible."

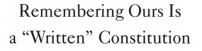

Remembering Ours Is
a "Written" Constitution

SO THIS IS A BOOK about what is "in" the United States Constitution but cannot be *seen* when one reads only its text. This is, of course, a paradoxical subject, given the unquestionable importance of the written text. Much is made, and rightly so, of the United States having a single, uniquely identifiable, *written* Constitution. Its very writtenness makes our Constitution stand apart from what people mean when they speak, for instance, of "the constitution" of a nation like the United Kingdom, in which thickly layered and long-settled customs and traditions—buttressed by a number of texts, both ancient (like the Magna Carta) and modern (like the European Union conventions on human rights)—together describe and delimit the structures and powers of government and so define a "constitution" that in some respects resembles our own.

And yet, while the United Kingdom's "constitution" of custom and tradition is accorded special status in the system of laws and practices within which ordinary affairs are conducted, the fact that it lacks the formality and concreteness of a unique written text seems of a piece with the recognized power of the British Parliament to alter the structure of government or its relationship with the people and their "rights" merely by enacting a law, the supremacy of which is treated as axiomatic. Indeed, this very plasticity might be said to be a defining feature of the British "constitution," under which Parliament reigns supreme.

When nations around the world debate whether to draft and embrace written constitutions as foundations of their legal and governmental systems, their people routinely treat the written character of whatever integrated constitution they might adopt as a central point of resemblance to the Constitution that they admire for having guided the United States of America from its inception in 1789 to the present, through its radical transformation during and in the immediate aftermath of the American Civil War.

The fact that we purport to follow and be bound by the Constitution that was proposed in 1787, ratified in 1789, and formally amended just 27 times (or was it 26? or perhaps just 23?) is due, in large part, to the fact that it *is* a single and singular text, one writing, that memorializes the commitments defining us over the course of time in a way that neither our physical territory nor the multiple ancestral origins of our nation can. Indeed, the physical writing itself—from the parchment signed in Philadelphia in 1787 and still carefully preserved at considerable expense in the National Archives to the numbered copies of the original that circulated physically throughout the several ratifying states—is almost instinctively treated with a devotion ordinarily accorded only to an object of national veneration, rather than any mere statute.

The Variable Role of Interpretive
Judicial Precedent

MERE STATUTORY ENACTMENTS—even those few that, over time, have assumed a nearly iconic status—are often perceived as being constituted entirely by the rules, principles, and structures that their words put in place, usually as seen through the lens of successive judicial interpretations. The fact that such statutes are not written in stone but can be amended at any time by mere majorities of the current House and Senate makes courts reluctant, paradoxically, to revisit previous interpretations of what the statutes mean. That, in turn, makes those to whom the statutes are addressed read them with the "gloss" furnished by those prior judicial interpretations. Thus, although it may seem counterintuitive, the great difficulty of formally amending the Constitution to overturn a Supreme Court interpretation of its meaning, something our nation has done just four times in its history, in contrast with the relative ease of formally amending an act of Congress for such a purpose, has led to a practice in which judicial interpretations of the Constitution tend—with the exception of certain "superprecedents" of the sort we will shortly encounter—to be more amenable than judicial interpretations of federal statutes to revision in subsequent judicial decisions.

Of course, early judicial interpretations of federal statutes do not *invariably* "stick" until Congress revisits the relevant statutory language. Title VII of the Civil Rights Act of 1964, for example, has turned out to be an important prohibition of on-the-job sexual harassment taking a wide range of forms. The language of the statute itself certainly did not dictate any such development. Nor did the legislative history or the history of postenactment judicial opinions construing the statute: the initial opinions were, if anything, hostile to sexual harassment claims. Nor, finally, was the statute changed by Congress to inaugurate this development. Most of the credit for conceptualizing "sex harassment" as a form of gender discrimination covered by the statute as originally drafted goes to a single individual, Catharine A. MacKinnon, who worked out the details of what sorts of conduct Title VII should take seriously as a form of discrimination, showed that enforcement would be practical, and demonstrated convincingly that prohibiting workplace sexual harassment was a matter of decency and good sense, despite some of the difficulties it would entail. Ordinarily, however, the early judicial interpretations become more firmly fixed in the case of statutes than in the case of the Constitution.

In all likelihood, our most iconic federal statutes, if preserved physically as originally signed by the president, would have considerable value as historically interesting artifacts. But the interest those few statutes—such as, perhaps, the leading Civil Rights Acts (like Title VII), the Sherman Antitrust Act, and the National Labor Relations Act—would attract is not comparable to the near-fetishism with which many regard "The" Constitution of the United States: its precise, physically embodied words are central to our very sense of who we are and aspire to be as a people. The frequently voiced observation that the Constitution is America's "civil religion"—its one unifying, if recognizably imperfect, scripture—appears to address the written text and what ordinary citizens might make of it more than the gloss that generations of judicial rulings have placed on it. Although law school courses in constitutional law typically focus on the unfolding succession of such rulings—and often spend shockingly little time on the Constitution itself, both as seen through the student's own eyes and as perceived by the non-judicial branches—not many people would confuse the Supreme Court's sequence of pronouncements on constitutional matters with "The" Constitution. This is so even when those pronouncements are delivered with rare unanimity and in a voice suggestive of imagined infallibility.

There was, to be sure, one occasion (in a justly celebrated case, *Cooper v. Aaron*, arising out of a state governor's resistance to a judicial order to integrate the public schools) on which the Supreme Court went so far as to say that one of its own landmark rulings—*Brown v. Board of Education*—was *itself* the "supreme Law of the Land," a status accorded by Article VI of the Constitution only to "This Constitution, and the Laws of the United States which shall be made in Pursuance thereof; and all Treaties made…under the Authority of the United States." Some observers praise how heroically the Court's opinion in *Cooper v. Aaron* seized the mantle of history. Others take the Court to task for what seems to them the presumptuousness and self-importance of its proclamation. From one perspective, just as a lawful executive order issued by the president trumps any contrary state law or state executive action under the Supremacy Clause of Article VI, so a Supreme Court opinion that is the premise for orders issued by lower courts should count as a "law" of the United States if the courts issuing the orders are exercising jurisdiction constitutionally conferred by Congress. And it may be that the Supreme Court's proclamation in *Cooper v. Aaron* meant no more than that. From another perspective, just as Abraham Lincoln's suspension of habeas corpus in advance of Congress's authorization during the Civil War reflected his defensible conclusion that nothing less would save the Union and thus the Constitution, perhaps the Supreme Court's decision in *Cooper* to treat *Brown* as *part* of the Constitution itself and not just as an opinion *about* the Constitution reflected a no less defensible conclusion that what the Union stood for could be saved only by taking *Brown* as the law of the land.

What it means to take *Brown* as the law of the land is, of course, another matter altogether. In June 2007, in *Parents Involved in Community Schools v. Seattle School District*, the Supreme Court divided closely over the constitutionality of plans voluntarily adopted by a number of local school districts around the country that took the race of individual students into account as a tie-breaking factor in some instances in deciding which students to assign to which public schools. The plans attempted to increase the racial diversity of those schools, making their racial composition more closely mirror that of the local public school population as a whole. The Court's plurality opinion, written by Chief Justice John R. Roberts, proclaimed that school districts that took race into account for the purpose of "integrating" their schools violated the meaning of *Brown* every bit as much as had the school districts that, in the 1950s and earlier, took race into account for the very different purpose of forcibly separating the races and ensuring that white children would not have to attend grades K–12 with their African American counterparts. A fifth vote for the invalidation of the school plans in *Parents Involved* was provided by Justice Anthony M. Kennedy, who shared the Chief Justice's basic antipathy to race-conscious measures but left the door open just a crack for the possibility that better-designed integration plans might pass constitutional muster.

Both in the opinions supporting the Court's result and in the impassioned dissents, as well as in much of the public commentary about the case, the controversy was framed in terms of which justices were faithful—and which had betrayed—the meaning of *Brown*. *Brown* was treated as a precedent to be understood and enforced rather than one to be revisited and perhaps even revised; in other words, it was treated as though it were part of the Constitution itself—something to be deeply understood and carefully applied but certainly not abandoned or even marginally adjusted.

But that is the exception that proves the rule: Although a handful of Supreme Court decisions have attained status as "superprecedents" that would be nearly unthinkable for any subsequent Court to overrule, virtually no Supreme Court ruling besides *Brown*—with the possible exception of the decision that is regarded as having permanently established the power of judicial review, *Marbury v. Madison*—has achieved a status essentially comparable to that of the Constitution itself. That is a phenomenon that again attests to the power of the written word in our constitutional constellation: If the Constitution is a nearly sacred text, there is an unbridgeable gap between the one set of *Words* that constitutes it and the mere collections of *words* of those who interpret and apply it.

This is not to deny that a considerable number of Supreme Court precedents construing various parts of the written Constitution come to occupy a privileged place in our law. Some decisions acquire that status by virtue of their gradual assimilation into the broader culture—such as the "*Miranda* warnings" that must be administered by police to suspects during custodial interrogation—and by the increasing accommodation to those decisions on the part of the organizations and institutions that initially resisted them, as well as by the growing sense that the parades of horribles forecast by those decisions' harshest critics failed to materialize.

Still other decisions acquire the rank of "semi-superprecedents," even as they remain perpetually controversial and never come to be accepted by more than a bare majority of the populace. Decisions of that sort, probably best typified by the 1973 abortion ruling, *Roe v. Wade*, become fairly entrenched in part because of how deeply they come to shape the expectations and life plans of influential segments of the population. Whatever the mechanism by which such peculiarly entrenched precedents come to occupy a special place in American life and law, very few people would describe them as so rooted in the constitutional culture as to become all but indistinguishable either from our Constitution's visible text or from what this book will come to describe as our invisible Constitution's bedrock postulates.

Interestingly, this collection of iconic but not quite sacrosanct precedents has a mirror image of sorts—one that takes the form of judicial opinions that have come to epitomize the inverse of what the Constitution and constitutional law should be—opinions like *Dred Scott v. Sanford*, *Plessy v. Ferguson*, probably *Lochner v. New York*, and, for most of us, *Korematsu v. United States*. Those decisions, described in order, proclaimed slaves and their descendants incapable of full citizenship in the United States or in any state (*Dred Scott*); endorsed racial apartheid as the epitome of equality as long as the separate facilities into which the racial minority was herded were "equal" to those from which they were invidiously excluded (*Plessy*); denied government the power to protect people from economic exploitation by those with greater bargaining power (*Lochner*); and defended the wholesale exclusion of Japanese American citizens from their homes and communities as a supposedly reasonable means of protecting the nation from military attack (*Korematsu*).

Those of us who try to teach the law of the Constitution find such "anticonstitutional" decisions at least as illuminating as the decisions that have become all but impossible to challenge. Like the abuses of the Crown so eloquently memorialized by Thomas Jefferson in the Declaration of Independence and the examples of tyrannical power recounted by the Constitution's framers in the process of formulating and defending the work product of their remarkable summer in Philadelphia, the paradigmatic examples of what the Constitution must never again be read to countenance furnish crucial sources of constitutional insight.

Yet, despite the obvious fact that such object lessons are to be found not within the Constitution's visible language but outside it, the common view is that anything not burned into the Constitution's unique text must have a more shadowy and dubious, and accordingly less legitimate, status in the law of the Constitution than that enjoyed by its words. The central role of the Constitution's written character gives that common view an almost irresistible force. Indeed, the singular centrality of the Constitution as the one written text that trumps all else gives rise to the major puzzle that this book addresses. For, at the very same time that the Constitution's tangible and self-contained writtenness appears central to its grip on our imaginations, *what holds us in its grip, and what we treat as its meaning, cannot be found in the written text alone but resides only in much that one cannot perceive from reading it.*

The "Dark Matter"

PHYSICISTS AND COSMOLOGISTS have come to believe that physically invisible "dark matter" and "dark energy" together define most of the universe we occupy. So, too—without meaning to press the analogy too far (given how mysterious the "dark matter" of physics remains, and how often its existence must simply be hypothesized in order to account for what would otherwise be disturbing mathematical anomalies)—I am convinced that the invisible Constitution is at the center of the Constitution's meaning and of its inestimable value. This book is about that claim. My hope is to nudge the nation's constitutional conversation away from debates over what the Constitution *says* and whether various constitutional claims are properly rooted in its written text and toward debates over what the Constitution *does*. Put otherwise, I hope to shift the discussion from whether various constitutional claims are properly rooted within the Constitution's written text to whether claims made in its name rightly describe the content, both written and unwritten, of our fundamental law.

PART II

Defining the Terrain

Invisibility Defined

IT IS MY PURPOSE, then, to make "visible" the Constitution's partial invisibility by setting before the reader the important respects in which the Constitution's commands, principles, and modes of operation and evolution go well beyond the words it contains. As we will see, that the Constitution's content cannot be captured by studying its visible surface is true in much more than a trivial sense.

When I speak of those elements of the Constitution that are only "trivially" invisible, I have in mind concepts and propositions that all but the most literal-minded and shortsighted reader would readily "see" and feel no need to defend in any elaborate way. Lawyers of every philosophical and ideological bent would describe anyone as "legally blind" who could not see, for instance, that, when the Constitution contains a command saying that "Congress shall make no law...abridging the freedom of speech, or of the press," the word "speech" must be understood to encompass not just audible or oral expression but visually readable, written, pictorial, and at least some gestural or otherwise symbolic expression as well, including music and dance and mime, as well as novels and pamphlets and posters and films and videos.

Similarly, the phrase "the press" must certainly be understood to include much more than the printing press as it was known to the congressional authors of the First Amendment in 1789 and to those state legislators who ratified it in 1791. On the other hand, whether "the press" should be taken to identify a collection of institutions and organizations, as some believe, or should instead be understood to refer to a set of journalistic and editorial functions, regardless of who performs them, as I believe it should, involves nontrivial arguments about what the underlying concept embraces. In resolving these substantive arguments, we must go nontrivially beyond the written Constitution. In that sense, we will be analyzing nontrivially "invisible" facets of the First Amendment.

The outer boundaries of the "trivially invisible" zone, I must concede, are necessarily blurry. Not everyone would agree, for example, that the "freedom of speech" extends to literally all symbolic protest—flag burning, for instance—and there would be at least as much disagreement over whether "freedom of the press" encompasses a special role for professional journalists or refers instead to a broad freedom, enjoyed by all who would exercise it, to gather and report whatever the reporter views as "news." And there remains even greater controversy over whether (and, if so, to what extent) any such freedom includes a privilege to keep secret the identity of one's journalistic sources, just as there was controversy for decades over whether the Fourth Amendment's ban on "unreasonable searches and seizures" encompassed wiretapping and electronic eavesdropping—technologies that the Supreme Court, over some dissent, concluded in 1967 were indeed within the Fourth Amendment's reach. But, however important are disagreements over the correct way to read particular provisions of the Constitution, such disagreements deal more with the meaning of the *visible* Constitution than with the existence and interpretation of those features of the Constitution that are essentially *invisible*.

I do not mean to denigrate the difficulty or significance of debate over the constitutional rules and principles that well-educated readers, familiar with standard modes of legal argument and with their application to the Constitution, can responsibly derive or infer from specific parts of the Constitution's text. Consider, for example, the principle that government may not engage in "viewpoint discrimination," penalizing or seeking to prevent expression or conduct on the basis of disagreement with the opinions or points of view the expression contains or the conduct expresses. It is this principle that lawyers would invoke to argue that someone who burns an American flag in order to dramatize his disagreement with current government policy could not constitutionally be punished for the offense of "flag desecration," defined to mean something like treating with derision or disrespect a cloth or other object bearing a pictorial representation of the stars and stripes. Such a flag burner might properly be punished for, say, trespass or arson if he engages in his protest on someone else's front lawn or in a place likely to cause someone's house to burn down. But he could not constitutionally be charged with or convicted for expressing an unpatriotic view of the flag or of "the Republic for which it stands."

Some people would disagree either with the constitutional status of the anti-viewpoint-discrimination principle or with this application of it. In fact, the Supreme Court's decisions overturning the convictions of flag desecrators divided the Court closely in each instance, with some justices whom one would ordinarily describe as "conservative" (e.g., Justices Antonin Scalia and Anthony Kennedy) siding with the majority and with some whom one would ordinarily describe as "liberal" (e.g., Justice John Paul Stevens) siding with the dissent. Regardless of where a reader might come down in a case like this, the argument would be about what appropriate modes of legal reasoning, applied to the text of the First Amendment, imply about the matter at hand. In effect, the argument would be over the correctness of extracting the anti-viewpoint-discrimination principle from that text. The argument would not be either a dispute about the constitutional principles that every reasonable reader would have to regard as implied by that text (what I have been calling "trivially invisible" principles) or a dispute about those genuinely "invisible" principles that *no* reasonable reader could claim to extract or infer from the text alone.

Of specific concern in this book is the latter set of constitutional principles and requirements—those that go beyond anything that could reasonably be said to follow simply from what the Constitution expressly *says*. At least some principles and requirements of this sort are not difficult to identify. In fact, the vast majority of educated citizens would probably include in their list of what the U.S. Constitution forbids or demands quite a few propositions of precisely this kind. I have in mind propositions of the following sort:

- Ours is a "government of the people, by the people, for the people."
- Ours is a "government of laws, not men."
- We are committed to the "rule of law."
- Courts must not automatically defer to what elected officials decide the Constitution means.
- Government may not torture people to force information out of them.
- In each person's intimate private life, there are limits to what government may control.
- Congress may not commandeer states as though they were agencies or departments of the federal government.
- No state may secede from the Union.

None of these propositions may fairly be said to follow from the Constitution's language by anything like standard "legal" arguments, although there may be room for dispute about how far from that language one must stray in order to stitch together a legal brief for one or another of the propositions. Yet their apparent detachment and distance from the Constitution's text does not prevent any of these propositions from being identified by nearly everyone as binding elements of our nation's supreme law. Especially dramatic in this respect is the proposition that no state may secede from the Union. That proposition, more obviously than any other, is written not in ink but in blood. It is not a proposition that could be defended in every imaginable national context—that of Kosovo, for instance, or perhaps of Tibet. But few would question its location at the heart of *our* Constitution. Yet none would be so bold as to pretend to "read" it in our Constitution's written words.

Nor would it be plausible to treat the antisecession principle, the anticommandeering principle, or the judicial review principle as facets of some universally valid body of divine, or "natural," or "higher," law. Nearly all of what scholars have written regarding what they routinely call the "unwritten Constitution," in a parade of articles and books spanning more than a century, has focused on the degree to which the Constitution's framers and ratifiers viewed such a body of "natural" law as real, objectively ascertainable, legally binding, and entitled to prevail over mere statutes and executive orders. And much of this writing over the past several decades has focused on the debate over the legitimacy of having a democratically unaccountable and deliberately counter-majoritarian institution resort to such "unwritten" law in order to strike down popularly enacted measures.

This book's focus differs in at least two respects. First, my discussion proceeds without presupposing any imagined body of "natural" law. As long ago as 1890, Christopher Tiedeman, a prominent proponent of having judges impose non-text-based limits on all government power, found it necessary to concede (in his book *The Unwritten Constitution of the United States*) that "there is no fixed, invariable list of natural rights," that such "rights vary and their characters change with the development of the ethical conceptions of the people," and that "the natural rights with which all men are proclaimed in the American Declaration of Independence to be endowed by their Creator, have been developed within the historical memory of man." Now, more than a century later and perhaps a bit wiser, we live in an era in which no system of beliefs in a universal, higher law could plausibly be regarded as a useful predicate for constitutional discourse and legal analysis. Most of the postulates and theorems that I see as constituting the invisible Constitution are far too historically contingent and institutionally specialized to count as serious candidates for "natural law" canonization.

Second, this book's inquiry is independent of the debates about how active or passive a role judges in particular should play when enforcing their views of what the Constitution, written or unwritten, visible or invisible, means in the face of contrary views taken by the elected branches of government. Acceptance of judicial *review*, whose existence I regard as one of the unstated axioms of our Constitution, is entirely consistent with a rejection of judicial *supremacy*, as many throughout our history have argued. The Supreme Court could say, as *Marbury v. Madison* so famously put it, "what the law means" in ruling on the controversy before it in a way that binds all parties to that controversy—and it could do so without deference to Congress's or the president's views that the Constitution means something quite different—without reaching a conclusion that would necessarily be binding on the entire government, in controversies involving other parties, for all time to come.

A parade of energetic scholars has in our own time developed the case for limiting judicial review to varying degrees, and at the very least for returning to what is claimed to be the nation's long tradition of rejecting judicial supremacy. Others have countered with forceful arguments linking the need for stability and the dangers of social chaos to the difficulties of having each department of government pursue its own reading of the Constitution within its own sphere of responsibility. Interesting and important though this never-ending debate surely is, I am not enlisting this book in that battle. Recall our very first example—that of a late-ratified amendment whose valid ratification, and whose alleged violation, no individual would be likely to have standing to contest in the federal courts. That should remind us that the challenge of understanding and abiding by the "invisible" Constitution is one that must be confronted by all who are bound by the Constitution, not just by the Supreme Court and the rest of the judicial branch. Coping with that challenge is a task quite independent of the judiciary's proper role.

This is manifestly the case with many of the most fundamental of the Constitution's provisions—including, to identify just one prominent instance, the provisions dealing with the impeachment and removal of the president for the commission of what Article II, section 4, calls "Treason, Bribery, or other high Crimes and Misdemeanors," and entrusting to the Senate "the sole Power to try all Impeachments"—a task to be performed with no contemplated participation by the judicial branch beyond that identified in section 3 of the same article, which specifies that "when the President of the United States is tried, the Chief Justice shall preside."

But even on matters with respect to which the prospect of judicial review carries with it the possibility that judges will second-guess, and may be permitted to pronounce final judgment on, the constitutional views reflected in the bills Congress enacts and the president signs or vetoes or embodied in the executive actions the president takes, it bears emphasis that, under the second clause of Article VI of our Constitution, all "Senators and Representatives...and the Members of the several State Legislatures, and all executive and judicial Officers, both of the United States and of the several States," are to "be bound by Oath or Affirmation, to support this Constitution." Despite the habitual buck-passing that goes on with respect to constitutional issues, with lawmakers and others doing the bidding of their constituents and leaving to the courts the task of taking the Constitution seriously, the responsibility reposed by Article VI cannot properly be lifted from the shoulders of nonjudicial officeholders by pointing to the duty of the judiciary to "say what the law is."

Returning, then, to the list of principles enumerated earlier, I should make clear that the list is meant to be merely suggestive, not exhaustive. And the principles listed are of several different kinds. Of particular note, only two of the eight (the fifth and sixth) involve what might be called substantive human rights. This book, therefore, goes well beyond an exploration of what are typically described as "unenumerated rights," which tend to arise in arguments in support of abortion rights, rights of sexual choice, or the right to die. This book, in other words, is not a selective brief in support of rights widely associated with the cultural and political Left.

Some of the principles on the list, like the last two—the anticommandeering and the antisecession principles—take the form of crisp, black-and-white rules that don't really involve matters of degree. Others, like the first three—the popular sovereignty principle, and the two versions of the legality principle—likewise don't involve matters of degree but are global characteristics of our system as a whole rather than sharp, specific prohibitions. And still others, like the second set of three—the judicial review principle, the antitorture principle, and the privacy principle—are prohibitory rather than systemic but do involve matters of degree and ambiguities of definition. How much courts might regard themselves as bound in various settings by what the political branches conclude the Constitution means without wholly abdicating their constitutionally essential function is a matter for ongoing debate; what constitutes "torture" is to some degree up for grabs at any given time; and where the boundaries of intimate private life end and society's legitimate concerns for the effects of personal behavior on others begin is anything but a fixed, uncontested, bright line. What seems incontestable, however, is that the invisible Constitution dictates that there be *some* such boundary, however shifting. And that there must exist at least *some* limits of decency on the kinds and degrees of pain the state may inflict on people seems axiomatic, at least absent a constitutional amendment obliterating all such limits.

That closing observation—the observation about amending not just the visible constitutional text but the propositions of the invisible Constitution—is worth pausing over. In describing the eight propositions enumerated above as "bedrock" principles, I do not mean to suggest that they are necessarily unamendable. To identify a proposition as part of the nation's "Constitution," albeit not of the Constitution's text, is not synonymous with treating that proposition as incapable of being lawfully repudiated by the textually sanctioned methods of constitutional amendment through Article V. An amendment allowing torture in certain circumstances, or one permitting Congress to command local governments to enforce certain federal laws, might be *substantively* objectionable, but neither amendment could plausibly be said to be beyond the pale as a *constitutional* matter if adopted in accordance with Article V.

Conversely, it may well be that *some* properly adopted formal amendments could themselves be deemed "unconstitutional" because of their radical departure from premises too deeply embedded to be repudiated without a full-blown revolution. Thus, for instance, an amendment repealing the Article IV guarantee of a "republican" form of government and simultaneously making membership in Congress a matter of heredity, rather than of election by "the People," might well be deemed void regardless of its process of adoption, as might an amendment that repudiates the rule of law or abandons the indissoluble character of the Union. But even a legal positivist who is uncomfortable with the idea of *any* duly enacted amendment being deemed "unconstitutional" should be able to embrace the notion that certain principles are so foundational to our legal and political order, have so long been regarded as indispensable to its legitimacy, and are so logically central to our governmental system's coherence that their binding status—at least until they are in fact repudiated by a textual amendment—is unimpaired by the fact that they are not stated in, or even plausibly inferable from, any part of the Constitution's text.

I also do not mean to suggest that the invisible Constitution exists as some Platonic or Kantian thing-in-itself apart from all our reasoning about it (at least on one interpretation of Kant). Indeed, we come to know this invisible Constitution only through reasoning to its contents, and in a certain sense we might speak of "constructing" it through our reasoning. At the same time, however, the contents of the invisible Constitution are not radically indeterminate—we cannot find in the invisible Constitution anything and everything we might wish.

Thus, there are certainly some propositions that have the same *form* as those listed above and that might conceivably be parts of *some* Constitution but that could not fairly be described as parts of *our* Constitution. That claim is important to establish, lest anyone imagine that the very idea of an "invisible" Constitution is so cloudy and formless that essentially *any* worthy candidate for future inclusion in the invisible Constitution could be said to be part of *our* Constitution in 2008 and beyond.

Not Necessarily an *Ideal* Constitution

CONSIDER THE CLAIM THAT the federal government, under our Constitution, owes to every U.S. citizen travel at public expense to and from any nation of that citizen's choosing as part of the right to be informed about world affairs; or the claim that our Constitution forbids the deployment by the United States, whether offensively or defensively, of any weapon of mass destruction; or the claim that every person in the world has a right under the Constitution to become a permanent resident of the continental United States. One could coherently argue for or against including propositions of that sort in a constitutional republic like ours. But arguing that those propositions are correctly deemed part of the Constitution we have today would be pointless—rather like arguing, to borrow an idea from the zany cartoonist Alan Stamaty, that the Constitution entrusts to the directors of the National Zoo the exclusive power to enact federal laws to govern the nation. Thus the set of propositions contained in the invisible Constitution I have in mind, while encompassing a list of indefinite length and scope, is indeed bounded and does not include whatever one might want it to include.

An influential law review article with the tongue-in-cheek title "Our Perfect Constitution" once accused a number of supposedly "liberal" constitutional scholars (including me, as it happens) of acting as though the U.S. Constitution is a "perfect" constitution and of smuggling into its meaning essentially every command and prohibition that we would personally choose to include in an ideal constitution for our nation. In so doing, that article confused some scholars' disagreement with particular then-recent trends in constitutional interpretation with an undisciplined willingness to "read" their social and political preferences into our Constitution. That confusion was rhetorically useful for the article's purposes, but it led to a mistaken conclusion.

Perhaps the examples offered above of theoretically *possible*, but plainly incorrect, statements of what our Constitution contains are too obviously over the top to be informative. Were the contents of the invisible Constitution to include only such broad and general maxims as all in our society intuitively accept—and to exclude only laughably absurd examples—the utility and significance of noting its existence would be questionable. An important goal of this book is to show that this is not so, and that we may, and do, reach conclusions about the more controversial contents of the invisible Constitution— conclusions that we may evaluate, and accept or discard, in accordance with criteria that go beyond mere personal preference.

Just as competing interpretations of the Constitution's *visible* text are subject to a number of nonarbitrary, although contestable, criteria of validity, so is the illumination of the invisible Constitution subject to nonarbitrary, although contestable, constraints. Accordingly, a significant task of this book will be to explore the modes of reasoning through which legal thinkers describe and dispute the contents of the invisible Constitution. Specifically, we will investigate in Part V a number of distinct methods by which these nontextual features of the Constitution have themselves been constructed and designed in the past.

Constitutional Axioms and
Constitutional Theorems

REASONING ABOUT THE INVISIBLE Constitution's contents must, of course, be channeled to some degree by subjective considerations. But that reasoning must at the same time be disciplined and driven by more than desired results. In that process, it may be helpful to draw on the distinction between axioms and theorems in a logical system. Axioms are the foundational propositions whose truth is to be assumed or taken for granted, while theorems are those propositions that can be derived from these basic axioms using accepted rules of logic. In a certain sense, the visible text of the Constitution might be said to contain the explicit axioms of our constitutional law and theory, and those general rules or principles that can be inferred from the Constitution's visible text might be said to comprise a set of theorems constituting a significant part of that body of constitutional discourse and doctrine. The principle against viewpoint discrimination discussed above, for example, is a member of this set, fairly derivable (although, of course, not without some controversial steps) from the First Amendment.

But it is the contention of this book that our constitutional canon—the set of general constitutional rules and principles on which we typically rely in reaching conclusions about what the Constitution requires in particular cases—includes much that cannot be inferred simply from the visible constitutional "axioms" alone. Part of this "invisible" matter is itself axiomatic in character: it takes the form of foundational postulates, difficult if not impossible to infer from propositions still more elemental or basic. But part of the invisible matter is less in the nature of an axiom or a postulate than a theorem, being itself inferable from more basic building blocks of the constitutional system.

To say that the invisible Constitution contains or implies rules that cannot be inferred from the visible text alone is emphatically not to say that the invisible Constitution bears no relation to the visible text. Indeed, most of the modes of reasoning to the contents of the invisible Constitution involve arguing in one form or another from its visible text (but not in a way that could be considered "mere logical inference"). At the same time, the Constitution's "dark matter" may be seen to animate and undergird significant portions of its visible text. And in some cases, as I shall explore here, it is the invisible constitutional principles that all but dictate the meaning widely ascribed to the visible text. Accordingly, we might say that the visible text of the Constitution does not contain all that is axiomatic or foundational in constitutional theory.

The Politics of Constitutional Invisibility

THE INVISIBLE CONSTITUTION this book discusses is commonly derided by both the American Left and the American Right as nothing but the disguised repository of the other side's political preferences—even while the Right and the Left alike invoke that invisible Constitution when it suits their aims. A standard technique used by nearly everyone engaged in constitutional debate is to denounce an opponent's constitutional claim as unsupported by the Constitution's explicit words. Thus, for example, when some liberals contend that the Constitution includes some version of a "right to privacy," and move from that contention to an argument for constitutionalizing the right to abortion or any number of other controversial rights, many conservatives immediately counter that no such privacy right is mentioned in or derivable from the Constitution's text and conclude that those who claim to "find" it there must be calling on "activist" judges to invent rights that adhere to some liberal agenda. Or, equally, when some conservatives contend that the Constitution protects state legislatures from being directed by Congress to enact certain laws dealing with commerce among the states, or protects state and local executives and administrators from being required by Congress to implement and enforce federal statutes dealing with gun control or missing children, many liberals equally invariably counter that no such guarantees are included in or inferable from what the Constitution says and conclude that such guarantees must be parts of the Republican Party platform, not the United States Constitution.

If this book is correct, then both sets of objections are wide of the mark, for both rest on the mistaken premise that the "true" Constitution contains nothing beyond what one can see in or readily infer from its written text. And both sets of objections are made with at least unconscious hypocrisy—an equal opportunity offense in political discourse. But I would not suggest that arguments about the legitimate claims of an invisible Constitution lack political valence. On the contrary, the consequences of according fuller recognition to what I am calling the invisible Constitution may, for the short-term and even mid-term future, not be what a liberal or progressive thinker about the Constitution might find to his liking. Put bluntly, the rhetorical device of pretending that the invisible Constitution is a mere figment of the other side's imagination would probably be more useful for liberals than conservatives these days, given that the more conservative features of that invisible Constitution are more likely to be advanced by the right-leaning jurists that currently control the Supreme Court and most of the federal judiciary. This is all the truer in light of the current disposition of most liberal jurists to favor nothing beyond incremental changes in judicial interpretation, which stands in stark contrast to the greater boldness of their conservative counterparts, at least on the Supreme Court.

On the other hand, liberals may find acceptance of the invisible Constitution useful in combating a conservative campaign to dismantle those bodies of constitutional principle—such as those pertaining to privacy rights—that have been championed mostly by the American Left. And at any rate, the option of asymmetric blindness, with an astigmatic and selective failure to see the constitutional elements most ardently embraced by the Right while urging recognition of the constitutional elements most helpful to the Left—or vice versa—is both unrealistic and ethically problematic. However sympathetic I might be to some of the results toward which a general denial of the invisible Constitution's reality would point, truth has its claims. And I have faith that, in the long run, the costs of pretense dwarf any possible benefits.

This Book's Mission:
Making Invisibility Visible

I HAVE TWO MAIN GOALS in what follows. First, I want to show, both by concrete example and by theoretical argument, the *reality* and *reach* of the invisible Constitution. Second, I intend to exhibit the various modes of reasoning through which we may arrive at and explain its contents. But arguing for a single "correct" version of the contents of the invisible Constitution is a task well beyond the scope of this book, as is the task of championing some version of the Constitution—of a "Constitution in exile," as some call it—that has ostensibly been wrongly abandoned along the way and is in need of restoration.

This is not to say, of course, that my beliefs about the substance of the invisible Constitution do not figure occasionally in what follows. Much of my argument for the reality of the invisible Constitution will involve showing how particular "invisible" constitutional principles have shaped not only outcomes in particular cases, but the trajectory of constitutional interpretation as a whole. And I hope to illuminate the ways the invisible

Constitution itself is in turn shaped by shared premises through a number of distinct processes of synthesis and analysis—of building up and breaking down.

Although the construction of a detailed model of the invisible Constitution that I might be inclined to advocate is not the primary aim of this book, I certainly hope to shed light on some essential features of the invisible Constitution I believe in and to contribute to the reader's understanding of it. By "understanding" the invisible Constitution, I mean developing some familiarity with its broad outlines, with the structural ideas it embodies, with the characteristic ways it unfolds and changes over time, and with the kinds of values to which I believe it is linked—values that are not inherently "liberal" or inherently "conservative" but are broadly committed to the dignity of the human person and the flourishing of humane aspirations.

There are, of course, entirely different visions of the good that a nation's collective aspirations might encompass, and I make no pretense to having discovered either a universally applicable normative template for the good society or a permanently valid descriptive formula for America. But many such alternative visions—in some of which the individual citizen counts for little and the end might justify the means—are alien to the American Constitution as I understand and have sought to explicate it.

Within the framework of *this* Constitution, my aim is to render more transparent the patterns of argument and analysis through which branches of the great tree of constitutional structures and protections have taken shape. As I hope to show, the vital force that flows through those branches has, over the course of our history, created a whole that is greater than the sum of its individual parts. Some branches might be prematurely trimmed or even cut off—as has occurred when the justices of the Supreme Court, to whom most of us have come to entrust the most influential exegesis of the Constitution, have taken wrong turns in their explication of the Constitution's meaning, finding in a particular phrase a limitation or an extension that the spirit of the Constitution as a whole is not best understood to embrace.

When such a wrong turn is taken—as it was, in my view, during the last several decades of the nineteenth century with respect to the Supreme Court's interpretations of some parts of the three Civil War amendments—a side effect is that other branches of the overall constitutional structure may end up bearing more weight than they can convincingly support. So, for instance, the Supreme Court in 1873, in the Slaughterhouse Cases, artificially constricted the meaning of the Fourteenth Amendment's guarantee that "*No State shall make or enforce any law which shall abridge the privileges or immunities of citizens of the United States.*" It did so by reading the words "privileges or immunities" to exclude the great bulk of what the American people have appropriately viewed as their fundamental rights—and of what the people who wrote and ratified the words "privileges or immunities" assumed those words would protect from state action. The upshot was that the bulk of those rights ended up being protected as forms of "liberty"—"liberty" that the Fourteenth Amendment says no state may abridge "without due process of law."

We will later explore the difficulties that squeezing "liberty" onto that branch of the constitutional structure have entailed. For now, it suffices to note that the essential idea that animates the Fourteenth Amendment—that, in their encounters with the state, persons are guaranteed a set of fundamental rights beyond those protected elsewhere—was powerful enough to survive the dubious turn taken by the Supreme Court in its interpretation of the written Constitution in the 1870s.

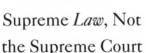

Supreme *Law*, Not
the Supreme Court

NOW THAT THIS BOOK'S subject has been defined, the time seems right to locate it more precisely in relation to the debate, as old as the nation itself, about the role of the Supreme Court in imposing its understanding of the Constitution on the other federal branches and on the state courts through the exercise of judicial review. It's a serious error to equate an inquiry into what the Constitution means—including the inquiry this book undertakes into the contents and meaning of what I've been calling the invisible Constitution—with a discussion of how free the Supreme Court should feel (or how much it should feel obligated) to impose its answers to such questions of meaning on political actors equally sworn to uphold the Constitution who have reached directly contrary conclusions in addressing the same questions.

Whether we are talking about the meaning of some part of the Constitution's text—like the definition of the federal judicial power in Article III or of the Free Speech Clause in the First Amendment—or about some unwritten axiom of the Constitution's plan, the issue of whether and when courts, including the Supreme Court, should treat the considered views of other government actors as conclusive, as merely relevant, or as altogether irrelevant at least when self-serving, is a complex one. Nearly all of the writing about that issue—writing that proposes reducing our nation's dependence on judicial review, taking the Constitution away from the courts, reposing greater trust in an informed and energized electorate, becoming less fearful of the people, and the like—addresses a set of questions essentially perpendicular to those explored in this book. On the one hand, some of the questions on which the Constitution's text is silent—such as the questions of how far Congress may subordinate the states as separate sovereigns, or of how far government may intrude into the intimate details of personal life—are probably better entrusted to the independent federal judiciary than to officials who must stand for reelection. On the other hand, some of the matters that the Constitution's entirely visible text squarely addresses—such as the question of just what constitutes an impeachable offense—are probably best left for final resolution to an institution other than the Supreme Court, particularly the Senate. This book is not about those institutional choices; it is much less about the Supreme *Court* than it is about the supreme *law*.

Thus, it is immaterial for this book's purposes that the issue of judicial review happens to preoccupy much of current legal academic scholarship (as well as our popular legal discourse), with many scholars continuing to defend judicial review vigorously while a number of others, at both ends of the liberal-to-conservative spectrum, argue cogently in favor of reining in the judiciary in the name of a number of theories, including popular constitutionalism, institutional competence, and adjudicative pragmatism. For the key point is that this book is about the architecture and content of the invisible Constitution—regardless of *who* is interpreting it, or by what institutional process. As such, my argument neither takes nor presupposes a stand on the question whether or to what degree the federal courts are the final and supreme authority on the Constitution's meaning. But I must qualify this disclaimer by noting that I believe a truly wholesale—and undeniably radical—rejection of the practice of judicial review in its entirety *would* violate what I see as a core, if textually invisible, principle of our Constitution. I will be better able to explain this book's qualified agnosticism about judicial supremacy after a brief overview of the controversies concerning judicial review.

Any story of judicial review does best to begin with Chief Justice John Marshall's pronouncements in *Marbury v. Madison* in 1803 that "it is emphatically the province and duty of the judicial department to say what the law is," that "a law repugnant to the constitution is void," and that "courts, as well as other departments, are bound by that instrument." It is common ground that, although earlier rulings took for granted the power of judicial review, it was with these words that Chief Justice Marshall first affirmed the power of the federal courts to review and invalidate acts of Congress in light of the judiciary's independent interpretation of the Constitution. What is open to vigorous controversy is whether Marshall intended, or whether his reasoning supports, an argument for the judiciary's unique status as the *supreme* interpreter of the Constitution.

It is important to understand that the debate about the judiciary's proper role in interpreting and enforcing the Constitution really involves two conceptually separate issues: while *judicial review* concerns the federal courts' entitlement to pass on the constitutionality of statutes and executive actions in cases arising before them, *judicial supremacy* concerns whether, when there is interbranch conflict about what the Constitution requires, the judiciary's interpretation is determinative and, as such, binding on the other branches beyond the case at hand. It is quite possible to endorse the power of judicial review while repudiating the notion of judicial supremacy. If the existence and supposed legitimacy of judicial review are sometimes mistakenly taken to imply the supremacy of the judiciary's constitutional conclusions, the reason may be a worry about the possible instability of treating each department of government as having the last word about constitutional questions raised within its own proper sphere of action.

If, for example, the president deems a particular federal criminal statute unconstitutional notwithstanding the Supreme Court's refusal to strike it down by reversing convictions for the statute's violation, the president under this "departmental" view would remain free to forbid his Justice Department to bring prosecutions under that statute, and free as well to pardon anyone who had been convicted of violating the statute under a prior administration—as President Thomas Jefferson did with respect to individuals convicted during the administration of President John Adams for violating the infamous Alien and Sedition Acts of 1789. Or if the Supreme Court were to uphold the constitutionality of a federal statute authorizing each state's governor to exempt any of that state's citizens who are enrolled in the U.S. military, on the citizen's written request, from deployment by the military in some increasingly unpopular combat engagement abroad (say, the military occupation of Iraq in 2008), a president who disagreed with that holding could properly instruct the armed forces, in his capacity as commander in chief, to disregard the challenged statute and any state governor's attempt to invoke it on a constituent's behalf—although the president would remain bound to obey the Court's judgment as to every individual who had been a party to the lawsuit resulting in that judgment and thus a specific beneficiary of the Court's decision in the case unsuccessfully litigated by the president.

Of course, if the Court were to stick to its guns and refuse to reverse course in the face of repeated challenges to its constitutional position that the statute in question was not an impermissible usurpation of the president's Article II responsibilities as commander in chief, presidential persistence would eventually become a wasteful exercise in futility—unless the president chose actually to defy the Court's judgments and to rely on the fact that it is the chief executive, and not the Court, who wields the power of the sword. It is the prospect of such confrontations—or at least of persistent conflict between the judiciary and the political branches and of the instability and unpredictability such ongoing conflict would entail—that has led some scholars to the conclusion that one branch or another must have the final say, in the normative and not merely chronological sense, on the Constitution's meaning. And while some academics have made a forceful case—based largely on the need for stability—that the judiciary should be the decider, others have suggested that the legislature, as the representative of the people, is the preferred candidate.

This brings us to the real heart of the debate about judicial supremacy, which is the perceived tension between constitutionalism and democracy. On the one hand, there lies the Constitution as "superlaw"—as "the people's" attempt to bind themselves through time to certain core principles that cannot be rejected or supplanted by means of ordinary majoritarian voting—or, as some have argued, to make solemn public commitments and not merely to express their intentions and expectations. On the other hand lie the claims of popular sovereignty and the notion that the constitutional interpretations of government actors, including the courts, should all be subordinate to the contemporary constitutional vision of "the people themselves."

In addition to such broadly philosophical attacks on judicial review in the name of "popular constitutionalism," some academics have proposed a radical curtailment of judicial review on strictly consequentialist grounds. On the view taken by such scholars, the crucial considerations in deciding whether and to what degree the federal judiciary should oversee the constitutional conclusions of other actors in the system are not what some have called "high-level claims about constitutionalism, democracy, or the nature of law" but are instead empirical judgments about "whichever interpretive methodology is most likely to have the best effect over all." These scholars argue that a low judicial profile is likely to produce the best overall results, in terms of the Constitution's own values, except where the clearest and most specific constitutional texts are involved. The ensuing form of judicial modesty would in fact be even more limiting than that famously proposed in 1893 by James Bradley Thayer. Whereas Thayer advocated that the Supreme Court enforce constitutional norms through judicial review only in cases of clear error, a proposed abolition of judicial review except where the texts to be construed are entirely unambiguous would eliminate in one fell swoop the better part of the Court's constitutional doctrine in elaborating and implementing the powers of the three federal branches vis-à-vis one another and vis-à-vis the states, as well as its role in enforcing pretty much the entirety of the Bill of Rights and the Fourteenth Amendment.

Although I have no need in this book to take a stand on the question of judicial supremacy—or even, for that matter, on the role of judicial review, although I do in fact treat a relatively robust form of the latter as presumptively desirable—it remains the case that, in considering the ways the invisible Constitution has taken shape over time, we will find ourselves relying heavily on illustrations drawn from the development of constitutional doctrine by the Supreme Court over the centuries. But the reason is simply that the Court has, as a matter of undeniable historical fact, been the institutional agent most deeply, consistently, and publicly engaged in explicating and making real the Constitution's requirements.

The Constitution's *Architecture,*
Not Its "Construction"

IT WOULD BE PRESUMPTUOUS—and inaccurate—to suggest that
this book is the first to address the gulf between the Constitution as
nearly all of us understand it and the text of the written Constitution.
Authors who have written about the unwritten Constitution have
been drawn to that topic principally by the question of legitimacy:
how, in a democratic society, can the government be bound by rules
and principles that the American people never formally approved?
Because the invisible Constitution was not promulgated pursuant
to the Constitution's own ratification procedure as specified in its
Article VII or by the new Constitution's own formal amendment
process as specified in its Article V, these authors have attempted
to develop alternative theories to explain the process by which the
invisible Constitution properly attains recognition as legitimate and
binding.

The most prominent of these theories belongs to Bruce
Ackerman, whose inspired *We the People* volumes argue that our
Constitution—not the text, but the Constitution as we understand

it—was constructed at three historical moments: at the time the Constitution was ratified, after the Civil War, and during the New Deal. Professor Ackerman insists that none of these constructions was "legitimate" under the law as it formally existed at the time. The Articles of Confederation, as we noted earlier, could be amended in accord with their own terms only by unanimous consent, but the newly proposed Constitution merely required 9 of 13 states for ratification. And amendments enacted pursuant to Article V of the Constitution must receive approval by three-fourths of all state legislatures, but many states of the former Confederacy were not permitted to vote freely on the three "Civil War Amendments." Finally, the New Deal revolution that washed away the laissez-faire theories embodied in the Court's *Lochner* era did not produce a single formal amendment to the constitutional text: not a word was changed or added.

Despite the lack of textual formality, each of these historical epochs, according to Professor Ackerman, represented a "constitutional moment" that transformed our nation's "higher law." Each qualified as such a "moment" because each featured a sharp battle between two divergent views of constitutional law—the Federalists against the Anti-Federalists, the Union against the Confederacy, and the New Deal against the old guard. When "the people," acting in carefully orchestrated institutional patterns, decisively rejected the old vision and approved the new—either directly (as in 1787 to 1789) or by supporting the politicians who espoused them (in 1866 and 1936)—the new principles became part of our Constitution. For Ackerman, what I would call the invisible Constitution represents the judiciary's attempt to synthesize the principles embodied in these three very different versions of higher law.

Standing in partial opposition to Ackerman is his no less talented and imaginative colleague Akhil Reed Amar. As a committed "constitutional textualist," Professor Amar rejects the theory that the

Constitution can be amended informally, without any change in its official text. His highly original work of scholarship *America's Constitution: A Biography* argues, however, that what constitutes the Constitution's text has been misunderstood by historians and legal scholars alike. By viewing the Constitution in historical context, by attributing globally transformative meaning to each textually promulgated constitutional change, and by giving more textual weight to the post-1865 formal constitutional amendments, Amar reads the written Constitution as a far more progressive text than the Constitution imagined by conservative textualists. Thus, for Amar, the process of constitutional change is driven by formal amendments—but by formal amendments more energetically and progressively understood. For example, while Ackerman claims that *Lochner* and its scores of judicial progeny may have been good law under the pre–New Deal Constitution, Amar argues that the Sixteenth Amendment, empowering Congress in 1913 to enact income taxes, should have been understood to eviscerate *Lochner*'s premises because it constitutionalized the proposition that Congress may lawfully redistribute wealth from the rich to the poor.

Located between Ackerman and Amar are scholars less troubled when constitutional change is effected by gradually shifting judicial interpretations. Those writers are indeed willing at times to defend such incremental change as a *more* legitimate source of constitutional guidance than the highly imperfect "consent of the governed" derivable from the state ratifications of the eighteenth and nineteenth centuries or the fictitious "consent" of more recent generations. These students of the Constitution are accordingly more receptive to the notion that the Constitution evolves in a manner reminiscent of the common-law tradition. Thus, they argue that constitutional change need not receive authoritative approval by "the people" so long as it represents a tradition of reasoned judge-made responses to real-world events.

Much more than a single volume could be written analyzing the merits and weaknesses of each of these theories—and of their spin-offs and competitors. But, rather than focusing on the historical or institutional processes that might help to legitimate the nontextual (and the textual but linguistically dubious) *transformations* through which the invisible Constitution has passed during the course of its long history, this book concentrates on the overarching and largely invariant *architecture* of that Constitution—the frameworks, patterns, buttresses, arches, keystones, and other building blocks that determine its overall shape and structure. It's a focus that makes sense once one accepts the existence and persistence of that invisible Constitution as an inescapable given, a phenomenon without which no visible Constitution could either become the supreme law or achieve concrete meaning.

To illustrate the distinction between the Constitution's construction and its shape, we can take a quick look at the contributions of the Warren Court and the Rehnquist Court to the invisible Constitution. None of the following decisions could reasonably be said to derive directly from the Constitution's text: Both *Miranda v. Arizona* (holding in 1966 that police officers must inform criminal defendants of their constitutional rights to silence and to an attorney before engaging in custodial interrogation) and *Katz v. United States* (declaring in 1967 that the Fourth Amendment protects the justifiable expectations of privacy held by *people*, rather than protecting places) exemplify the Warren Court's belief that the Constitution protects those suspected of crime from law enforcement excesses—and that those excesses may take more subtle forms than overtly forcing someone to be a "witness against himself" in a "criminal case," as expressly forbidden by the Fifth Amendment, or undertaking "unreasonable searches and seizures" of "persons, houses, papers, and effects," as expressly forbidden by the Fourth Amendment. Similarly, both *City of Boerne v. Flores* (barring the federal government in 1997 from nullifying state laws under the enforcement clause of the Fourteenth Amendment unless the federal law under challenge was "congruent and proportional" to a widespread pattern of constitutional violations by states) and *Seminole Tribe of Florida v. Florida* (finding in 1996 that Congress cannot abrogate state sovereign immunity acting pursuant to its Article I powers) are prototypical examples of the Rehnquist Court's view that the Constitution places strict, although not textually based, limits on federal legislative power.

The architecture of the invisible Constitution that emerged from the Warren and Rehnquist Courts—however the processes of judicial deliberation proceeded, and whatever the historical dynamic may have been—assumed a perhaps surprisingly constant form, a form to be examined in some detail in the fifth and final part of this book. But even before developing the half-dozen models that readers will find set out in that part, it's worth noting that, while those models don't purport to explain how the Warren Court or the Rehnquist Court arrived at their conclusions, the models do aim to expose the framework and display the architecture of the rules both Courts formulated to describe their reasoning and its implications. Thus both the Warren Court in *Miranda* and the Rehnquist Court in *City of Boerne* saw themselves as creating prophylactic rules that gave "breathing room" to core constitutional principles. Similarly, each Court—Warren in *Katz* and Rehnquist in *Seminole Tribe*—looked deep underneath the Fourth and Eleventh Amendments to discover the underlying rationale for their respective inclusion in the written text. (Those who doubt that conservatives played a part in constructing the invisible Constitution should examine Chief Justice Rehnquist's *Seminole Tribe* opinion. In a quotation that originally appeared in another case, but could serve as a testament to the existence of the same mode of construction as that used in *Katz*, Rehnquist wrote, "we have understood the Eleventh Amendment to stand not so much for what it says but for the presupposition...which it confirms.") The Constitution that emerged from both periods had a thicker protective bubble of prophylactic rules and a stronger bond to the foundational principles that underlie the textual guarantees.

That the Constitution when interpreted by the Rehnquist Court had the same basic architecture as the Constitution when construed by the Warren Court illustrates the fact that the *shape* of the invisible Constitution has remained reasonably similar across different ideological eras. The invisible Constitution, it seems, is not the legal equivalent of Play-Doh, a formless body that can be molded in any way by whoever touches it. Instead, those who construct the invisible Constitution tend to their work within the fixed shapes that already exist.

That the invisible Constitution evolves in a recurring architectural pattern—even as its substance and meaning change—should not be surprising to those who have read the scholarship of political scientist Stephen Skowronek, whose book *The Politics Presidents Make* argues that two structural dimensions create four basic models of presidential leadership. The first dimension is whether the "previous established commitments" of the governing regime are vulnerable or resilient. The second dimension is whether the president is opposed to or affiliated with those established commitments.

Of course, any armchair historian could tell you that the presidencies of Abraham Lincoln, Franklin D. Roosevelt, and Ronald Reagan were quite different from one another, just as the decisions in *Miranda* and *City of Boerne* reflected very different political circumstances and judicial assumptions. But that we can find *structural* similarities between things that are *substantively* different tells us something very important about the phenomenon we are examining and trying to map.

PART III

Explorations beyond the Text

Invisibility Exemplified:
The Moving Finger Writes

TO PURSUE OUR EXPLORATION of the invisible Constitution, it helps to focus on how the Constitution's visible surface—its text— is formally amended only in a forward-moving manner that never backspaces to erase a word that went before. This simple fact provides what might be a rather surprising illustration of an important but invisible dimension of the Constitution: its "time's-arrow" rule of unidirectional construction.

This little-noted feature of how the Constitution is written over time—one that has been so long taken for granted as to escape scrutiny—exposes respects in which even what the Constitution's words expressly *say*, or at least appear to say, at any given time is not invariably binding. One dramatic example draws on the fact that the Constitution still contains in its opening article the odious phrase identifying each slave, although not named as such, as counting for just three-fifths of a person when seats in the House of Representatives are allocated among the states of the Union. Although the opening two sections of the Fourteenth Amendment, ratified in 1868, overrode the legal effect of that 1789 formula, it still remains visible today in Article I, right where it was from the beginning.

This observation rests on an important dimension of the Constitution's reality, one not described in the text. That dimension is the indelible quality of every word of that text, in stark contrast with the mutability of the text of the typical statute, which is ordinarily erased in whole or in part when amended or repealed. Our normal practice is to *add* text to the Constitution without addressing or touching earlier text that may be rendered inoperative or altered in its operation by what we have added. Thus, the Twelfth Amendment, which radically altered the method of selecting the president and vice president, said nothing about the portions of Article II's text that the Twelfth Amendment transparently superseded—under which the runner-up in the Electoral College automatically became vice president, as did Thomas Jefferson when his arch-rival John Adams became president in 1796.

Not even the very rare instances of formal repeal in our constitutional history, as with the Twenty-first Amendment's explicit repeal of section 1 of the Eighteenth Amendment (the Liquor Prohibition Amendment), result in the removal of the repealed language from newly minted versions of the Constitution that roll from the commercial presses on an ongoing basis, let alone the small number of original copies of the United States Constitution located in various federal depositories. I am reminded of the lines in Omar Khayyam's *Rubaiyat*: "The moving finger writes and, having writ, moves on. Nor all your piety nor wit shall lure it back to cancel half a line, nor all your tears wipe out a word of it."

The Twenty-first Amendment serves also to illustrate how elements of the invisible Constitution may assume an indelibility comparable to that of the text itself. Among the most important powers delegated to Congress by Article I of the Constitution is, of course, the power conferred by section 8, clause 3, *"To regulate Commerce with foreign Nations, and among the several States, and with the Indian Tribes."* That congressional power did not subtract from the states the authority to regulate commercial activity within their own borders, subject to the proviso that such regulation would be void (under the Supremacy Clause of Article VI) to the degree it actually conflicted with legislation validly enacted by Congress under its Commerce Clause power.

The Supreme Court under Chief Justice John Marshall recognized that even when state laws did not conflict directly with any act of Congress, such local power over intrastate or "internal" commerce could well be exercised in ways that would threaten the cohesion of the Union. This might happen, for example, if states were free to enact laws governing internal commerce that operated to erect what amounted to trade barriers against products or services from other states, or to discriminate against such products or services. The centrifugal force of such laws, and of the countermeasures they would likely invite from states whose businesses were adversely affected, might be more than Congress, where inertia was likely to prevail, could be counted on to handle. From this recognition emerged, over the course of roughly a century, something that came to be known as the "dormant commerce clause," by which the Supreme Court meant to identify what it took to be the negative implications, even when Congress was inactive or "dormant," of that national body's overarching responsibility for regulating interstate and foreign commerce: Congress, in which the people of all the states were represented, remains free to regulate commerce among the states in ways that Balkanized sectors of the economy in the interests of localism. And Congress may, if it chooses, adopt national blueprints for economic regulation in which states are in effect licensed to erect trade barriers or to engage in discrimination against their neighbors. But such state or local obstructions to the free flow of commerce are deemed to violate the "dormant commerce clause" in the absence of affirmative congressional authorization. Although some justices have from time to time challenged this (obviously invisible) "dormant commerce clause" as an illegitimate fiction of the judicial imagination, it had become a seemingly permanent feature of the constitutional landscape by the early years of the twentieth century and remains so today.

Enter the Twenty-first Amendment, which, in repealing the Eighteenth Amendment (the "Prohibition" Amendment) in 1933, gave states broad power to police the importation of liquor "for delivery or use…in violation of [their] laws." Did this replacement of a nationwide ban on liquor production and distribution with express authorization of state-by-state antiliquor measures displace the dormant commerce clause? The question was posed by state laws regulating the sale of wine from out-of-state wineries to in-state customers. The challenged laws permitted in-state wineries to sell wine directly to consumers in the states involved while prohibiting out-of-state wineries from doing so, or at least making direct sales economically infeasible for many wine producers outside the regulating states. By construing the "aim of the Twenty-first Amendment" quite narrowly—"to allow States to maintain an effective and uniform system for controlling liquor by regulating its transportation, importation, and use"—the Supreme Court in 2005, in *Granholm v. Heald*, concluded that the "Amendment did not give States the authority to pass nonuniform laws in order to discriminate against out-of-state goods, a privilege they had not enjoyed" prior to the amendment's passage, under the dormant commerce clause.

Rejecting precedents from the mid-1930s to the contrary, a closely divided Court in *Granholm* held that "the Twenty-first Amendment does not supersede other provisions of the Constitution and, in particular, does not displace the rule that States may not give a discriminatory preference to their own producers." The gist of the dissenting opinions by Justices Stevens and Thomas, together speaking for the four justices in dissent (Stevens was joined by Justice Sandra Day O'Connor, and Thomas by Chief Justice William H. Rehnquist, as well as Justices Stevens and O'Connor), was that the latter "rule" was no "provision" of the Constitution but was merely part of the "unwritten" Constitution that could surely be erased by an explicit "Amendment that the Nation ratified."

Justice Stevens, at the time the Court's most senior member, came close to pulling rank by doubting the ability of "those members of the younger generations who make policy decisions" to recall the attitudes that gave rise both to the Eighteenth Amendment's ratification in 1919 and to its repeal by the Twenty-first Amendment in 1933. His brief dissenting opinion urged "special deference" to the understanding and views "of judges who lived through the debates that led to the ratification of those Amendments," foremost among whom, he said, was Justice Louis D. Brandeis, the author of the 1936 decision that the majority in *Granholm* essentially overruled. Thus did Justice Stevens explain his vote to join what he called the "persuasive and comprehensive dissenting opinion" of Justice Thomas and to dissent from what he saw as the deviance by the majority in the opinion written for the Court by Justice Kennedy. Interesting and colorful as the warring views about liquor regulation were, more interesting still was the majority's insistence on a principle that in effect elevated the invisible Constitution to a status fully equal to that of the text that is visible to all.

The practice of leaving the Constitution—both in its visible manifestations and in its invisible dimensions—intact to the degree possible, even when new provisions might in theory be treated as erasing what had gone before, serves as an antidote to collective amnesia about national missteps. By preserving even unwritten and wholly implicit constitutional principles, so long as they have not been formally repudiated in an amendment's text, we sometimes give the constitutional vision of the past a status so privileged that only the most focused and manifestly deliberate national decisions to revise that vision can operate to usher in a new regime. And by keeping even textually superseded language (like that of the Eighteenth Amendment) intact and fully visible in each circulated copy of the official text, we undermine efforts to sanitize or otherwise rewrite our troubled history, as those in power throughout the world are wont to do with theirs.

Those two tendencies might be in some tension with one another, as in the liquor case, where retaining the force of the dormant commerce clause absent its express replacement supported the majority's decision to invalidate various state laws as impermissibly discriminatory, while retaining the memory of what had led to the Eighteenth Amendment along with its replacement, the Twenty-first, supported the dissent's insistence that the challenged state laws should have been upheld. However that tension might be resolved in various contexts, both of the facets of indelibility noted here are significant features of how the Constitution must be understood—no less so for themselves being unspecified in any portion of the visible text.

Cleo's Claims

WHAT WE HAVE JUST EXAMINED represents but two facets of something broader than either: the essentially universal recognition that, even though nothing in the Constitution's text says so, *all* of its text and structure must be understood with an eye to its unfolding history—to the history of events and attitudes that might help explain the ends Congress sought to achieve in proposing it to the states for ratification; to the history that surrounded the drafting process in Congress and the ratification process in the states that might help explain what those who voted for the final draft, and those who voted for ratification, thought they were approving (and what those who voted against that draft, or against ratification, thought they were opposing); and to the history of the text's early application and enforcement, as well of its interpretation by various institutions over the course of time—up through, and for many readers focusing on, the present. And, although the absence of anything in the text directing readers to consult this history certainly has not prevented "originalists" or "textualists" from making historical arguments whenever the text has been even arguably ambiguous (and sometimes even to counteract the effect of seemingly unambiguous text), it would be hard to find any school of thought about the interpretation of constitutional language or structure that would dismiss history's claims as simply beside the point.

Nobody could hope to read and apply faithfully any set of purposive rules—from the Constitution to a state statute to the rules for taking a college exam or the rules of a little league softball game—without knowing something about the history that preceded those rules and spurred their adoption, and maybe even the history of how (and by whom) those rules have been interpreted and enforced, including how and why they might have been changed in the time since their adoption.

A garden-variety example from a less exalted plane than constitutional interpretation should help make the point. Suppose a college has a rule that says "All debts must be paid in full by the student within a week prior to graduation day; if a debt is left unpaid, the student's graduation will be postponed to the next regular graduation date following full payment of any such debt." If we learn that this rule was promulgated when local bookstore owners and other vendors to students became angered at university administrators for handing out degrees to students who then left town with large unpaid debts for books and other supplies, that discovery should presumably bear negatively on how we assess a student's argument that the rule refers only to the student's debts to the school itself. If we then learn that the rule was adopted only after a *different* rule—one expressly referring to "debts *to the school or to local merchants*"—had been proposed but roundly rejected on the ground that this rule would be too difficult, or socially inappropriate, for the school to undertake to enforce, that information would no doubt give the argument a nudge in the student's favor.

If at this point school administrators point out that seamless Internet links between town and gown have developed in the time since the rule was initially adopted so that the original reasons for limiting it to debts owed to the school itself have evaporated, how much that will hurt the student's position will depend on whether we think rules of this sort always retain their "original meaning" as reflected in the authors' specific expectations or believe instead that such rules express more general principles or concepts that need to be adapted to changing circumstances if they are to remain faithful to their original purposes. Deciding what the relevant "history" here is, as well as discovering the facts pertinent to that history, will entail making fundamental choices about what fidelity in historical and purposive interpretation means, about what kind of rule we are dealing with, and about the appropriate frame of reference through which (and the appropriate level of generality at which) to understand the history bearing on that sort of rule. And for none of those choices should we expect much guidance from the text—from the visible Constitution.

That is certainly the case for the most famously contested inquiry into the purposes of a constitutional provision—the inquiry into just what the Equal Protection Clause of the Fourteenth Amendment was to mean with respect to various ways of taking race into account in making governmental decisions, either about individuals or about institutional arrangements. Among the current understandings of what that language meant, one that appears to be ascendant is the view expressed by Justice Scalia during the December 2006 oral argument of *Parents Involved in Community Schools v. Seattle School District,* decided by the Supreme Court in 2007. Addressing counsel for the respondent school district in midargument, Justice Scalia asked whether this "area of the law...doesn't have some absolute restrictions." Counsel for the school district noted in response that "There are many areas of the law, certainly in the First Amendment and the Fourth Amendment, that have considerable flexibility," whereupon Justice Scalia pounced with this retort: "What about the Fourteenth? I thought that was one of the *absolute restrictions*, that you cannot judge and classify people on the basis of their race. You can pursue the [integrationist] objectives that your school board is pursuing, but at some point you come against an absolute, and aren't you just denying that?" Counsel's effort to deny that the text or history of the Equal Protection Clause supported any such one-dimensional principle was, as the history of that case soon made clear, unavailing.

Less controversial (at least now) than the ahistorical effort to attribute to the Fourteenth Amendment an absolute bar against any consideration of race, however individualized and benign, and however integrationist the purpose, is the effort made in *Brown v. Board* itself to read in the Fourteenth Amendment at least a strong presumption against the government's use of race to segregate and subordinate a racial minority. Perhaps surprisingly, for those who have not immersed themselves in the relevant history, even that isn't a slam dunk. Although some enterprising scholars, including Judge Michael McConnell of the U.S. Court of Appeals for the Tenth Circuit, have sought to make the argument that the concrete expectation of those who wrote and ratified the Equal Protection Clause was that legally mandated public school segregation of the races would be deemed to violate the Fourteenth Amendment, I believe that the more persuasive argument has been made by those many scholars who reluctantly concede that this was not a widespread expectation—but who go on to argue, building on the work of the legal philosopher Ronald Dworkin, that the relevant inquiry is *not* what the original drafters and ratifiers of the Amendment imagined or even expected the concept they wrote into the Constitution would come to require, but *what concept they intended to enshrine* by the language they used, and *what that concept, rightly understood, had come to demand.* And if, as the great Charles Black argued so eloquently, the concept they intended to enshrine was that the subordination of one race by another through the force of law was to be forbidden, then that ideal entailed an end to the forced separation of African American students from white students in public schools once it became plain to us, as it perhaps had been less plain to our forebears, that the social meaning of such forced separation could *only* be the subordination of African American students on the basis that they were not "good enough" to mix with their white student counterparts.

Rightly understood, then, the Constitution comes packed with a thick, non-self-defining history, which follows it through time and which succeeding generations must of necessity unpack, doing so in light of what they have in the intervening years and decades come to understand about the concepts that the Constitution's history and structure, as well as its text, show it to have embodied. This is a dimension of the invisible Constitution that necessarily evolves over time, and in a direction that is crucially path-dependent and that cannot ever simply retrace its steps so as to erase what has gone before.

Sometimes, to be sure, a later addition simply repudiates its predecessor. But there are also important possibilities for extension or generalization, leading to retrospective reconsideration of earlier versions of the Constitution. A number of scholars have argued persuasively that the Nineteenth Amendment, prohibiting denials of the right to vote "on account of sex," and the Fifteenth Amendment, banning voting rights restrictions "on account of race, color, or previous condition of servitude," change our expectations when we read the Fourteenth Amendment. That amendment's entirely general guarantee of "the equal protection of the laws" itself discloses no particular substantive concerns, no sense of the concrete problems the constitutional language might especially aptly address. An amendment drafted in 1866 and ratified in 1868 refashioning states as constitutional actors following the Civil War was surely shaped in important part by the circumstances of former slaves caught in the maelstrom of Reconstruction terror. But did the constitutional response extend past guarantees of core legal protections to encompass entitlements to political participation? Section 2 of the Fourteenth Amendment addresses this matter in so painfully oblique a manner that the question is more raised than answered.

But the Fifteenth and Nineteenth Amendments, and later the Twenty-fourth and Twenty-sixth (enfranchising first African Americans and then women, and later banning poll taxes and protecting rights to vote from the age of 18 upward), make clear that voting is itself constitutionally "core" in what the Constitution had become by 1964 or at the very latest 1971, if not by 1920. And the conjunction of the Fifteenth and Nineteenth Amendments confirms that not only is race—more precisely, the legal consequences of American racial consciousness—a constitutional problem but also gender: the legal consequences of American assumptions about the relationships of men and women. Constitutional law, we all know, has proceeded accordingly—as evidenced in both judicial understandings and popular expectations.

The "relation back" of the Fifteenth and Nineteenth Amendments—the effect of these amendments on our understanding of the Fourteenth Amendment—is not something either automatic or magical. It reflects, rather, a new sequence of questions put to the Constitution's reader, invisible within the wording of any one of the three constitutional amendments, but plainly evident once the amendments are read together. "Equal protection of the laws" thus references particular concerns about legal instruments or actions that incorporate American assumptions about race and gender. Are those concerns in some sense similar—or are they just two items on a list?

If race and gender pose problems that are at least partly of a piece, are race and gender unique in this regard? We have come to understand that, often at least, the troubling ways law borrows our culture's presuppositions about race and gender have important things in common—although there are also important differences. The Supreme Court treats both racial and gender classifications as triggering some version of "heightened scrutiny," although proceeding somewhat differently in each context. Especially outside the courts, people debate the ways in which concerns about legal uses of race and gender should likewise mark as constitutionally troubling other legal appropriations of social, cultural, or supposedly "natural" categories. These discussions are especially intense at present with regard to the law's uses of sexual orientation and of appearance and apparel. Thus, we appear to be in the midst once more of the recurring debate, plainly fraught with racial and other overtones, about the proper height of the waistline for pants worn by teenage boys—too low now, too high in the ethnically charged "zoot suit" controversy of several generations ago.

Constitutional history, however, is not hermetic. Reactions to events, large and small, also work to reorient constitutional readers, revealing new problems or opportunities. We all know, obviously, that the Civil War—the enormity of the undertaking, the horror of its huge casualties on both sides—recast constitutional assumptions. Slavery, it came to be understood, must be abolished, not simply contained. Fundamental assumptions had to be rethought and the Constitution therefore changed. Lincoln's Gettysburg Address, his Second Inaugural Address, and the Thirteenth Amendment followed.

The Great Depression—cataclysmic in different ways—also left its mark on constitutional understandings. And there have been many other thought-churning events. The great civil rights marches, beginning with the Montgomery Boycott and culminating in the

March on Washington—with Martin Luther King Jr. functioning as Lincoln's analog—inaugurated an era in which increasingly robust modes of dissent, demonstration, and discourse came to the fore as broadly accepted forms of free speech, assembly, and petition—both in judicial proceedings and in popular understanding.

More examples, of course, could be listed. There is always—in our reading of the Constitution—a complicated back and forth. Sometimes the progression of provisions—the Constitution's own internal history—initiates analysis; sometimes, we know, events exterior to the succession of constitutional texts reinforce or redirect our attention as readers. All of this is as much a part of what the Constitution tells us as the text itself. It is invisible—but, once recognized, unavoidably evident.

Reflect again on how the Constitution's latest textual layers, even when they do not expressly refer to those that came before, are sometimes understood as operating implicitly to modify the meaning even of explicit and formally unamended patches of text—patches that remain to be read in the document as though unaffected by what was in due time to follow. Such exercises in what amounts to a version of time travel—back to the future—highlight the respect in which the Constitution resembles not just an archeological dig but also the night sky. Justice Jackson once wrote of the "fixed star[s] in our constitutional constellation." His metaphor seems singularly apt—although for a reason he might not have had in mind. The points of light that punctuate the night sky, like the discrete provisions of the Constitution's text, form patterns that speak to poets and philosophers more perhaps than they do to physicists or astronomers. The task of connecting the dots inevitably calls for human insight and imagination. It is of necessity far more than a scientific exercise.

If you've ever been lucky enough to gaze star-ward from a place like rural Montana on a clear night, then you have seen not only nearby planets and stars but also distant galaxies whose light left on the trip from unimaginably far away to your own eyes in some instances tens or hundreds of millions of years ago. The single tapestry of star-glittered sky that we witness as we look out at the universe thus represents not one simultaneous reality but a large number of different realities, each accessible to us only across great chasms of space and from its own locus in time, but all reaching us at the same moment to populate the space-time composition that is the night sky.

This character of what we observe as an intertemporal collage connects the night sky with the Constitution. For the Constitution, too, is composed of elements drawn from, and reflecting the concerns of, strikingly different eras in our history. Like the sky we see at night, it retains as though still vital and unchanged any number of features that might—like supernovae that have collapsed into invisible black holes long before their light reaches our eyes—have long since been erased or transformed. Readers of the Constitution must project patterns onto its provisions and make rulings in the name of invisible structures—structures that conservatives and liberals alike can only describe as the "tacit postulates" of the constitutional plan.

Doubling Back: The Holistic
Reading Rule

THE DISCUSSION OF THE three-fifths formula set out in the section before the last illustrates an invisible proposition *about* constitutional law more than it suggests an invisible proposition *of* constitutional law. That is, it tells us something important about how we are to proceed in *reading* what the Constitution's text says—but it *doesn't* display a substantive command or constraint that, although unwritten, itself operates in the same way that a textually explicit constitutional provision would. Nonetheless, the way the three-fifths formula evaporates without ever being expressly repealed illustrates the operation of an important, albeit unwritten, principle in understanding the Constitution's meaning. Beyond that, it illustrates a circumstance in which the Constitution *no longer means what its text seems to say*. Treating the text in a holistic way, the evaporation of the three-fifths formula and of the way it insulted slaves and their descendants symbolically while rewarding the slave masters politically exemplifies an application of the unwritten rule that, although time's arrow moves in but one direction, later-enacted provisions supersede earlier ones to the degree they are logically irreconcilable.

For another application of the same unwritten rule, consider the effect of the First Amendment's Freedom of Speech and Press Clauses on the provision of Article I, section 8, clause 8, empowering Congress "*To promote the Progress of Science and useful Arts, by securing for limited Times to Authors and Inventors the exclusive Right to their respective Writings and Discoveries.*" While conferring exclusive copyright or patent privileges on authors and inventors operates to some degree to encourage some actors to write and/or invent, such grants of exclusive rights necessarily serve also to prevent would-be authors and inventors from borrowing protected expressions and ideas in attempts to fashion their own creativity and expression. Should the First Amendment be understood to displace or qualify the power affirmatively conferred on Congress by the Patent and Copyright Clause, notwithstanding the absence of any reference to that clause in the First Amendment? To what degree is a presumption against implied constitutional repeal or restriction operative to limit the effect of the latter on the former? To what degree, on the other hand, should a priority for later over earlier provisions be presumed? A priority for limit-setting provisions over power-granting provisions? A priority for the specific over the general? Some other rule or principle of reconciliation or harmonization?

My interest here is not in offering answers to these clearly "constitutional" questions but in making clear the need to ask them. My aim is to underscore that while the text of the written Constitution alone cannot provide the answers, they must be drawn from a body of law and thought having an unavoidably "constitutional" character.

Consider also the Fourteenth Amendment's express provision for penalizing any state that denies "the right to vote" to "any of the male inhabitants of such State, being twenty-one years of age, and citizens of the United States." That language, dating to 1868, has been neither repealed nor amended, much less erased. But after the Nineteenth Amendment in 1920 prohibited the abridgment "on account of sex" of the "right of citizens of the United States to vote"—and after the Twenty-sixth Amendment in 1971 prohibited the abridgment "on account of age" of the "right of citizens of the United States, who are eighteen years of age or older, to vote"— wouldn't it seem wrong to continue to read the 1868 language as though it still penalizes states only for the disenfranchisement of *21-year-old males* rather than for the disenfranchisement of *18-year old males or females*?

If one were to answer that question in the affirmative, then section 2 of the Fourteenth Amendment would mean something that its visible text appears to deny. If, on the other hand, we were to read the penalty section of the Fourteenth Amendment in a way that makes it cohere with the Nineteenth and Twenty-sixth Amendments, we would have *added* a penalty never duly enacted by "We, the People of the United States." Moreover, it is by no means clear that constitutional authority to add that penalty belongs to whichever branch of the national government—presumably either Congress or the judiciary—would purport to exercise the power to do so.

One could argue at some length about this particular structure or rule. But it is not among this book's purposes to decide whether the partial disenfranchisement of the state in my hypothetical example is indeed required by the Constitution rightly understood—or to debate the question of which branch of government is empowered to provide a definitive answer. The real point is that the proposed use of the Nineteenth and Twenty-sixth Amendments to modify the meaning of the Fourteenth would in fact represent consider-ably more than the erasure of one qualifier—"male"—and the recalibration of another—replacing "twenty-one years of age" with "eighteen years of age." It would, in truth, represent the creation (or, on another view of the matter, the recognition) of *a constitutional structure nowhere to be found in the Constitution's text*. If it were indeed a structure we believe the Constitution is best understood to have put in place, then it would be part of what I have called the "invisible Constitution."

Two Types of Extratextual Norms

AT THIS POINT it is crucial to emphasize that either accepting or refusing to recognize such a penalty requires reliance on notions nowhere to be found in—and not reasonably derived from—the visible text of the Constitution. For the interpretive principle under which one would hold the penalty to be triggered—doubling back to harmonize earlier portions of the text with later additions—is not present in or implied by the Constitution's text. But the principle underlying the opposite conclusion—that no penalty would be triggered in such circumstances—would likewise have to be located outside the text. *Either* of the underlying constitutional metaprinciples—rules for how the Constitution's text is to be read—must be discovered outside the text itself. And in fact, as I'll argue further below, while there is nothing incoherent in the idea of a constitutional text that itself contains a number of particular interpretive rules, a written Constitution containing a *complete* list of rules for its own interpretation is a logical impossibility.

What is most notable about the disenfranchisement penalty problem is not just how any way of answering it requires an appeal to extratextual *interpretive principles*, but how any answer ends up generating extratextual *substantive rules*. These are the two types of extratextual norms to which this section's title refers. The idea that the invisible Constitution in fact embodies certain *substantive* principles central to defining both the structure of government and the rights of persons—and that those norms are parts of the Constitution *actually in force* rather than of some merely *possible* Constitution—is likely to be among the most controversial of the propositions put forth in this book.

Interestingly, however, this proposition will seem more controversial to constitutional specialists than to ordinary educated citizens. Many well-informed nonspecialists wouldn't be phased by the idea that there is an invisible Constitution whose contents are no less part of our supreme law than are the rights and rules visibly enumerated in the Constitution's text. Plenty of well-informed folks, after all, are at least generally familiar with the fact that the very *text* of the Constitution points proudly to the existence of constitutional protections for rights nowhere spelled out in that text. Anyone who has ever read the text would have encountered the Ninth Amendment: *"The enumeration in the Constitution, of certain rights, shall not be construed to deny or disparage others retained by the people."*

And any reader of the text would have encountered as well the words of the Tenth Amendment: *"The powers not delegated to the United States by the Constitution, nor prohibited by it to the States, are reserved to the States respectively, or to the people."* Taken together, those twin textual provisions would seem to ordinary readers to imply that states and individuals alike are repositories of rights not to be located anywhere in the Constitution's text. And that pair of provisions would lead ordinary readers to the conclusion that our invisible Constitution can contain *neither* any substantive delegations of power to the national government, nor any substantive subtractions of rights from individuals, that are not to be found in or reasonably derivable from textual provisions contained in the visible Constitution.

It is mostly the constitutional specialist who would be inclined to discount that conclusion, pointing to the decades—indeed, centuries—during which the Ninth and Tenth Amendments were dismissed as mere tautologies or, as one Supreme Court nominee famously said of the former amendment if not of the latter, as mere "inkblots." But students of the Constitution who are unencumbered by the cynicism of expertise would properly resist marginalizing the text of those two crucial amendments. Whether one takes one's cues from the Ninth and Tenth Amendments as textual proof of an extratextual Constitution or instead treats those provisions as inconclusive and looks to other sources of constitutional wisdom, one would be hard pressed to defend a wholly text-based Constitution. The next few sections set forth a variety of examples designed to underscore how much of what virtually all of us take for granted— and rightly so—as features of our Constitution would evaporate if we were to treat the invisible Constitution as unreal. One way of seeing the strikingly limited reach of the Constitution's visible text, in comparison with the Constitution as a whole, is to realize that even if the text contained no Ninth or Tenth Amendments, we would have little choice but to act as though something equivalent were there. That the consequences of a purely textual Constitution would be unthinkable, some might say, hardly proves that the invisible Constitution is more than wishful thinking. Perhaps so; it depends to a great degree on what counts as "proof" in this realm. But without venturing too far into the domain of epistemology, those who have become convinced of the invisible Constitution's reality can at least take considerable solace from how much of what all of us *think* we know would dissolve if that Constitution were unreal after all. And it remains the case that the written Constitution does indeed contain the Ninth and Tenth Amendments.

Beyond that, as we shall see, the idea of a self-contained body of fundamental law, and certainly of a Constitution whose text is complete in itself, is a grand illusion. But first we will consider several examples designed to highlight the necessity of positing relatively concrete elements of the Constitution beyond its text—elements more in the nature of constitutional "provisions" than of meta-constitutional "rules of construction" of the sort we have already encountered both in the unidirectional rule and in the holistic reading rule.

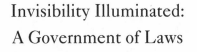

Invisibility Illuminated:
A Government of Laws

LET'S IMAGINE A CITY ordinance making it a crime for someone to purchase or rent a house or apartment in the city, or to stay overnight as an owner's or renter's guest in such a house or apartment, without first obtaining the written approval of at least two-thirds of those living within 500 feet. Whether viewed from the perspective of the outsider looking in or of the person who wishes to sell or rent to an outsider or to invite someone to spend the night, any such rule effectively makes an important part of every person's liberty hostage to the whims and prejudices of all who happen to live nearby. Let's assume that any resulting deprivation of any person's sale, purchase, rental, or sleepover opportunities—seemingly, forms of "liberty" and/or "property"—followed from a flawless process, and that the same was true of any penalty that might be imposed for violation of the ordinance. On those assumptions, in no *procedural* sense would "due process of law," as demanded by the Fourteenth Amendment to the Constitution, have been violated. Nor would any *substantive* facet of personal liberty particularly singled out by the Bill of Rights (or by any other specific constitutional provision), such as freedom of speech or the free exercise of religion, have been sacrificed. After all, the restricted, excluded, or penalized person will not have been prevented from, or punished for, doing anything defined in terms of any speech, religious exercise, or other distinctly protected activity in which that person might have engaged.

What, then, would lead most of us to agree that the hypothesized ordinance would be unconstitutional? One answer, I believe, is that such a law would violate the underlying principle that ours is a "government of laws, not men." But where is that principle to be located in our constitutional canon?

In the Supreme Court's landmark 1958 ruling in *Cooper v. Aaron*, leaving no doubt that it meant to enforce the holding of *Brown v. Board of Education* even against recalcitrant state governors who had not been parties to the *Brown* litigation, Justice Felix Frankfurter wrote: "From their own experience and their deep reading in history, the Founders knew that Law alone saves a society from being rent by internecine strife or ruled by mere brute power however disguised." Justice Frankfurter then quoted from Roscoe Pound's article "The Future of Law": "Civilization involves subjection of force to reason, and the agency of this subjection is law." But it was the text of the Massachusetts Constitution of 1780, as drafted by John Adams, and not the text of the U.S. Constitution, that made the principle explicit, explaining that the separation of legislative, executive, and judicial powers in the Commonwealth of Massachusetts, and the use of each pair of powers to check the third, was meant "to the end it may be a government of laws and not of men," a phrase echoed famously in John Marshall's great opinion in *Marbury v. Madison* nearly a quarter century later.

To make one person's liberty depend entirely on another person's whim—or, as in this instance, on the collective privately held wishes of everyone who happens to live within a circle of specified radius around the place where someone wants to spend the night as another's guest or to purchase or rent a dwelling from a willing seller or landlord—obviously violates that principle. If the vote of exclusion were viewed as a form of local legislation, then it would seem to offend the ban of Article I, section 10, against any state's passage of "any Bill of Attainder." But in fact, the vote could not plausibly be so viewed, for the ordinance operates not by constituting those who live within the specified radius as a political subdivision or a polity, in which the occupants are expected to express their policy preferences in their capacities as citizen-voters, but by inviting those who live there to act as members of something akin to a mob in simply blackballing the would-be newcomer or guest. Thus the exclusion of an individual for failure to obtain the requisite super-majority vote of those living in the area would be pursuant to power but not to law. The proposition that ours is a government of laws, not men—that we live under the "rule of law"—is, to be sure, not terribly specific, but it is telling in its frequent invocation both by courts and by ordinary citizens in describing something both readily understandable and absolutely fundamental about our political system. It is a principle that, by just about any imaginable account, would have to be reckoned *part of our Constitution*.

Invisibility Elaborated:
Government of the People,
by the People, for the People

THINKING ABOUT WHAT'S WRONG with the hypothetical law discussed in the previous section reveals yet another invisible constitutional principle at work. As originally posed, recall that our imaginary law would have made an individual's liberty and access to property depend entirely on the whims of *private individuals*, legally and politically accountable to no one but themselves. But even if those private individuals were to be defined by the ordinance as "special city deputies" and the vote of exclusion were to be designated a species of "spot zoning," the decisions of those wishing to exclude an individual would not be checked by anything resembling a democratic process, whether direct or representative. No such process would regulate their exercise of discretion or impose on them any duty to explain that exercise. There would be nothing to prevent the would-be owner, renter, or guest from being blackballed on an entirely arbitrary and unpredictable basis, not to mention the risk that it would be imposed on an invidious basis such as race, religion, political ideology, or some other criterion constitutionally forbidden to actors representing the government.

A premise of our system is that good will, altruism, and empathy are insufficient safeguards against such arbitrariness and oppression—whether suffered at the hands of purely private individuals, of specially deputized individuals or groups, or of a genuinely public official. When our statesmen have invoked "the better angels of our nature," they have done so in order to inspire popular attitudes and aspirations, but without lulling themselves into the Panglossian belief that our institutions might safely operate on the premise that those better angels would remain ascendant. To safeguard individuals and groups against the abuse of power, our system depends on structures that make all those whom we entrust with power vulnerable to *losing* that power at the hands of those over whom they wield it. "No taxation without representation," after all, was one of the most bitter battle cries of our Revolution, a central complaint catalogued in our Declaration of Independence.

"Government of the people, by the people, for the people" carried that theme into our founding documents when Abraham Lincoln appealed to such government in the Gettysburg Address. But nearly half a century before that canonical address, a far more mundane precursor of the same theme was centrally expressed in one of the greatest and most enduring rulings of the Supreme Court presided over by Chief Justice John Marshall. In 1819, the Court reviewed the validity of a special tax enacted by the legislature of Maryland, levied directly on notes of the Bank of the United States. To be sure, this was a case about a mere tax on banknotes, not to be equated with the extraordinary, horrific events so indelibly marked by Lincoln's great speech on the battlefield at Gettysburg. But sometimes the quotidian marks the profound as deeply as does the apocalyptic. As the Marshall Court held in the landmark case of *McCulloch v. Maryland*, the tax's fundamental infirmity was that it imposed a special financial burden on a group of citizens—those who lived in the United States but outside of

Maryland—who lacked the political power to sanction (by denying reelection) the lawmakers doing the burdening.

The Court's famous conclusion was that only Congress, in which citizens of the entire nation were represented, could impose, or authorize imposition of, such a nationwide tax burden. Nor would judicial invalidation of the Maryland bank tax take from the State of Maryland any power it possessed before entering the Union, for the power to tax the instruments and instrumentalities of the Union arose only from the Constitution that gave birth to the United States of America. The Maryland tax was therefore unconstitutional, not because it violated any express textual command of the Constitution but for a more fundamental reason that underlay the Constitution as a whole.

Less obviously, perhaps, but no less surely, than Maryland's decision to raise revenues from those whom its government did not represent and to whom its government did not have to account, the decisions of the property owners living within the charmed 500-foot circle to secure their own well-being by restricting the liberty of their neighbor to sell or rent to the unwanted person, or to invite that person to spend the night—as well as their decisions to restrict that person's liberty—would be unchecked by anyone to whom the owners wielding the veto had to answer or owed their unearned power. Nor would judicial invalidation of the ordinance purporting to entrust the owners with such unchecked authority take from them any power they possessed independent of the city's extraordinary legal provision. Surely there was no "state of nature" in which the owners possessed a power to invoke the machinery of the state to preserve the exclusivity of their small circle.

Like *McCulloch v. Maryland*, and in a manner reminiscent even of the Gettysburg Address, our hypothetical case would undoubtedly be governed by a defining principle drawn from the invisible Constitution: the principle that ours is a "government of the people, by the people, for the people." Even when the structure of federalism and the realities of federal-state relations are not implicated, as they were in *McCulloch v. Maryland*, and even when the core principles of freedom, slavery, and the Union are not at stake, as they were at Gettysburg, the proposition that ours is a government that derives its legitimacy both from its character *as* a "government" and not simply as a mass of individuals, and from the "consent" of the governed, remains a vibrant constraint on all of law and on all the powers that law delegates to individuals and groups.

The scare quotes around the word "consent" are required because, of course, few (if any) of us have meaningfully consented to most of the exercises of power that this principle purports to sanctify. In some contexts, that qualification becomes crucial and cannot be relegated to the margins of analysis. But for the most basic purposes, the idea is deeply rooted that the results of popular voting, mediated by the reasoned processes of law, enjoy a constitutional legitimacy that is absent when the results are decreed by the unreasoned fiat of individuals or groups chosen by, and answerable to, no one but themselves.

Why? Where does the constitutional status of that simple idea come from? There are a few textual points reflecting it, but examining them merely confirms that the broad principle at issue here cannot be extracted from the text alone but must instead be interpolated from features of the Constitution that remain invisible.

Consider the Constitution's statement that government may not deprive "any person of life, liberty, or property, without due process of law." That rule is applicable to the federal government by virtue of the Fifth Amendment and to the states by virtue of the Fourteenth Amendment. In my hypothetical example, it was a duly enacted "law" that delegated to private individuals, each acting in his or her own interest, the power ultimately wielded against the property and liberty of others. Might it nonetheless be said that the resulting arrangement failed to accord "*due process* of law" because the individuals it empowered were neither politically nor legally accountable to anyone for the way they chose to exercise the power over liberty and property with which they were entrusted? True, the same might be said of jurors in the typical civil or criminal case, but at least in the case of jurors, there is an appointed or elected judge who instructs them on the legal rules they are to apply to the evidence that they are directed to consider, controls the introduction of such evidence in accord with a body of legal rules, and exercises control over the jury's deliberations and its verdict by preventing the entry of any judgment that no reasonable person could reach on the basis of the evidence lawfully admitted, as viewed through the prism of the applicable legal rules and as weighed under the applicable standards of proof. No remotely similar apparatus constrains the exercise of power by the individuals in my imaginary scheme. But where does the Constitution tell us that either the notion of "law" or the concept of "due process" precludes the unconstrained placement of power in private hands, where the repositories of the power thereby entrusted meet whatever qualifications the law imposes? After all, those who are eligible to cast a ballot in the next presidential or congressional election wield considerable, and potentially momentous, power over the lives, liberty, and property of us all—even if less directly and visibly than in the case I have hypothesized.

Maybe the answer lies not in shoehorning into the phrase "due process of law" a complex rule about how power over others is to be organized but in looking elsewhere in the Constitution's language. One might, in particular, point to the Constitution's demand in Article IV, section 4, that the "*United States shall guarantee to every State...a Republican Form of Government.*" A reader would not need too much imagination to construe that guarantee as embodying a rule forbidding the open-ended delegation of direct governmental authority over others' lives to private individuals neither elected by the people nor appointed by anyone so elected. But linguistic moves of that sort could be criticized as results-driven and ultimately question begging. While there is undoubtedly a commitment to a "Republican Form" of government in the text of the Constitution, the central meaning of that commitment has proved extraordinarily elusive. John Adams, for one, admitted that he "never understood" this clause; he went so far as to suggest that no one ever did or will. Even setting aside disputes over the precise content of the provision, it would be very hard to say that this clause embodies some unique vision of popular sovereignty and representative government held by the Constitution's authors or ratifiers—a vision in which the people would exercise control over their rulers and would subject themselves to the sense not of a single publicly unaccountable individual or group of individuals but to that of "the People" as a whole.

Far and away the most candid explanation of why the posited law—which would itself, after all, presumably have been promulgated at the municipal level by a duly elected or appointed body—would offend the Constitution is that it would violate a principle nowhere written into the text or implied by it but nonetheless central to its being: the principle of democratic accountability. The importance of having a government that derives its powers not from a divine or otherwise external source of law but, in some complex yet still meaningful sense, from the consent of those to be governed has been taken for granted as a starting point throughout the nation's history.

During the debates at the Constitutional Convention of 1787, as well as the debates over the Constitution's ratification in the states between that time and 1789, those who supported the proposed Constitution had to demonstrate that the document paid sufficient heed to the revolutionary generation's demand for representative government, at least in the sense that, in dealing with others as governed, we are obliged to see them also as governors, so that no individual could properly "govern" another without a public reason in principle applicable if the circumstances were reversed—a kind of "golden rule" that embodies a principle of equal respect. And while concerns about a tyrannical Crown might now seem passé, this bedrock postulate has continued to inform interpretation of the Constitution. Indeed, the principal Supreme Court rulings that resurrected the postulates of federalism between 1990 and the early 2000s relied in no small part on the way various challenged arrangements—especially those in which the central government in Washington "commandeered" state government—obfuscated lines of authority in ways the Court's majority believed would frustrate political accountability and mutuality of respect.

Invisibility Further Illustrated:
Suspending Habeas Corpus

USING LEGALITY AND DEMOCRATIC accountability to constrain power assumes that someone other than the power holder is in position to examine its use. To make the point most clearly, imagine yet another example. Suppose the president issues an executive order proclaiming that "the United States has been subject, since the terrorist attacks of September 11, 2001, to a war against American civilians by international terrorists" and that this war constitutes an ongoing invasion of American territory in which the public safety requires the "indefinite detention," at places outside the United States but subject to U.S. jurisdiction and control, of "any person, whether or not an American citizen, whom the President designates, on the basis of whatever information he deems sufficient, as an unlawful enemy combatant who either is engaged in international terrorism against the United States or is in possession of knowledge bearing on the details of one or more terrorist plots to murder American civilians" and authorizing the "interrogation of any such detained individual, by whatever persons and using whatever methods the

President deems necessary and appropriate, not in order to punish the detained individual but solely to extract whatever knowledge that individual might possess, for the limited purpose of preventing the successful execution of any such terrorist plots."

The executive order specifies that "neither the knowledge thereby extracted, nor anything learned with the assistance of that knowledge, may be used as evidence in any criminal prosecution of the individual from whom the knowledge is extracted pursuant to this order, to the degree that the method of extraction entailed coercively overbearing the detainee's will."

Finally, the executive order states that

> no state or federal court shall have jurisdiction to entertain a writ of habeas corpus or to conduct any other judicial proceeding the purpose of which is to review the legality of such an individual's detention, or of that individual's interrogation or other treatment, nor shall any court have jurisdiction to grant any form of relief to any such individual in order to prevent, to terminate, to alter the conditions surrounding, or to provide any remedy in respect of, any detention or interrogation carried out pursuant to this order, inasmuch as the sole remedy available to any such individual is to be the review on appeal of any judgment of conviction or sentence resulting directly or indirectly from such detention.

Some readers will recognize that, in its essence, the exercise of power contemplated by this order was that authorized by Congress in the Military Commissions Act of 2006. In the hypothetical example, however, Congress is assumed to have enacted no such provision; the imagined order, much like orders President George W. Bush is widely believed to have issued prior to the enactment of the 2006 Act, represents a freestanding exercise of executive power, rather than an exercise of power delegated to the president by Congress. What difference, as a constitutional matter, does the presence or absence of congressional authorization make? Article I of the Constitution, in section 9, clause 2, states: *"The privilege of the Writ of Habeas Corpus shall not be suspended, unless when in Cases of Rebellion or Invasion the public Safety may require it."* Nothing in the text specifies who is to determine whether the nation is suffering a case of "Rebellion or Invasion" in which "the public Safety may require" suspending the writ of habeas corpus, the time-honored device by which the judicial branch examines the legality of an individual's executive detention and of the way that individual is being treated. Nor does anything in the Constitution's text specify which branch of government may, based on such a determination, "suspend" the privilege of the Great Writ.

Many, including the justices of the Civil War–era Supreme Court, have argued that the very placement of the Suspension Clause in Article I of the Constitution, which is generally concerned with "all legislative Powers" granted by the Constitution and thereby "vested in…Congress," automatically means that *only* Congress may exercise, or authorize the exercise of, the power to "suspend" the availability of habeas corpus. But that conclusion hardly follows either as a linguistic or as a logical matter. Indeed, Article I, section 8, clause 10, says that "Congress shall have Power…To…punish Piracies and Felonies committed on the high Seas, and Offenses against the Law of Nations," but that language has not been thought to deprive the president as chief executive from carrying out lawful punishments for such piracies, felonies, and other offenses. And Article I, section 8, clause 14, says that "Congress shall have Power…To make Rules for the Government and Regulation of the land and naval Forces," but that language has not been thought to prevent the president as "Commander in Chief of the Army and Navy of the United States," under Article II, section 2, clause 1, from promulgating such military rules. If, as nearly everyone seems to agree, it is the case that habeas corpus may be suspended only by, or pursuant to, an act of Congress, then the reason is not the words or arrangement of the Constitution's text but a principle more properly located in the invisible Constitution.

Moreover, even if we modify the hypothetical example by introducing a suitable act of Congress—say, the Military Commissions Act of 2006—so that the president is no longer acting solely under his own steam, the Constitution would become a largely hollow set of promises if we accepted the notion that the president, armed with congressional permission, could at any time (or for all time) proclaim the United States to be subject to an ongoing "Invasion" in which "the public Safety" requires the elimination of all judicial scrutiny, through the writ of habeas corpus or otherwise, of the circumstances and conditions leading to the detention of anyone the president or his underlings designated, in effect, a terrorist enemy of the United States (or, perhaps, an innocent person who happens to possess important information about what the terrorists are planning).

The availability of judicial review to test the constitutional validity of any ensuing conviction or sentence imposed on a detainee seems immaterial to the law-free zone within which anyone could be plunged by the hypothesized executive order, whether with or without congressional authorization. After all, a principal complaint of most of those caught up in such a scheme of preventive or inquisitorial detention would likely be that no charges have been lodged against them, and that no trial from which either an acquittal, or a reviewable conviction and sentence, might emerge is on the horizon. Yet one could point to nothing in the Constitution's text—beyond the inconclusive language of the Due Process Clause—supporting the conclusion that the Constitution can abide no such black hole in legal space. One would have to resort yet again to an axiom of the invisible Constitution to sustain that proposition.

What, finally, of the use of "whatever methods" of interrogation the president deems "necessary and appropriate, in order not to punish the detained individual but solely to extract whatever knowledge that individual might possess" to assist in preventing the slaughter of innocent Americans? The Constitution's Eighth Amendment states: *"Excessive bail shall not be required, nor excessive fines imposed, nor cruel and unusual punishments inflicted."* Were we to grant that retribution could suffice, all by itself, to justify ratcheting up the level of pain or suffering that may be inflicted on an adjudicated wrongdoer, there would be no limit to how horrible a regime of pain we might permissibly choose to inflict. To avoid going down that terrible road, we must refuse to take this exit altogether. And to grant this much is to conclude that the deliberate infliction of added pain or suffering in the process of putting a prisoner to death, for the sole purpose of punishing that prisoner more severely, would violate the Eighth Amendment's prohibition.

That proposition was recently tested in the Supreme Court in the context of lethal injection protocols for capital punishment that arguably inflict gratuitous pain and paralyze the prisoner so that neither movement nor screams of pain are possible. But even if we were to conclude that inflicting physical pain or mental agony for its own sake is constitutionally proscribed, nothing would follow for the kind of torture contemplated by the hypothesized executive order. For by hypothesis the purpose of the harsh methods of interrogation authorized by that order, with or without congressional permission, is not to impose more severe punishment on one who has *committed* a great wrong but, rather, "to extract...knowledge" from the detainee—even perhaps a detainee innocent of any wrongdoing for which "punishment" would be in order—so as to *prevent others from committing* such a wrong and thereby to protect innocent lives.

Many informed students of this gruesome subject are convinced that information extracted through torture—that is, through levels of pain, suffering, or fear that the subject predictably will be unable to endure for long—is invariably too unreliable to use. If this were true, it would render the policy underlying the executive order unwise. But stupidity in itself is not unconstitutional. Moreover, this logic works only when an admission of guilt is being extracted—which is the reason that torture-extracted "confessions" have long been deemed inherently unreliable. But in the context of *prevention* rather than *punishment*, the torturer's objective is not to obtain the detainee's agreement to an accusation of guilt that the torturer already believes to be true or in any event knows is what he wants to hear, but to learn from the detainee something the torturer manifestly does not yet know. So, for example, information extracted by torture pointing to the location of a weapon of mass destruction or to a code enabling officers to disarm such a weapon might have obvious utility, especially if the detainee recognizes that providing information that proves useless would simply lead to still worse torture.

Thus, if governmental use of torture (surely including techniques, like simulated drowning, that put the detainee in protracted fear of impending death and cause extreme suffering even if they inflict no permanent injury and perhaps even no acute pain as such) is categorically forbidden by the Constitution, then that prohibition must rest on considerations other than the claim that torture is invariably useless. Nor does the Fifth Amendment's ban on compelled self-incrimination apply to forbid the use of torture if the extracted information is employed solely to prevent future terrorist attacks. It follows that, if the very use of torture to extract information violates the Constitution—as those who see a policy condoning such torture as an affront to everything America stands for believe it does—it is the invisible Constitution and not anything in the text that it violates.

Federalism—and "the Right of the People to Keep and Bear Arms"

IT SHOULD GO WITHOUT SAYING that liberals aren't the only ones who would suffer buyer's remorse were we to accept a text-only Constitution as our lot. Consider an act of Congress—the "Above-Average Gun Violence Act"—that requires any city in the United States with a higher-than-average annual per capita rate of violent crime involving the use of firearms to enact, within one month of the Justice Department's release of the relevant annual figures, a gun control law (i.e., a law regulating the purchase, sale, and possession of firearms) that has been submitted to, and approved by, the attorney general, who in turn is directed to approve no gun control law that is not "at least as strict as that of the city or county in the United States with the lowest annual per capita rate of violent crime involving the use of firearms." Would such a congressional enactment be constitutional? Can the question be answered by looking at the imaginary statute on its face, or would the answer depend on whether the statute was being applied to a city other than the nation's capital, the District of Columbia?

As to the District of Columbia, there would be no difficulty finding an affirmative source of the authority being exercised by Congress. It would be the text of Article I, section 8, clause 17, stating that "*Congress shall have Power To . . . exercise exclusive Legislation in all Cases whatsoever, over such District (not exceeding ten Miles square) as may, by Cession of particular States, and the Acceptance of Congress, become the Seat of the Government of the United States.*" Whether acting directly, or through power it has delegated to the District of Columbia government, Congress is affirmatively authorized to regulate economic and social life throughout the nation's capital, and thus to direct those whom it entrusts with governmental power over Washington, D.C., to adopt the firearms measures specified in the Above-Average Gun Violence Act—subject, of course, to any limitations we conclude the Second Amendment imposes on laws enacted by Congress.

As for other cities, it is at least strongly arguable that Congress, acting pursuant to the Commerce Clause, would be exercising one of the "powers . . . delegated to the United States by the Constitution," as the Tenth Amendment requires. The inclusion in the statute of firearms "possession" along with "purchase" and "sale" would, at least under modern precedent, be justified by the power of Congress, conferred by Article I, section 8, clause 18, "*To make all Laws which shall be necessary and proper for carrying into Execution the foregoing Powers,*" on the theory that Congress could reasonably deem federal control of possession essential to effective enforcement of a federal ban on purchase and sale—a theory articulated most recently by Justice Scalia in connection with the congressional ban on the possession as well as sale of marijuana, even under close supervision by a state that permits medically licensed marijuana use.

At most, however, this analysis establishes that the imagined federal statute falls within the *affirmative authority* of Congress under the Constitution, leaving open the question whether the statute nonetheless runs afoul of some negative constitutional prohibition.

The most obvious one would seem to be the Second Amendment: *"A well regulated Militia, being necessary to the security of a free State, the right of the people to keep and bear Arms, shall not be infringed."* Does the statute "infringe" that Second Amendment right?

There is precious little judicial precedent, but a mass of academic writing addresses the meaning and scope of the Second Amendment, with a majority of scholars concluding that it is only each state's "well regulated Militia" that the Second Amendment protects from federal interference, and a minority arguing that the preamble's reference to the necessity of a "well regulated Militia" should not render irrelevant or totally dilute "the right of the people"—even as individuals unconnected to any organized state military force—"to keep and bear Arms." Sorting through this body of precedent and scholarship would be well beyond the point of this book; it suffices here to recognize that neither pole in this ongoing debate can point to decisive textual support for its conclusion and that both must rely on sources of meaning well beyond the visible text.

A District of Columbia statute undergoing judicial challenge as of the writing of this book raises the question whether, whatever else it might mean, the Second Amendment has either no application or at most a far less robust application to congressional measures to regulate firearms traffic, possession, and use *in the nation's capital.* Even if the preamble of the amendment is not read to limit its reach to weaponry in the hands of state militias as such, that preamble might well be read to limit the amendment's reach to federal control of firearms in the hands of citizens in the several states, as opposed to federal control of firearms in distinctly federal territories, and especially in the seat of the federal government. If that reading were adopted, then the imagined statute would seem to pose no great constitutional difficulty in its application to the District of Columbia. But what of its application to New Orleans or Dallas or Los Angeles? The next section turns to those questions.

States as Sovereigns?

EVEN IF WE START with the assumption that the hypothetical statute's application to cities other than Washington, D.C., does not violate the Second Amendment—either because we read the Second Amendment as having no application to individual gun ownership unrelated to state militias, or because we read it as applying to such gun ownership but requiring only that the regulation at issue be "reasonable"—there remains a serious problem with the hypothesized federal statute, although it is not a problem identifiable in terms of the Constitution's text. That problem is to be found in the way the statute commandeers the law-making apparatus of state subdivisions—cities, counties, and towns—rather than directly regulating the people who live in those subdivisions. The statute, it may be argued, treats the states and their municipalities as though they were mere agencies or departments of the federal government—boxes on the organizational chart of the national bureaucracy—rather than honoring their status as quasi-autonomous bodies.

That, at least, was the argument that prevailed in a closely divided Supreme Court in several decisions rendered in the 1990s when Congress sought to command states to enact measures to control radioactive material generated within those states and, in another case, to command local law enforcement officers to enforce certain background-check provisions of the Brady Act, a federal gun control statute passed in 1993. In striking down those commands as unconstitutional, the Court's majority conceded that nothing in the Constitution's *text* prohibited the commandeering either of state and local law-making machinery or of state and local executive decision-making and law enforcement machinery. It was, rather, something in the "tacit postulates" of the constitutional scheme—that is, something in what this book calls the invisible Constitution—that stood in the way of congressional efforts to absorb state and local government into the machinery of federal lawmaking and law enforcement.

Part of the dissenting justices' argument was that the basic functions of federalism—including its purpose of avoiding unduly concentrated national power—would be better served by permitting Congress to command state and local action than by insisting that Congress regulate on its own and use a nationwide army of federal officials to enforce every federal regulation. The dissenters also questioned the majority's argument that political accountability was frustrated by such schemes of congressional commandeering. At the heart of the dissent, however, was the suggestion that even if the majority had its history and policy right, that would not justify such a departure from the Constitution's text. And absent a text-based limitation on Congress, the dissenters suggested, the Constitution leaves Congress free to exercise any of its expressly or implicitly delegated powers however it deems best.

To the degree that this dissenting position might be understood as a disagreement about the precise *content* of the invisible

Constitution, one might either find it persuasive or deem it unconvincing. A reasonable argument can be made either way. But if one were to view the dissenters' position as challenging the very *existence* of binding constitutional postulates that are not textually grounded, their position would be utterly wrongheaded. For the dissenters surely would not have denied the existence of binding nontextual constraints imposed by the Constitution on the exercise of governmental power against individual human beings; their constitutional jurisprudence has regularly built on such nontextual constraints as those entailed by variations on the "right to privacy" explored in Part IV. But to deny that the Constitution contains any significant nontextual constraints on federal power vis-à-vis state and local governments, while insisting that it contains a rich array of nontextual constraints on governmental power vis-à-vis individuals and private associations such as couples and families, is to adopt a strangely lopsided and analytically incoherent framework for constitutional understanding. If one can read the invisible Constitution through the left eye, one should be able to read it through the right as well.

To explore further the invisible Constitution's tacit postulate that the several states and their subdivisions are "sovereign," let's suppose that the legislature of Massachusetts were to make it a criminal offense for anyone, anywhere in the United States, to deny or disparage, orally or in writing, the validity of a marriage lawfully performed in Massachusetts between two people of the same sex. No one would doubt that this state statute violates the Constitution. Is it a violation of the First Amendment's command that "Congress shall make no law...abridging the freedom of speech?"

Well, not exactly. Massachusetts, after all, is not "Congress." But couldn't Massachusetts be deemed to be acting as an *adjunct* of Congress, inasmuch as Article I says "*All* legislative powers herein granted shall be vested in a Congress of the United States?" No, most people would respond, because the legislative power of a state such as Massachusetts is not among the "legislative powers *herein granted*," being instead a power neither "delegated to the United States by the Constitution, nor prohibited by it to the States," and thus a power "*reserved to the States* respectively, or to the people," to quote again from the Tenth Amendment.

How do we *know* that the power of a state legislature to enact binding laws is *not* among the powers "granted" by the United States Constitution but is, rather, an attribute of statehood? Nothing in the Constitution's text *tells* us. It seems to be an unwritten postulate of the Constitution's structure that the states do not in fact derive their law-making powers from the federal Constitution. This unwritten postulate would insist instead that each state enters the Union as a self-governing polity already equipped with whatever inherent attributes of sovereignty—including a functioning set of law-making, law-enforcing, and law-interpreting organs—it possessed before its entry. To be sure, the Constitution itself imposes certain new limitations and roles on those preexisting organs. But it is not the Constitution that *creates* such state organs as their legislatures, or that empowers them to function in their distinct governmental capacities. In short, the law-making powers of Massachusetts or of any other state are not *bestowed* on them by the United States or by the Constitution but inhere in what it means to be a "State" as the Constitution uses that term.

It follows that when a state legislature—or the state's populace, acting collectively pursuant to a referendum-creating provision of the state's constitution—enacts a law that would abridge freedom of speech or religion or violate some other prohibition that would come into play if Congress had been the author of the law in question, we cannot plausibly argue that the power being exercised was law-making power created or vested *by the Constitution* and therefore conferred by Article I on Congress—power being exercised, the argument would have gone, either pursuant to Congress's will or at least at Congress's sufferance. So it follows that the First Amendment, and the rest of the Bill of Rights, is not rendered applicable to state enactments by any constitutional alchemy that converts states into "federal" entities in drag.

PART IV

The Content of Liberty and Equality and the Boundaries of Government Power

The "Substantive Due Process" Conundrum

IF THE "ADJUNCT OF CONGRESS" theory fails to furnish a solution to the puzzle of why principles of free speech bind a state such as Massachusetts in the example just hypothesized, what theory might furnish that solution? As I noted earlier, ever since the mid-1920s, the answer has been the Fourteenth Amendment, section 1, which provides in relevant part that *"No State shall make or enforce any law which shall abridge the privileges or immunities of citizens of the United States;...nor shall any State deprive any person of life, liberty, or property, without due process of law."*

As between the Privileges or Immunities Clause and the Due Process Clause, one might guess that the former should have played a more important role in ensuring rights such as freedom of speech against state abridgment. But one would be wrong. The Supreme Court, in a series of decisions tracing to the early 1870s, gave an exceedingly narrow (and now increasingly doubted) interpretation to the phrase "privileges or immunities," so the somewhat contorted avenue used by the legal profession, including the Supreme Court, to import freedom of speech into the panoply of rights protected by the Fourteenth Amendment against the states has entailed saying that the freedom to speak one's mind is part of one's "liberty," which the Fourteenth Amendment says no state may deny "without due process of law."

That the freedom to speak is a facet of "liberty" seems uncontroversial enough. But the text protects "liberty" not in general but solely through banning its deprivation "*without due process* of law." So, what if the "process" used to prevent someone from speaking, or to penalize someone for having spoken, is just as fair as anyone could wish? That is, what if the state law abridging freedom of speech is applied through the most elaborate and careful trial procedure imaginable, complete with a full and fair opportunity of the target to mount a defense? Even so, it has been thought possible to say that the person penalized for speech has been "deprived of…liberty…without due process *of law*" if the enactment purporting to authorize the penalty merely had the *form* of a "law" but did not count as *real* "law" within the meaning of the Due Process of Law Clauses of the Fifth and Fourteenth Amendments. Arguably, an act of Congress purporting to make all criticism of the incumbent congressional leadership a felony punished by lengthy imprisonment not only would offend the First Amendment but also would supply no "law" sufficient to imprison an alleged offender consistent with the Fifth Amendment's Due Process of Law Clause. If this is so, then perhaps state legislation purporting to make all criticism of the state's chief lawmakers a punishable felony likewise would not count as a "law" for purposes of the Fourteenth Amendment's ban on deprivations of life, liberty, or property without due process of law.

Some have complained that recognizing what amounts to "substantive due process" in this manner is linguistic nonsense, as oxymoronic as the phrase "pastel red greenness." One response has been that the phrase "due process of law" includes not only the

procedural-sounding words "due process" but also the arguably substantive concept of "law" itself. Not every imaginable exercise of
brute force by government, surely, counts as "law." But to describe
a ban on expressing unpopular opinions, or a prohibition against disapproved forms of worship, or a restriction on the use of contraceptives, as something other than "law" when it is inscribed in a duly
enacted piece of legislation and takes the form of a comprehensible,
even if odious, directive to private citizens, seems a stretch. Less
linguistic legerdemain, and thus less grammarian grumbling and
semantic dismay, would have been occasioned had people read the
phrase "privileges or immunities of citizens of the United States"
to encompass, among other things, such liberties as the "freedom
of speech," and thus to treat the Privileges or Immunities Clause
of section 1 of the Fourteenth Amendment as essentially enlarging
the reach of that freedom (and others) from rights initially protected
only against Congress (and, given Congress's exclusive law-making
powers, against the entire federal government) to rights protected,
as of 1868, against the states as well.

In any event, the practice of treating the due process of law guarantee as a central source of substantive limits on state governmental
authority has a long pedigree and seems unlikely to be abandoned
in the foreseeable future. Indeed, the practice dates at least to 1857,
when the phrase "due process of *law*" in its Fifth Amendment
incarnation was first applied to invalidate an act of Congress in
the infamous *Dred Scott* decision, in which the phrase was taken to
encompass a set of *substantive* limitations on the permissible *content*
of government's commands or penalties.

Although the Civil War and the amendments enacted in its aftermath thoroughly repudiated *Dred Scott*'s horrific holding that persons of African descent who were either slaves or the descendants
of slaves could not be citizens of any state and had "no rights which
the white man was bound to respect," neither the war between the

states nor the Fourteenth Amendment was thought to have altered *Dred Scott*'s importation of substantive content into the notion of "law" as it appeared in the Fifth Amendment's prohibition against federal action depriving any "person...of life, liberty, or property, without due process of law." Put otherwise, those who wrote and ratified the Fourteenth Amendment's Due Process Clause were using the same language that had appeared in the Fifth Amendment at a time when the Supreme Court had plainly understood that language substantively, albeit in a *particular* substantive manner that the authors and ratifiers obviously chose to repudiate in the opening words of the Fourteenth Amendment.

It is fairly common for opponents of judicial declarations that "substantive due process" protects individuals with respect to one or another particular claim of right, such as reproductive freedom, or a right to die with dignity, or the right to control the upbringing of one's children, to invoke the ghost of *Dred Scott* as ammunition against such protection. They typically argue that sticking to the Constitution's text would have prevented the travesty of *Dred Scott* and that, more generally, sticking to that text would prevent judicial usurpation of what should be state (and sometimes federal) legislative authority. Even setting aside the complex debate over whether *Dred Scott*'s profound misstep was overdetermined by the antebellum Constitution itself, this argument overlooks the cataclysmic consequences that would result from "sticking to the text"—which, in this context, would mean sucking all substance (as opposed to procedure) out of the Due Process Clauses of the Fifth and Fourteenth Amendments.

To stick to the text is to say, for example, that a state may imprison someone for speech with which its officials disagree, provided that the law making that speech illegal is written clearly, and provided the person charged with violating it receives a procedurally fair trial. And to stick to the text is to say that the federal government may segregate the schools of the District of Columbia by race, or may arrest people on the basis of their ancestry or their sexual orientation, without even demonstrating some special need to do so. For there is nothing in the text of the national Constitution prohibiting Congress from depriving persons within its jurisdiction of the "equal protection of the laws." Only the states confront an Equal Protection Clause in our Constitution, and only Congress confronts a Free Speech Clause.

In order to impose an equality requirement on Congress parallel to the equality requirement that the Fourteenth Amendment's Equal Protection Clause imposes on the states, the Supreme Court found it necessary, in *Bolling v. Sharpe*, to hold that Congress deprives public schoolchildren of their "liberty" .without "due process of law" when it forces racial minorities to attend schools of their own and forbids racial mixing in the public schools of the nation's capital. That is, the Court had to read "due process of law" to include a purely substantive, and not merely a procedural, component—something it had been doing with respect to the Fifth Amendment's Due Process Clause ever since the 1940s, although in a way most people now would criticize as tragically insensitive to the realities of racial discrimination, as when the Supreme Court decided the Japanese curfew and relocation cases *Hiribayashi v. United States* and *Korematsu v. United States*.

In the latter half of the twentieth century, the Court continued to follow the trajectory of *Bolling* by interpolating a substantive requirement of equality into the Due Process Clauses of the Fifth and Fourteenth Amendments. Illuminating the strengths and shortcomings of this reading is *Loving v. Virginia*, in which the Court in 1967 declared unconstitutional Virginia's statute forbidding whites and blacks to marry, in part because that ban violated the Fourteenth Amendment's Due Process Clause by depriving individuals of a fundamental liberty—in this case, the freedom to decide whom to marry—on the basis of a racial classification that embodied a judgment of "white supremacy."

However much we might agree with the outcome of the case—and it is a decision I should say I have always applauded—the Court's reasoning points to an important limitation inherent in reading a demand for "equality" into the Due Process Clauses: All those clauses forbid is the deprivation of "life, liberty, or property" without "due process of law." The prohibition says nothing about the withholding of privileges, opportunities, or benefits that fall outside that triumvirate. If it is to remain tethered to the constitutional text, the reading of "due process" essayed by the Supreme Court in *Bolling* necessarily extends only to equality in deprivations of *liberty*, *property*, or *life*.

Those categories were stretched in the 1970s, in the context of claimed deprivations without adequate process, to cover government-created "entitlements" to retain such things as public employment, public housing, or public welfare when the governing rules creating the entitlements in question stated that one would not lose the jobs or other benefits at stake unless specified objective facts were first established. But, at roughly the same time, the ban on deprivation without due process of law was contracted to exclude government-imposed grievous personal burdens that neither qualified as "liberty" or "property" deprivations in the more restrictive senses used in older common-law jurisprudence nor fit within the "new property" categories that had been created to cover welfare checks, food stamps, and the like. For example, individuals publicly blacklisted by the government as unworthy of trust but not in fact deprived of particular employment or contractual opportunities, or individuals fired by government from public jobs not protected by civil service–like forms of tenure or job security, were out of luck when it came to invoking the new, entitlement-based precedent.

And even in the days when the three substantive categories ("life, liberty, or property") were regarded as sufficiently encompassing to cover essentially any serious personal injury positively inflicted by government, the ban on imposing such injury without "due process of law" was not seen as tantamount to a ban on denying anyone any affirmative opportunity or benefit without due process. Thus, when the issue involved who should be eligible for public welfare or public housing or public employment in the first instance, or when it involved who should be eligible to vote for which offices or in which federal legislative districts, those who sought a textual justification for imposing an equality requirement on Congress looked in vain, for the Fifth Amendment's Due Process Clause—being confined to governmental deprivations of life, liberty, or property—provided no solace. If there is a deep conviction that Congress may not deny equal treatment before the law—not just when depriving some of liberty or property enjoyed by others but also when allocating federally created opportunities among would-be beneficiaries—then that conviction must reflect more than an incorporation of equality norms into the substance of the Due Process Clause ban on lawless deprivations of individual life, liberty, and property. It must in addition reflect our understanding of the content comprising the Constitution's invisible "dark matter."

The Jagged Road to Equality

NOT ONLY DOES THE CONSTITUTION lack a textual basis for imposing on Congress a broad equality requirement that goes beyond a demand for equality in the deprivation of life, liberty, or property. Beyond that, the Constitution lacks a textual basis for much of what is commonly attributed to the very notion of "equal protection of the laws." Early judicial decisions interpreting the U.S. Constitution and the even older Constitution of the Commonwealth of Massachusetts—which contains the capacious declaration that all men are "born free and equal"—tended to regard such equality guarantees as commanding nothing about the substantive *content* of legislative enactments but as requiring only that, whatever the laws might be, they must be *applied and enforced* equally. The "equal protection *of the laws*" was taken to mean less than the "protection of *equal laws*." And to be "born free and equal" was likewise taken to mean nothing about the *kinds* of laws in respect of which equality was to be enjoyed. It was on that reading of the Massachusetts Constitution that the state's highest court ruled in an 1849 case,

Roberts v. City of Boston, that racial segregation by law in the public schools implicated no equality principle as long as the law segregating the races was not itself so transparently irrational as to constitute a deprivation of liberty without due process—a ruling that foreshadowed the U.S. Supreme Court's quite similar pronouncement in its now infamous "separate but equal" decision of 1896, *Plessy v. Ferguson*.

Depending on the level of generality at which one examines the understanding of those who wrote and ratified the Fourteenth Amendment, one can find historical evidence for a wide range of possible understandings of the equality concept that the amendment was meant to enshrine. At the level of specific expectations of what the amendment would do, there is little evidence to support the claim that people understood it to bar, for example, racial segregation by law in railroad cars of the sort involved in *Plessy* or racial segregation by law in schools of the sort involved more than half a century later in *Brown v. Board of Education*. On the other hand, at the level of more general and abstract understandings of what the amendment meant, a powerful case can be made that the use of law to subordinate one race to another was to be forbidden.

But, levels of generality apart, it is difficult on any view to credit the proposition, advanced from time to time by jurists as distinguished as Supreme Court Justice Scalia (during the oral argument of the *Parents Involved* case), that the Equal Protection Clause of the Fourteenth Amendment states an "absolute restriction" against any government consideration of race in the treatment of individuals, whatever the purpose. For unlike the Fifteenth Amendment, which expressly prohibits racial disenfranchisement, the Fourteenth says not a word about race, making it all the more remarkable not only that Justice Scalia could have said what he did but also that Chief Justice Roberts, writing in 2007 for a plurality of the Supreme Court in *Parents Involved* striking down voluntary public school integration plans that take the race of pupils into account when assigning students to schools, could purport to "read" in the Fourteenth Amendment a flat, exceptionless ban on *any* governmental use of an individual's race, fully equating the deliberate separation of African American children from their white classmates with the intentional use of race to integrate the races in the public schools.

It is not my purpose here, however, to examine that 2007 ruling in any detail, much less to explain my disagreement with it. My purpose, rather, is to underscore the degree to which nearly the entire debate over the meaning of the equal protection guarantee—even in the historically central context of race, and certainly in the many other contexts in which the meaning of equality has been disputed, from gender to nationality, from age to disability, from marital status to birth status, from sexual orientation to bodily integrity—has been a debate not so much over what the Constitution's text says, or even over what its disarmingly simple and spare language on this subject originally meant, as over the Constitution's invisible, unstated presuppositions about the purposes of demanding various forms of equality under law in various realms of our public life, and about the permissible means of attaining such equality.

The Reapportionment
Revolution

THE INFLUENTIAL LEGAL PHILOSOPHER Ronald Dworkin
divides equality claims into two categories: claims to be "treated
as an equal" and claims to "equal treatment." The former category
encompasses concerns about whether the *lines drawn* by government, regardless of what substantive benefit or opportunity is being
distributed or what burden is being imposed, function to subordinate
some groups to others and deny to some the full dignity and equal
respect that all persons are due from government. The second category, in contrast, involves *the substance of what is being distributed* and
concerns universal equality of access to a few special opportunities.
With respect to those particular opportunities—principally, voting
for elected officials and invoking the jurisdiction of the courts—
the mere absence of insulting lines and invidious classifications is
insufficient. Instead, "equal treatment" requires each individual to
receive an *equal share* of whatever the state makes available.

The Constitution's text is famously silent with respect to the principles of classification that the Equal Protection Clause (or the equality

component of the Due Process Clause) mark as presumptively invidious or "suspect." Nothing in the Constitution actually *says* that government classifications expressly based on race (or gender) call for special, much less overwhelmingly compelling, justification. Although the Constitution contains amendments expressly forbidding the use of race, gender, ability to pay a poll tax, and age (above the age of 18), it contains no provisions making these classifications impermissible, either absolutely or presumptively, in areas other than voting. So, too, the text says nothing about what government-provided benefits or opportunities are to be handed out, if at all, on a "one person–one unit of opportunity" basis. Thus the Constitution's text certainly does not identify access to the polling booth, or access to the courtroom, as "goods" whose unique role in our legal and political structure require their equal per capita distribution throughout the polity. It contains no text suggesting that, with respect to voting or judicial access (or any other "fundamental" lever of political power), an equality principle of any sort—and certainly not the principle known as "one person, one vote"—should be imposed on the states and cities, let alone on the federal government.

Yet ask any person if our Constitution permits an apportionment scheme in which representatives in either chamber of a state legislature or in the U.S. House of Representatives are chosen in equal numbers (usually one per district) from districts containing wildly differing numbers of voters, and you will surely receive a resounding no for an answer. It may be because the Supreme Court so decreed over four decades ago and has incanted the formula so repeatedly ever since, but the "one person, one vote" principle, applied both to the apportionment of state legislatures and to the drawing of lines for congressional districts, has attained an all but mythical status as a bedrock constitutional principle on which our democracy is built.

The vast majority of people would certainly be inclined to agree with the once controversial statement of Supreme Court Justice

William O. Douglas that "the conception of political equality from the Declaration of Independence, to Lincoln's Gettysburg Address, to the Fifteenth, Seventeenth, and Nineteenth Amendments can mean only one thing—one person, one vote." And few people (other than specialists in voting theory, many of whom would strongly dissent) could be found today who would dispute the once highly contested statement of Chief Justice Earl Warren declaring the "one person, one vote" principle to be "the clear and strong command of our Constitution's Equal Protection Clause" and adding that it "is an essential part of the concept of a government of laws and not men. [It] is at the heart of Lincoln's vision of 'government of the people, by the people, [and] for the people.'" Lofty words indeed, but words obviously not grounded in the Constitution's text—even as amplified by its founding history.

Indeed, although the Supreme Court could at least point to the words "equal protection" when imposing its version of the "one person, one vote" theory on state legislatures and local governments, when it came to congressional districting, the Court had to rely, in the 1964 decision *Wesberry v. Sanders*, on a much more amorphous constitutional text: Article I, section 2's specification that members of the House of Representative shall be chosen "by the People of the several States." It would be difficult to argue seriously that the "one person, one vote" principle is implicit in the words "by the People," which themselves contain no hint of a restriction on *how* the people are to choose their representatives and no intimation that one person's vote must "count" (roughly) as much as another's, particularly in the specialized sense in which the reapportionment cases deploy the principle of giving equal "weight" to equal numbers of voters—a principle that the hardwired malapportionment of the U.S. Senate, in which tiny Rhode Island and gargantuan California both have exactly the same number of senators, conspicuously violates.

My purpose here certainly isn't to question the reapportionment decisions and their complex progeny—about whose legitimacy, wisdom, and consequences an enormous amount has been written with exceptional insight by such scholars as Heather Gerken, Lani Guinier, and Pamela Karlan and whose core holdings I have always applauded. My purpose is simply to highlight how far beyond the visible Constitution one must reach in order to support anything like the principles for which those decisions stand. Yet most people today would regard those decisions, and even the bumper-sticker slogan in which they are usually encapsulated—"one person, one vote"—as more fundamental to our Constitution than any number of detailed rules one could quickly locate in the document. Indeed, most people would probably think of "one person, one vote" as expressing a principle less related to the drawing of district boundaries in order to ensure roughly equi-populous legislative districts than to a more abstract notion of equal citizenship—even of equal dignity and concern for each member of the political community. And most people would dismiss the conspicuous departure of the two-senators-per-state rule from the principle of the reapportionment decisions as an obvious anomaly that sheds no light on the principle itself—an anomaly without which our republic could never have gotten started, and one that might wisely be abandoned now by a constitutional amendment altering the composition of the Senate after first amending the Constitution to change Article V's requirement that "no State, without its Consent, shall be deprived of its equal Suffrage in the Senate."

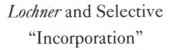

Lochner and Selective
"Incorporation"

As I showed earlier, the language in the Fourteenth Amendment prohibiting state action that deprives anyone of life, liberty, or property without due process of law seems always to have been understood to contain not only *procedural* limits on how states might go about applying their rules of conduct to particular individuals but also *substantive* limitations on *which conduct* by individuals any state may choose to forbid or to penalize—just as the Supreme Court in 1857 had construed the Fifth Amendment's Due Process Clause counterpart of the same language to contain such substantive limitations.

It has taken little imagination to posit that those substantive limitations and procedural requirements might draw their primary inspiration, if not their entire content, from the several constraints imposed on federal action by the Bill of Rights. So, for instance, a law enacted by any state purporting to outlaw statements denying or disparaging the validity of a same-sex marriage lawful in that state—to return to the hypothetical example with which Part III ended—would be deemed to conflict with the Due Process Clause of the Fourteenth Amendment, inasmuch as that clause "incorporates" the Free Speech Clause of the First Amendment. But the process of such selective incorporation—"selective" because it has never been generally agreed, although it has certainly been vigorously argued, that the *entire* Bill of Rights is "incorporated" against the states by anything in the Fourteenth Amendment—has followed a rather crooked path. Selective incorporation has been driven by casual and often frankly conclusory reference to the necessary preconditions of "ordered liberty," not by any careful excavation of relevant history from the drafting and ratification of the Fourteenth Amendment, or by any rigorously analytical dissection of what those preconditions might be.

However well established this process of "selective incorporation" seems to be, it is worth remembering that the process by which freedoms such as those of speech and religion have come to represent substantive sources of limitation on the law-making and law-enforcing powers of the several states is not truly different in kind from the now much more controversial, and in most quarters quite thoroughly discredited, process by which economic liberty—most prominently, "liberty of contract"—became the centerpiece of the substantive limits on state and federal regulatory authority. During the "*Lochner* era"—lasting from the 1890s until 1937 and so named after the era's most famous case, *Lochner v. New York*—restrictions of contractual freedom by which legislatures established, for instance, wage and hour and other protections for workers, were routinely invalidated as unwarranted departures from the liberty recognized as implicit in the Due Process Clauses (and as unacceptable departures from principles of federalism when the legislature involved was Congress).

In *Lochner* itself, the Supreme Court invalidated, as a violation of the Fourteenth Amendment's Due Process Clause, a law of New

York State prohibiting anyone's employment as a baker for more than 10 hours per day or 60 hours per week. The Court's majority was unwilling to credit the state legislature's judgment that longer hours for bakers could endanger the public's health by yielding bread of lower quality. It also dismissed the legislature's supposed concern with the health of the bakers themselves as a meddlesome interference with the autonomy of adult males well positioned to make their own trade-offs between health risks and financial rewards. With those health concerns set aside as incapable of justifying the legislation, the Court concluded that the challenged law represented a form of class legislation designed to benefit workers at the expense of owners and held that rearranging time-honored common-law rights of property and contract for any such purpose was beyond the limited powers entrusted to government by the American people.

Similar reasoning was employed by the Court in the ensuing decades to hold unconstitutional scores of state laws designed to protect laborers or consumers as well as a more limited set of congressional measures with similar objectives, holding the latter to be violations not only of the Due Process Clause of the Fifth Amendment but also of the Constitution's division of authority between the federal government and the states, even when the federal legislation at issue manifestly regulated "commerce among the several states" and thus fell within the letter of Congress's Article I, section 8, clause 3 law-making power.

The edifice of doctrine represented by *Lochner* was vulnerable from the start to forces both from within the doctrine and from the society and political economy in which it had to operate. Internally, it contained fissures that threatened to become gigantic faults capable of swallowing it as a whole, because the decision to second-guess legislative judgments about some empirical matters but not others seemed unprincipled. Contrast the Court's presumption of contractual autonomy and self-sufficiency on the part of workers and consumers generally with the willingness of the Supreme Court from the start to treat children, adult women, and workers in isolated, inherently dangerous situations as exceptional cases for which legislatures could enact protective rules. Those precedents could not easily be limited to the groups that judges initially singled out for supposedly appropriate paternalism. And externally, the doctrine came under pressure from the growing perception that the society as a whole had a compelling interest in preventing vast inequalities in bargaining power from reducing some sectors of the population to poverty while shamefully enriching others.

The Great Depression dealt the *Lochner* vision of the Constitution a deadly final blow, as more and more judges, never too far removed from the population as a whole in basic sensibilities, came to see an insistence on laissez-faire not as a logically inevitable outgrowth of a "natural" law of private property and contract but as a politically arbitrary formula for allowing wealthy business interests to exploit their workers and customers to the point of requiring taxpayers as a whole to come to the rescue of those most dramatically victimized. At the same time, the Court came to the conclusion that its decisions limiting the ability of Congress to deploy its powers over commerce to achieve distributive and other concededly social and moral ends—as well as to protect the national economy from the ripple effects of initially local disturbances— had become indefensible. With a switch in view by the least conservative member of the five-justice block that had held back the tide of economic change, Justice Owen R. Roberts, the Court dramatically altered its course in the spring of 1937, bringing to an abrupt end the entire construct that had prevailed for nearly four decades and that had come into increasing tension with a rising tide of political conviction that states and the federal government alike should have the latitude to restrict the rapacious extremes of uncabined and unreconstructed capitalism. Thus *that* version of the invisible Constitution went into exile—and it has remained in virtual eclipse since, giving the entire "substantive due process" enterprise something of a foul odor.

But the enterprise itself—an enterprise of which "selective incorporation" is but an unusually enduring variant—never died and, in most respects, appears to remain alive and well. Even in the most famous of the dissents in *Lochner,* that of Justice Oliver Wendell Holmes Jr., the opposition to substantive due process had been couched not in terms of an insistence that "due process of law" had no substantive bite but in a far more modest register. For Justice Holmes, the point was that although the "Fourteenth Amendment does not enact Mr. Herbert Spencer's Social Statics" and thus leaves state legislatures and Congress free to moderate the excesses that flow from imposing Darwin's "survival of the fittest" onto society, what amounts to a political Darwinism nonetheless survives all. For "the word liberty in the Fourteenth Amendment is perverted when it is held to prevent the natural outcome of a dominant opinion, unless"—and that was indeed a huge "unless"—"it can be said that a rational and fair man necessarily would admit that the statute proposed would infringe fundamental principles as they have been understood by the traditions of our people and our law." Aha: "fundamental principles," not derived from the text of the visible Constitution but from "the traditions of our people and our law."

From Liberty of Contract
to Forms of Self-Government

THE STRUGGLE IN CONSTITUTIONAL discourse from 1937 to the present—a struggle that is likely to endure well into this century—is all about convincing one another, and of course first persuading ourselves, that we have identified "fundamental principles" and "traditions of our people and our law" more defensible and enduring than the common-law roots of the *Lochner* era's worship of contract and property. As we have seen, one possible alternative source of sustenance has been the Bill of Rights and the points of reference it identifies—speech, religion, self-defense, and the like. But liberty is more than a series of isolated points, as I will suggest in greater depth when exploring what I call the "geometric" model for building the invisible Constitution in Part V of this book.

Quite apart from the points of light singled out in the Bill of Rights, there is a bright source of illumination to be found in a slightly revised understanding of what the *Lochner* era sought to protect. That era drew its central inspiration from the regime of private contract, a regime we know was of special concern to the founding generation, as reflected in its ban, in Article I, section 10, of any state "Law impairing the Obligation of Contracts." Chief Justice Marshall thought that this provision imported against the states a substantive body of higher law respecting the autonomy of bargaining parties, leaving to state legislatures only a limited role in policing the permissible boundaries of contractual arrangements. But, in the only such instance during his 34 years as chief, Marshall was outvoted in the 1827 case of *Ogden v. Saunders*, in which the majority concluded that the Contract Impairment Clause restricted only *retroactive* legislative impairments of contractual obligation.

The Court in that case, over the dissent of the great chief justice, held that contracts derive their "obligation" not from a body of higher law antedating and transcending the written Constitution but from the positive law of the jurisdiction in which any given contract had been concluded. It followed from that positivist view of the matter that a jurisdiction's substantive restrictions on the kinds of contracts it deemed valid and enforceable and the kinds it would not enforce—for instance, contracts to work in a bakery for 12 hours a day or 80 hours a week—were, in essence, incorporated by reference into any contracts made within that jurisdiction after the effective dates of those restrictions. On that view, enforcing such restrictions could not, by definition, "impair" the "obligation of contracts." Such impairment could be accomplished only by applying contract restrictions retroactively. And, in *Home Building & Loan v. Blaisdell,* the Supreme Court in 1934 went a major step further and concluded that every contract impliedly incorporated in its terms not only the explicit restrictions then in effect on allowable contractual arrangements in the jurisdiction where the contract was concluded, but also the background "postulates of the legal order." According to the Court in *Blaisdell*, one of those postulates was, in effect, that, when things get really tough, all bets are off. This meant that laws relieving debtors from the literal enforcement of the terms of their mortgages or other loans likewise impaired no "obligation of contracts," even when they were applied retroactively, because they simply carried out the threat implied from time immemorial by the background law of the place where the loan contracts had originally been made.

Readers will recall how the artificial truncation of the Fourteenth Amendment's Privileges or Immunities Clause—its interpretation by the Supreme Court in the Slaughterhouse Cases to encompass only uniquely *federalism*-related rights—contributed to the infusion of the Fourteenth Amendment's Due Process of Law Clause with substantive content. So too, the truncation of the Contract Impairment Clause by the *Blaisdell* gambit contributed to the trajectory whereby that substantive content—the "liberty" that could not be abridged "without due process of law"—came to focus on *contract* as a core facet of liberty. Conceived not as a mere product of the positive law of the jurisdiction in which it is made, a contract—or, more broadly, a reciprocal relationship or network of relationships—is a kind of private government, depending, at times, on external mechanisms of official enforcement but often achieving its cohesive effects through the internal system of reciprocal trust and interdependence that such a network fosters.

If self-government writ large is the overarching theme of our Constitution, as many believe it to be, then it is not too great a stretch to think of contractual relationships as paradigmatic forms of self-government: self-government writ small. From that perspective, we can see the Impairment of Contract Clause as a shield against a particularly egregious form of government intrusion into such an autonomous regime, but not as the exclusive shield. Government intrusions that do not take the form of upsetting settled expectations predicated on a formal exchange of promises but that nonetheless impose the larger community's norms on the internal choices of mutually interrelated partners would, from this perspective, require unusually strong justification if we were to understand the invisible Constitution to include a wide-ranging axiom of self-government. From such a perspective, the great error of *Lochner* was not that it treated the ban on deprivations of liberty without due process of law as having a substantive dimension—a treatment with strong historical warrant and with linguistic warrant as well—and not that it treated the regime of "private self-government" as centrally important to the substance of personal liberty, but that it committed the category error of applying that concept to asymmetrical relationships in which legislatures had rationally determined that serious inequalities of bargaining power rendered the element of "self"-government illusory and made the "liberty" of contract a thinly veiled cover for economic or social domination.

Taking this as the point of departure, and recalling the insistence of Justice Holmes in his *Lochner* dissent that "fundamental principles as they have been understood by the traditions of our people and our law" continue to constrain the allowable substance of government interference with what amounts to private self-government, we might be forgiven for concluding that, in circumstances of genuine reciprocity and equality, interpersonal arrangements are entitled, under the invisible Constitution of self-government, to presumptive protection from interference by the forces of government and officialdom.

Intimate Association and Private
Self-Government

WHAT THIS MIGHT WELL MEAN is exemplified by the stream of decisions, dating to the 1920s in the heart of the *Lochner* era and extending into the early years of this century, protecting various facets of personal privacy and autonomy—both in the context of traditional "families" and in intimate interpersonal contexts that are anything but "traditional"—from clumsy, or simply unthinking and intolerant, intrusions by state or local government. The authority of parents to "govern" their families by directing the upbringing of their children was accordingly protected in the heyday of *Lochner* from state laws demanding that parents send their children to public rather than private schools (*Pierce v. Society of Sisters*) and insisting that they not teach their children foreign languages (*Meyer v. Nebraska*). Although the Supreme Court's opinions in those cases rested in part, and somewhat artificially, on constitutional objections to the state's interference with the commercial arrangements involving property and contract that underlay the enrollment of students in private schools and the parents' hiring of foreign language teachers for their children, those opinions also emphasized the more profound intrusion represented by the state's attempt to standardize the upbringing of children, usurping parental control of the ideas and information that would shape the next generation. So those early decisions, despite their *Lochnerian* setting, had deeper roots and continue to be cited with approval in a time when *Lochner* itself is distinctly out of favor.

When the Supreme Court ruled in 1965, in *Griswold v. Connecticut*, that a state could not criminalize the medical provision of birth control devices so that married couples could have sex while minimizing the risks of pregnancy and childbirth, it spoke in cloudy terms about the "penumbras" of various amendments as the sources of its holding. But probably the most convincing ground of the decision was its vindication of the principle that, at least within a marital relationship that the state itself had legally approved, a usurpation of the prerogatives of self-government was afoot when the state sought to micromanage the details of the sexual and reproductive lives of the married couple, including the couple's actions in reaching out to a third party—there, a medical professional—for assistance in shaping their lives as they thought best.

When the Court extended that holding to unmarried couples soon afterward, in *Eisenstadt v. Baird*, it was recognizing that the axiom of private self-government that lay near the foundation of the invisible Constitution could not plausibly be limited to the relationships formally sanctified by the state through the institution of marriage. When the Court, just short of a decade later, struck down the conviction of a grandmother for violating a nuclear-family zoning ordinance by living with two of her grandchildren who were first cousins rather than siblings, in the 1977 decision *Moore v. East Cleveland*, it was affirming the principle that the variants of familial self-government could not be contained within a state-determined Procrustean form. And when the Court, four years earlier, had held in *Roe v. Wade* that a woman's control over whether she will continue a pregnancy and become a mother cannot be usurped without compelling justification by government until her fetus would be able to survive independent of her body, it was affirming the same principle, coupled with and amplified by a principle of self-ownership the nub of which is that our bodies are our own and are not to be harnessed by government to involuntary servitude on behalf of others, even if those others are members of the human species whom we have ourselves conceived. What makes the abortion ruling so controversial even today is less the difficulty of accepting the starting premise that a woman's liberty as a self-governing person is deeply implicated than the difficulty of deciding just when the larger community, expressing its will through government, is entitled to trump that liberty in the interest of protecting the innocent unborn.

When no such incommensurable countervailing interest as the survival of the fetus is at stake, there is far less excuse for constitutional interpreters to hesitate before recognizing the decisive relevance of personal self-government to the validity of state or federal laws dictating to mature adults the people with whom they may have various kinds of physically noninjurious intimate relations, or instructing such adults as to the form that their personal relationships may assume and the permissible anatomical arrangements through which their mutual attraction and intimacy may be expressed.

Consider in this light the Supreme Court's 1986 decision in *Bowers v. Hardwick*, wherein a closely divided Court rejected an attempt to demand strict judicial scrutiny of a state's rationale for its law criminalizing oral and anal sex between consenting adults when challenged by a gay man who had been caught engaging privately in intimate sexual relations with another man. The majority opinion by Justice Byron R. White went out of its way to dismiss as "facetious" what it described as the "fundamental right to engage in homosexual sodomy"—not at all the right that the law's challenger was in fact claiming, or the conduct at which the challenged state law, which itself drew no gender distinctions whatsoever, was in fact aimed. Full disclosure requires me to acknowledge that, together with a talented young associate named Brian Koukoutchos and the incomparable scholar and advocate Kathleen Sullivan, I had briefed and argued that case on behalf of the gay man challenging the law at issue. I fully expected to lose in that challenge—not because I lacked confidence that the invisible Constitution of personal self-government should be understood to prevent the state from interfering in the consensual sexual intimacies of couples acting in private, regardless of their gender or sexual orientation, but because I sadly anticipated an unthinking reaction from a majority of the justices. I also hoped for—and, after the argument was over, fully expected—dissenting opinions that would lay the groundwork for an overruling decision before too many years had passed.

I was disappointed in neither expectation: The 1986 *Bowers* opinion was about as unthinking and outrageous as anyone could have anticipated, but the dissents eloquently voiced an analysis that prevailed, first in the court of history and later in the Supreme Court, whose 2003 decision in *Lawrence v. Texas*, in which I represented the American Civil Liberties Union as a friend of the Court, was the mirror image of *Bowers*. There, a majority led by Justice Anthony Kennedy not only overruled *Bowers v. Hardwick* but reached the unusual (indeed, I think the unprecedented) conclusion that *Bowers* had been wrong "the day it was decided" and that, by analyzing a gender-neutral Georgia statute as though it had targeted only gay sex, which the majority termed "homosexual sodomy," the Court in *Bowers* had itself violated basic constitutional axioms of equal respect and concern for same-sex couples while leaving untouched the presumed rights of opposite-sex couples.

The *Lawrence* decision did not rely on the fact that the Texas statute at issue drew a gender-based distinction. Unlike the concurring opinion by Justice O'Connor, the majority opinion by Justice Kennedy recognized that, until even a purportedly gender-neutral ban on private consensual sodomy was declared unconstitutional, a law whose cultural message was to condemn gay men, lesbians, bisexuals, and transsexuals would continue to relegate same-sex relationships to a shadowy, second-class status. In striking down the Texas law, the *Lawrence* Court also made no attempt to include oral or anal sex in some special catalogue of constitutionally protected anatomical positions. On the contrary, the Court noted that just as the *Griswold* decision had protected intimacy in the marital relationship rather than the mechanical act of engaging in heterosexual intercourse while wearing a condom, and just as the relational rights of personal self-government that *Griswold* had protected would have been demeaned had they been reduced to their anatomical or physiological components, so, too, the decision in *Lawrence* should be understood as protecting relational intimacy for homosexuals no less than for heterosexuals, and as doing so not just in the interest of individual liberty but, as well, in the interest of equal concern and respect.

The decisive fifth vote in *Bowers* had been cast by Justice Lewis F. Powell Jr. He took the unusual step, not long after his retirement from the Court, of telling a group of students at New York University Law School that he thought his vote in that case had been the one mistaken vote he had cast during his tenure as a justice. He and I had a spirited exchange of letters in the aftermath of that speech, the gist of which was that, while Justice Powell thought he had erred, he doubted that it had made much real-world difference, inasmuch as few cases of consensual oral or anal sex ever led to prosecution and conviction. What he seemed not to realize was that, while this may well have been so, the very criminalization of an act that, however misleadingly, was equated in the public mind with gay men and lesbians helped to reinforce the marginalization of these groups and furnished ready excuses for discriminating against them in employment, housing, adoption, immigration, and other social realms. That was a consideration that escaped neither the notice of Justice Kennedy in his majority opinion in *Lawrence* nor the notice of Justice O'Connor in her considerably narrower concurring opinion. In the end, even the very conservative Court before which that case had been argued saw the deep connection—in a virtual double helix—between liberty and equality and rendered a ruling that was uncharacteristically sensitive to the relational roots of substantive due process as a facet of the mostly invisible Constitution.

Maintaining Boundaries:
From Territoriality to Privacy

LET'S RETURN TO THE HYPOTHETICAL statute that purports to criminalize statements disparaging a Massachusetts same-sex marriage when made by anyone *anywhere in the United States*. Lawyers looking to challenge the "anywhere" feature of that statute as unconstitutional might well invoke the constitutional prohibition against any congressionally unauthorized attempt by a state either to target or to discriminate against interstate conduct or to control conduct occurring entirely in other states and involving no significant contact with the enacting state. That is a prohibition some have treated as implicit in the delegation to Congress, in Article I, section 8, clause 3, of "Power To... regulate Commerce with foreign Nations, and among the several States, and with the Indian Tribes." As noted earlier, it has been customary to treat that affirmative delegation of federal power to Congress as casting a shadow of negative implication that restricts the power of the states to regulate interstate commerce on their own—that is, without congressional authorization—giving rise to what has been called the "dormant" commerce clause, which in effect outlines a provisional set of prohibitions on what the state and local governments may do without an affirmative green light from Congress, and in this sense prohibits some kinds of state action when Congress has said nothing, having essentially "slept" on the matter.

The derivation of this prohibition would be difficult to defend as an actual interpretation of the visible text. Rather, it stands as yet another illustration of what I mean by the "invisible Constitution." As we noted earlier, by no means all commentators, and certainly not all sitting Supreme Court justices, regard that derivation as legitimate; some, including Justices Scalia and Thomas, have on occasion denounced the entire "dormant commerce clause" as little more than a fraud on the Constitution. But their view on this point is a clear outlier, and the analysis supporting such a principle seems quite solidly grounded. Accordingly, any extraterritorial applications of the hypothetical Massachusetts statute must be understood to represent state actions implicitly licensed by Congress insofar as they have any effect at all and have not been congressionally repudiated. Because the Commerce Clause would empower Congress to delegate to Massachusetts the power to engage in various kinds of nationwide legislative action, one might properly say that extraterritorial applications of the imaginary statute *either* are without effect because congressionally unauthorized *or* are violations of the First Amendment because congressionally authorized but subject to the constraints imposed by the First Amendment on all actions by Congress.

As this discussion illustrates, the *source* of a conclusion of unconstitutionality based on the extraterritorial feature of the law at issue would not be anything someone could straightforwardly "read" on the surface of the Constitution but would instead be something to be elaborated in the process of construing—or, perhaps more accurately, constructing—the Constitution's invisible but indispensable infrastructure.

To the degree that constitutional rights, powers, rules, and principles are linked to constitutional language in any sense, it is obviously possible to *describe* them all as "visible" on the Constitution's surface. To anyone determined to deny the existence of an "invisible" Constitution, that may be an appealing tactic. But the tactic obscures more than it illuminates, because it clouds what most people intuitively perceive at any given time as an innate difference between, on the one hand, elaborating the meaning of phrases like "freedom of speech" or "unreasonable searches and seizures" and, on the other hand, deriving constitutional structures and ideas from essentially unarticulated presuppositions surrounding and grounding the Constitution as a whole, with extratextual references doing essentially all the intellectual work.

Even if no "dormant commerce clause" doctrine were recognized, a challenger to the hypothetical law's application to conduct outside Massachusetts would probably invoke a general, overarching constitutional norm condemning extraterritorial legislation on the basis of an axiom regarding the boundaries of all government power. As a general proposition, we take it for granted that no polity may govern activity occurring entirely outside its borders, with some possible exceptions for authority that any jurisdiction might exercise over its citizens wherever they might travel.

This norm of territoriality bears a deep relationship to the core idea of limited government, which we will encounter again in the discussion of what I call the "gravitational" construction of unwritten constitutional rights. As the preceding two sections suggested, the most profound principle underlying both *Lochner*—where the relations in question were insufficiently reciprocal for the principle properly to apply—and the modern privacy decisions from *Griswold* to *Lawrence* is that public government in our system must respect the boundaries of private government when it does not involve situations of asymmetric power and subordination. Just so, the proposition that one state may not govern the internal life that takes place in another becomes an application of the same underlying principle that prevents any level of government from reaching into the private realm of intimate relationships to commandeer their details. And both of these propositions are facets of the same fundamental principle that prevents the federal government from commandeering the inner workings of the government of any state or municipality.

If we think of self-governing relationships, within communities that are not themselves enclaves of hierarchy and exploitation, as presumptively entitled, under the invisible Constitution, to protection from interference by government entities outside those relationships—interference that is unconstitutional absent unusually persuasive and narrowly tailored justification—then we have something like a "unified field theory" of much of the invisible Constitution as it has, by and large, actually evolved over the past seven decades or so.

Any reader unconvinced by the preceding discussion of this overarching theory, or even of the indispensability of *some* extratextual source for fundamental facets of the Constitution's meaning, would do well to return now to the most conspicuously visible evidence of invisibility in the Constitution's text: the Ninth Amendment.

PART V

Visualizing the Invisible

Once Again: The Ninth Amendment's Rule of Construction

THE CONSTITUTION'S TEXT NOTABLY includes one instruction directed expressly at inquiries about the existence of rights not textually specified—an instruction whose own meaning is, as one might expect, open to considerable debate. The Ninth Amendment directs that *"The enumeration in the Constitution, of certain rights, shall not be construed to deny or disparage others retained by the people."* That directive, remarkably, was all but forgotten for nearly the first 175 years of its existence, until it was resurrected by Justice William O. Douglas's majority opinion in *Griswold v. Connecticut*, the 1965 ruling discussed in the preceding section invalidating Connecticut's ban on the use of birth control for married couples, and elaborated in a way that gave it at least a linguistically plausible meaning in Justice Arthur J. Goldberg's concurring opinion in that same case.

As Justice Goldberg read it, the Ninth Amendment stated a rule of construction or interpretation that was binding at least on all federal officials, Supreme Court justices included, directing them not to draw negative inferences from the failure of the Constitution expressly to articulate a particular claim of right. Not itself a substantive font or source of rights, the Ninth Amendment was to be read as an authoritative obstacle to applying the "Inclusio unius est exclusio alterius" maxim when noting that a claimed right, such as a "right to reproductive autonomy," or a "right to die with dignity," has not been "enumerated" anywhere in the Constitution or its express amendments.

The Ninth Amendment's text itself points expressly to the existence of sources of law, sources on which claims of right may be grounded, that lie *outside* the Constitution's own textual boundaries. Even on the (I think implausible) view of some that the "rights" to which the Ninth Amendment refers—the rights "retained by the people" although not "enumerate[ed] in the Constitution"—are not themselves *federal* rights and might not even be *judicially enforceable* rights, the Ninth Amendment remains a confirmation, from within the Constitution itself, that the Constitution preserves the existence of some claims of legal right that cannot be located in, or straightforwardly derived from, anything written in the Constitution's text. It is in that sense a cry from within that there is something without, a ray of light from an illuminated part of the constitutional galaxy pointing to the existence of constitutional dark matter, although not defining what that dark matter might be. That the Ninth Amendment has been explicitly identified by the Supreme Court as a source of law in just two other plurality opinions—*Richmond Newspapers v. Virginia* (establishing in 1980 a right on the part of the press and the public to attend and observe criminal trials) and *Planned Parenthood of Pennsylvania v. Casey* (reaffirming in 1992 the core of *Roe v. Wade*'s enduringly controversial holding about the reproductive rights of pregnant women)—does not diminish the extent to which its "cry" has shaped the Court's jurisprudence on questions of "fundamental rights."

Those who go further still and invoke the Ninth Amendment as affirmative authority for some particular set of rights—rights to decent housing, nutrition, health care, employment, even a sound environment—go much farther than I would go in anchoring within the Constitution's visible text their visions of what the Constitution's preamble calls "Justice" and "the Blessings of Liberty." One of the Constitution's greatest twentieth-century expositors, the legal scholar and poet Charles Black, whose classic work *Structure and Relationship in Constitutional Law* is among this book's main sources of inspiration, took that step too far in the last book of his life, *A New Birth of Freedom,* which expanded on an earlier article he had written arguing that the Ninth Amendment might plausibly come to be seen as the well from which courts could draw economic and social rights of all sorts. Although I suspect I would find myself in sympathy with many of the outpourings of such a well, I would find it hard to convince myself that they were truly being drawn from the well rather than being poured into it. By making a wishing well of the Ninth Amendment, the scholars who invoke it substantively rather than confining it to its more modest but still valuable role of a rule of interpretation risk relegating it to vacuity. They play inadvertently into the hands of those, such as the scholar and former judge Robert Bork, who would treat the Ninth Amendment as a meaningless "inkblot," or those, such as the great constitutional theorist John Hart Ely, who thought the Ninth Amendment could not support arguments about privacy or other "unenumerated" rights any more than a clause proclaiming the existence of ghosts could sustain arguments in support of such entities in a time that no longer could take ghostly sightings seriously.

What nonetheless appears to make it possible for some readers of the Ninth Amendment to view it as a source of material rights, and for others to reduce it to a vacuous blur, is that neither the text of the Ninth Amendment nor any other textual fragment in the Constitution contains any directive as to just how the Ninth Amendment itself, which appears to state a rule about how to read the Constitution, is to be read. The amendment contains the words "shall not be construed," so it does announce itself as a "rule of construction." But whom it purports to bind; what is meant by its reference to the "enumeration in the Constitution, of certain rights"; what is the character of "others [i.e. rights] retained by the people"; what it would mean to "deny *or disparage*" such other rights—all of these issues are left unresolved by the Constitution's text. And that is the unavoidable fate of any rule (or set of rules) purporting to give readers a road map, or a recipe, for construing what they find when they look at a text such as the Constitution. One would otherwise need rules for construing the rules of construction, and then rules for construing those rules, and so on, ad infinitum. The process would be one of endless nesting and, were it ever to end, of self-reference, rife with all of the familiar paradoxes that circularity and self-reference entail.

The Inescapable Role
of Constitutional "Dark Matter"

THIS IS A GOOD PLACE to pause for a moment and consider the allure of a wholly visible, transparent, fully accessible, and entirely self-contained constitutional text—one needing no supplementation from outside its four corners and therefore one with the egalitarian appeal that comes with the absence of arcane or hidden meanings. Can anyone resist the magnetic pull of such a possibility?

To bring a visible image to mind, the reader might reflect on the title of a novel by Jonathan Safran Foer, *Everything Is Illuminated*. A constitutional text in which all was indeed illuminated and nothing hidden from view might seem more likely to be a structure for governance whose output all could accept as legitimate, even when they might disagree with some of the boundaries and interactions among the branches of government or with some of the rights generated by the structure to delimit or direct the action of any of those branches on the various spheres of private life. Illumination might generate transparency, and transparency should generate participatory access and potential acceptability.

Alas, it doesn't take much thought to expose the futility of such an aspiration. To begin with, a written constitution for a complex society cannot be expected to arrive by immaculate conception, unburdened by the baggage of an invariably contested and complex history. Our Constitution, for example, emerged from a constitutional convention called to consider amending the Articles of Confederation—in essence a troubled treaty among colonies, thenceforth designated states, that had only recently, after a protracted and bloody war, proclaimed and won their independence from the mother country. It proved to be a runaway convention, acting far beyond its original mandate to *revise* the articles and instead launching an entirely new nation, governed by a newly written Constitution that would become the binding law of the states that ratified it (once 9 of the 13 original states ratified). Whereas the Articles of Confederation proclaimed that they could be amended or replaced only by the unanimous consent of all 13 of its signatory sovereigns, the Philadelphia Convention abandoned the requirement of unanimity, thereby putting great ratification pressure on every state outside the first nine. Unanimity was eventually achieved, but only by adding a Bill of Rights, and only under the cloud cast by the founding violation of the articles themselves.

It would be too much to expect that this background would have no effect on the original understanding, in the ratifying states and beyond, of the 1787 Constitution's basic structure and core presuppositions. Indeed, it would be too much to expect that the even earlier backdrop formed by the Revolutionary War and the Declaration of Independence would be irrelevant in deciphering the words and phrases strung together to "ordain and establish this Constitution for the United States of America." Even so rudimentary a matter as the definitions of "legislative Powers" in Article I, of "The executive Power" in Article II, of "The judicial Power of the United States" in Article III, and of "States" and "the people" as those terms are used throughout the text must be supplied from outside the texts sent to the states in 1787 and on the other occasions when constitutional amendments were proposed.

Nor is the dependence of the text on matters obviously beyond it a function merely of the historical contingencies surrounding our Constitution in particular. It is, rather, the inevitable fate of *any* text designed to convey meaning to future readers, and especially of any text written to put a new polity on a purposive and enduring trajectory subject to various partially defined constraints. Metaquestions about how to read and integrate the several parts of any such text impress themselves on anyone charged with interpreting and applying it: What are we to make of provisions that appear to be superseded by others but have not been erased? How should we address apparent conflicts, gaps, or inconsistencies between some parts of the text and others? How are we to understand the history and controversy surrounding the various parts of the text? How should that understanding bear on the way those parts are construed and enforced? Against what baselines and expectations should we understand the institutions put in place by the text and identify their modes of interaction and the limits of their powers? As Cass Sunstein has shown with his usual insight and flair, this is an omnipresent question: Baseline bias—not just in cases like *Lochner* but routinely and ubiquitously—distorts analysis throughout the law. In an important sense, as Sunstein argues, ours is always a "partial Constitution." We cannot assess it, and therefore ourselves, unless we can discern its invisible structures, the networks of rails that otherwise guide our thoughts.

The Analogy to Gödel's
Incompleteness Theorem

WHAT WE HAVE BEEN DISCUSSING may be illuminated by a suggestive analogy provided by the famous incompleteness theorem of the great twentieth-century philosopher-mathematician Kurt Gödel, who established that any system of logic with a finite set of axioms rich enough to permit expression of the basic rules of arithmetic (such as $x + y = y + x$) will necessarily generate propositions that are true—in the specific sense that no counterexample will ever be provided to falsify them—but that cannot be proved by the logical rules of the system. That this astonishing truth was itself provable to the satisfaction of essentially the entire philosophical and metamathematical community was a source of dismay for some but of joy for many others, who understood that the import of the great theorem was *not* that truth or falsity could never be fully established even within the orderly world of mathematics but that the inability to prove certain propositions within a logical system could not be equated with their falsity. Indeed, in a larger logical universe within which the universe lacking the requisite proof was embedded, those propositions could indeed be shown to be true.

The astrophysicist and novelist Janna Levin, in her 2006 book *A Madman Dreams of Turing Machines*, explores the point with élan and insight. The proof of Gödel's theorem, put in nonmathematical terms, relies heavily on a process of assigning numerical formulas to logical propositions in such a way that it becomes possible to express in numerical terms the proposition "This theorem cannot be proved." This proposition, one can readily see, must simultaneously be unprovable (because if it could be proved, it would be false) and true. Self-reference is thus employed integrally in the theorem's proof. And in this way, both the theorem and its mode of proof might shed light on the theoretical possibility of a totally self-contained constitutional text.

Imagine, in particular, an unwritten metaconstitutional rule pointing to our Constitution and stating: *"In construing this Constitution, the reader must be confined to the enacted text."* If that proposition—itself a constitutional mandate—is correct, then, not being part of the "enacted text," the proposition being affirmed must be false. That self-contradiction, in turn, suggests that the proposition cannot be correct and, therefore, that any directive to confine oneself to the enacted text must be wrong. And reimagining the interpretive rule as itself part of the constitutional text does little to solve the problem—we'd still need to know how to interpret the interpretive rule!

I would be the first to concede that arguments of this kind, which may feel alien (and even alienating) to many of this book's readers, may be less than airtight and in any event may be a far cry from the mode of argument Gödel employed. That said, this line of thought, if appreciated at an intuitive level, should strengthen the conviction that hopeless circularity would result from an aspiration to make our Constitution, or any constitution, entirely self-contained so as to generate constitutional law entirely from within a constitutional text. And that in turn underscores the truth that what I have called the "invisible" Constitution—and have sometimes described as analogous to the "dark matter" of the modern cosmologist's universe—must of necessity supply and define a significant part of what we perceive as the Constitution's meaning.

Organizing the Constitution's "Dark Matter"

THAT THERE IS MORE "out there" than is encompassed in constitutional text, and that much of what is out there nonetheless counts as part of our Constitution, now seems plain enough. What remain to be addressed are the processes by which we might best visualize and articulate the rules, principles, and rights that are part of our Constitution but are not discernible in or directly derivable from portions of its text.

Any sensible inquiry into those processes must be driven more by history and culture than by analytic logic. How the Constitution's "invisible" rules and rights are to be elaborated is a question amenable in the first instance less to theory than to observation. I would identify six distinct but overlapping modes of construction in forming the invisible Constitution: *geometric*, *geodesic*, *global*, *geological*, *gravitational*, and *gyroscopic*. The first three are essentially constructive (in the sense that they entail building outward from or drawing links between portions of the Constitution's text), the last three deconstructive (in the sense that they entail imagining how the

Constitution would break down or fall apart unless certain assumptions were made).

My division of the methods of constitutional construction into these six categories reflects my sense of how best to conceptualize the mental processes involved in identifying (and, at times, self-consciously shaping) elements of the constitutional landscape. Although the groupings I propose here have not previously been identified and distinguished as such, they seem to me both a natural and an illuminating way to map the range of methods people have used in deriving constitutional principles of a nontextual character. The fact that the categories I have identified are so readily represented in the form of the illustrative diagrams I have drawn probably reflects nothing intrinsic to the methods in question; other representations are readily imaginable. These in particular reflect my attraction to paradox (here the paradox of using visual materials to describe what is invisible in the Constitution) and my distinctly "right-hemisphere" way of thinking about legal (and other) materials. And the fact that my list of methods has ended up being organized around the letter "*g*" will doubtless alert the reader at the very start that my aesthetic sense at times leads me to succumb to the allure of alliteration even at some loss in transparency of meaning.

Here are my drawings—one for each of the six ways of constructing the invisible Constitution—presented as I created them rather than in a professional rendition, in the belief that any resulting reduction in clarity will be more than offset by the gains in vibrancy and immediacy.

I. Geometric Construction

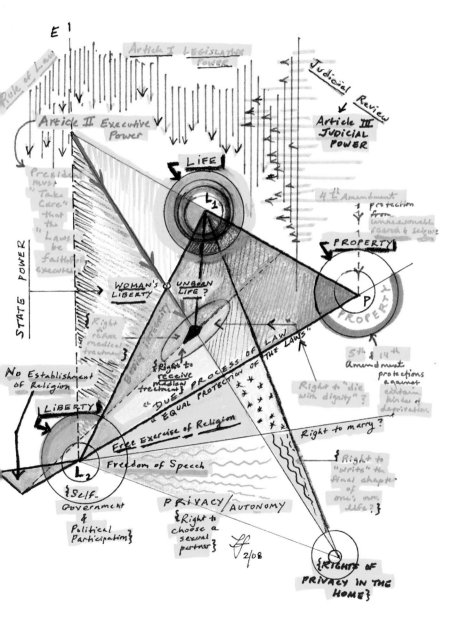

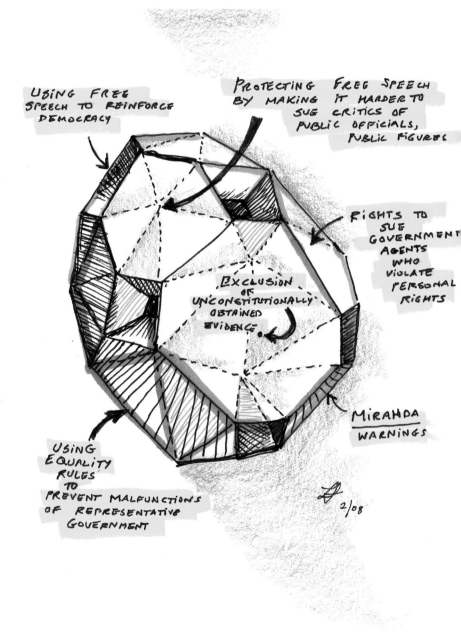

USING FREE SPEECH TO REINFORCE DEMOCRACY

PROTECTING FREE SPEECH BY MAKING IT HARDER TO SUE CRITICS OF PUBLIC OFFICIALS, PUBLIC FIGURES

RIGHTS TO SUE GOVERNMENT AGENTS WHO VIOLATE PERSONAL RIGHTS

EXCLUSION OF UNCONSTITUTIONALLY OBTAINED EVIDENCE.

MIRANDA WARNINGS

USING EQUALITY RULES TO PREVENT MALFUNCTIONS OF REPRESENTATIVE GOVERNMENT

2/08

III. Global Construction

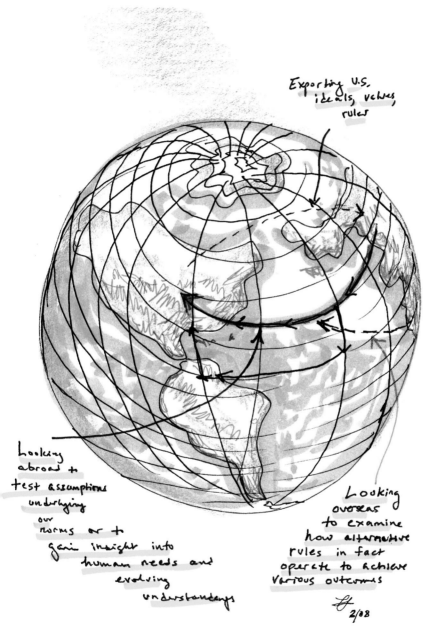

Exporting U.S. ideals, values, rules

Looking abroad to test assumptions underlying our norms or to gain insight into human needs and evolving understandings

Looking overseas to examine how alternative rules in fact operate to achieve various outcomes

2/08

IV. Geological Construction

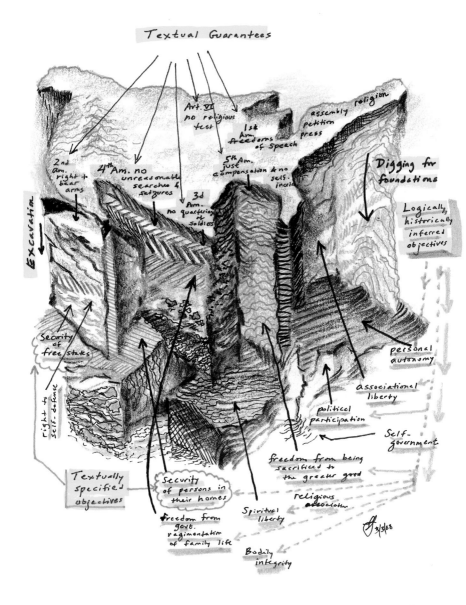

V. Gravitational Construction

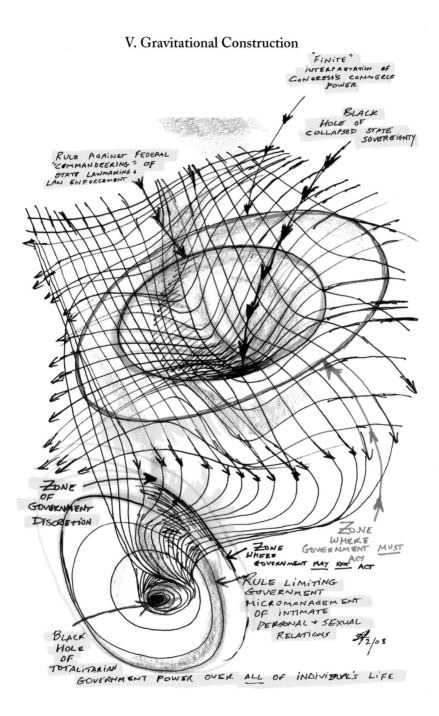

"FINITE" INTERPRETATION of CONGRESS'S COMMERCE POWER

BLACK HOLE OF COLLAPSED STATE SOVEREIGNTY

RULE AGAINST FEDERAL "COMMANDEERING" OF STATE LAWMAKING & LAW ENFORCEMENT

ZONE OF GOVERNMENT DISCRETION

ZONE WHERE GOVERNMENT MUST ACT

ZONE WHERE GOVERNMENT MAY NOT ACT

RULE LIMITING GOVERNMENT MICROMANAGEMENT OF INTIMATE PERSONAL & SEXUAL RELATIONS

BLACK HOLE OF TOTALITARIAN GOVERNMENT POWER OVER ALL OF INDIVIDUAL'S LIFE

VI. Gyroscopic Construction

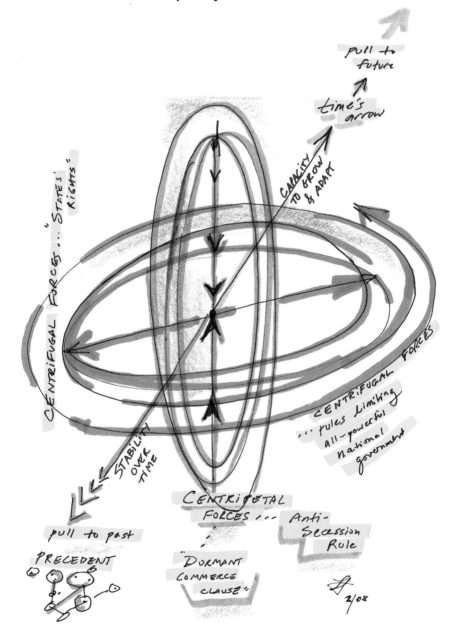

pull to future

time's arrow

CAPACITY TO GROW & ADAPT

CENTRIFUGAL FORCES... "STATES' RIGHTS"

CENTRIFUGAL FORCES ...rules limiting all-powerful national government

STABILITY OVER TIME

pull to past

PRECEDENT

CENTRIPETAL FORCES ....

"DORMANT COMMERCE CLAUSE"

Anti-Secession Rule

2/08

Geometric Construction

BY THIS TERM I MEAN essentially "connecting the dots" and "extending the lines." It is a technique Charles Black practiced with consummate skill and exemplified brilliantly in his slim but profound volume *Structure and Relationship in Constitutional Law*. Consider, for instance, the way the Due Process Clauses of the Fifth and Fourteenth Amendments protect "life," "liberty," and "property" from governmental deprivation "without due process of law." The Constitution's explicit identification and protection of those three substantive "points"—life, liberty, and property— from both federal and state deprivation strongly suggest a pattern that is easier to discern if one imagines a triangle connecting the three points of substance, rather than thinking of them in isolation as though the Constitution's authors and ratifiers had simply chosen three items to protect more or less randomly out of a pile of possibilities.

Then consider a fourth point, not on the plane determined by these three but identified by the command of Article II, section 3, that "The President...shall take Care that the Laws be faithfully executed." The pyramid defined by these four points taken together suggests, does it not, a lodestar of the invisible Constitution, one I discussed at the beginning of Part II: that "ours is a government of laws, not men"?

As Justice Robert H. Jackson expressed that postulate in his unforgettable concurring opinion in the Supreme Court's 1952 Steel Seizure decision, holding President Truman's takeover of the nation's steel mills unconstitutional, "The essence of our free Government is 'leave to live by no man's leave, underneath the law'—to be governed by those impersonal forces which we call law." Jackson recalled "a memorable Sunday in 1612 when King James took offense at the independence of his judges and, in rage, declared: 'Then I am to be *under* the law—which it is treason to affirm.' Chief Justice Coke replied to his king: "Thus wrote Bracton, 'The King ought not to be under any man, but he is under God and the Law.'" Those historic recollections define the axis *perpendicular* to the plane defined by "life, liberty, and property." Add that plane to the axis, and one has the enduring conclusion: The Executive is to be "under the law," which is to be made by the legislative branch. And, without such "law," no one is to be deprived of property, of liberty, or of life itself.

The rule of law implied for Jackson that the president could not, under the Constitution, take the property of the steel companies, however good his reasons, without authorization from an act of Congress. Justice Hugo L. Black put it this way in the Court's majority opinion in the Steel Seizure case: "In the framework of our Constitution, the President's power to see that the laws are faithfully executed"—actually, Justice Black should have said "the President's *duty* to see that the laws are faithfully executed"—"refutes the idea that he is to be a lawmaker.... The Founders of this Nation entrusted the law making power to the Congress alone in both good and bad times. It would do no good to recall the historical events, the fears of power and the hopes for freedom that lay behind their choice. Such a review would but confirm our holding that this seizure order cannot stand."

I would supply the link missing from that formulation (and from Justice Jackson's more memorable formulation as well) by invoking the Due Process Clause, without which it would have been difficult to assume, as both Justice Black and Justice Jackson did, that it is only pursuant to *law* that property (or life or liberty) may be taken for public use. Add that plane to the axis Justice Jackson traced to Bracton through Coke's answer to King James in 1612, and one completes the argument. What, after all, differentiated Harry Truman's seizure of property from Thomas Jefferson's congressionally unauthorized Louisiana Purchase? That purchase was an executive action Justice Jackson disposed of in a footnote, insisting that it furnished no precedent for President Truman's steel seizure. Why not? Because, Justice Jackson wrote, although "Mr. Jefferson acted without authority from Congress" and was subject to "rather academic criticism," the criticism was based "not upon [that] ground" but on the ground that neither the executive *nor* the legislative branch could point to any express grant of authority, vis-à-vis the states, "to expand the boundaries of the United States by purchase or annexation." That observation, as Jackson all but said, would not have doomed Jefferson's actions under the "implied powers" approach championed in Chief Justice Marshall's opinion in *McCulloch v. Maryland*—an approach that Justice Jackson embraced wholeheartedly when he wrote, elsewhere in the same opinion, that he would "give to the enumerated powers the scope and elasticity afforded by what seem to be reasonable, practical implications, instead of the rigidity dictated by a doctrinaire textualism," which could render the powers granted "almost unworkable, as well as immutable."

In any event, the constitutional command that President Truman violated but President Jefferson did not was a command concerning the use of government power to effect a deprivation of "life, liberty, or property"—not the use of government power to enlarge the nation. The geometric construction that limits the former does not limit the latter, a point vital to remember if it is claimed that the geometric method knows no bounds. And it seems only fitting that the shape of the geometric solution that ties the argument together should be a pyramid. After all, Justice Jackson began his great concurring opinion by musing: "Just what our forefathers did envision, or would have envisioned had they foreseen modern conditions, must be divined from materials almost as enigmatic as the dreams Joseph was called upon to interpret for Pharaoh."

Justice Oliver Wendell Holmes Jr. once observed: "A word is not a crystal, transparent and unchanged, it is the skin of a living thought and may vary greatly in color and content according to the circumstances and the time in which it is used." Thinking in this way of the plane determined by the vertices of the "life, liberty, property" triangle—and then of the pyramid formed from that triangle when the axis indicated by the Take Care Clause of Article II is included—it may be helpful to imagine the pyramid in Holmesian terms, even though doing so might bring it alarmingly to life, as "the skin of a living thought" stretched tight over an underlying substantive form that the history, both of the Fifth Amendment and of the Fourteenth as well as of Article II, helps us to identify and flesh out.

What is the Constitution, read across time, *getting at* when it commands government respect for the person at these three points, or along the three dimensions in which those points connect with the executive's duty to execute the law to form the pyramid we have been examining? Surely it is relevant in this connection to reflect on the particular *aspects* of life and liberty that are singled out for special protection in the Bill of Rights—such as "freedom of speech" and of "religion" in the First Amendment; a "right of the people to keep and bear Arms" in the Second Amendment; a guarantee "in time of peace" against government's "quarter[ing]" of the military "in any house, without the consent of the Owner," in the Third Amendment; a "right of the people to be secure in their persons, houses, papers, and effects, against unreasonable searches and seizures" in the Fourth Amendment; a right not to be "compelled in any criminal case to be a witness against" oneself in the Fifth Amendment; a protection against "cruel and unusual punishments" in the Eighth. What is one to make of this enumeration, informed but not exhausted by the particular abuses against which the colonists and constitutional framers railed?

As we have noted more than once, we know by virtue of the Ninth Amendment that "the enumeration in the Constitution of certain rights shall not be construed to deny or disparage others retained by the people." Whatever else this language might mean, it certainly cautions against any reading of the rights "enumerated" in the Bill of Rights that would treat those rights as a comprehensive and exhaustive list. The very fact that the Fifth Amendment also protects "liberty" in general—and not only "speech," "religion," and other *particular* liberties identified in the first eight amendments—from deprivation "without due process of law" reinforces the suggestion of a more capacious constitutional vision. As Justice John Marshall Harlan once wrote, dissenting from the Supreme Court's initial unwillingness to invalidate Connecticut's ban on birth control even by married couples in the case of *Poe v. Ullman*, "'liberty' is not a series of isolated points" but "a rational continuum which...recognizes...that certain interests require particularly careful scrutiny of the state needs asserted to justify their abridgment." To speak of filling out that "continuum" is another way to talk about connecting the dots to describe the living thought over which the "skin" of the Constitution's words is stretched.

So, for instance, because the First Amendment protects "freedom of speech" and "the right of the people peaceably to assemble," and because the Fourth Amendment protects—albeit only "against unreasonable searches and seizures"—the "right of the people to be secure in their persons, houses, papers, and effects," there is a strong case for treating as presumptively protected from government the choices adult individuals make about the identity of those with whom they share their homes and lives, and the details (anatomical and otherwise) of the ways they choose to interact expressively in their homes with other consenting adults. Decisions like *Griswold v. Connecticut*, the Court's 1965 holding that a state's criminalization of the use of contraceptives by married couples during sexual intercourse (extended to unmarried couples in *Eisenstadt v. Baird*) violates the Constitution, and *Lawrence v. Texas*, the Court's 2003 holding that a state's criminalization of oral and anal sex between consenting same-sex partners is similarly unconstitutional, represent applications of this presumption. And, as we saw earlier, both *Griswold* and *Lawrence* also represent extensions of an axiom of respect for self-government that pervades the Constitution and helps to undergird the line connecting the dots of the First and Fourth Amendments.

Plainly, nothing in the explicit text of the Constitution addresses the use of contraceptives in order to engage in sexual intimacies without risking pregnancy or the particulars of those intimacies in the privacy of the home. Equally plainly, unless it were both possible and desirable to restrict the reach of the Constitution to the isolated points evident on its written surface, the Constitution's silence on the specifics cannot end the debate about whether these decisions were right or wrong. Writing for the majority of the Court in *Lawrence*, Justice Kennedy opined:

Had those who drew and ratified the Due Process Clauses of the Fifth Amendment or the Fourteenth Amendment known the components of liberty in its manifold possibilities, they might have been more specific. They did not presume to have this insight. They knew times can blind us to certain truths and later generations can see that laws once thought necessary and proper in fact serve only to oppress. As the Constitution endures, persons in every generation can invoke its principles in their own search for greater freedom.

In truth, "the components of liberty in its manifold possibilities" probably represent no fixed set of freedoms about which it would, even in principle, be possible to be "more specific"—at least not if specificity is meant to indicate comprehensiveness and exclusivity. It was the general phenomenon of the government dictating the details of private interpersonal relationships that the Constitution, in this view, meant to prevent. When, as in the use of antisodomy laws to discriminate against and oppress gay men and lesbians, what had once seemed a suitable expression of the majority's moral code applicable to all was exposed as a tool of subordination and stigmatization, then a commitment to human dignity properly found expression in the interstices of specific constitutional protections. The "living thought" whose "skin" the pinpointed vertices of particular rights help to mark out becomes, from this perspective, the preservation of a core, inevitably contestable at the margins, of personal and interpersonal dignity, equality, and autonomy.

Time's Geometry

As justice holmes envisioned, a word is not static but rather "may vary greatly in color and content according to the circumstances and the time in which it is used." This suggests a fourth dimension to the skin we pull taut over word-points in the Constitution: time. Not simply time in the sense of the backdrop of history against which the authors and ratifiers of the Constitution and of individual amendments were writing, but time both as it transforms the meanings of words once used and as it adds further words as posts holding taut the skin we have stretched across the Constitution's landscape.

Thus it is, for example, that the ratification of the Fourteenth Amendment fundamentally altered the balance of state and national power, becoming an additional post to support the skins that had been stretched over words already enshrined in the Constitution, and informing the interpretation of those now-altered skins. And, as indicated earlier, the meaning of the Fourteenth Amendment itself has not remained static in constitutional history but rather has undergone its own evolution in response to significant events in our nation's past. The meaning and import of the Equal Protection Clause (and its role in a democratic government), for example, shifted with the Nineteenth Amendment's ratification in 1920 and again in both world wars as the cognitive dissonance between our racial discrimination and inequality at home and our fight for democracy and against racism abroad became intolerable. The comparisons and hypocrisies were not lost on Justice Frank Murphy, who wrote during World War II that statutory racial discriminations are "at variance with the principles for which we are now waging war," an observation that probably reveals more than a little about the psychodynamics of *Brown v. Board of Education*, coming as it did just eight years after our victory in World War II. In a similar vein, the Court's articulation of the "one person, one vote" principle arguably was informed by the Cold War era, during which there was a growing consciousness about what American democracy meant or should mean as contrasted with Communism, and a new rallying cry to look to the Constitution to reform the nation's tattered democracy.

A Libertarian Presumption?

RETURNING NOW TO THE "geometric" mode of construction discussed earlier, some readers of the Constitution have gone further
than simply connecting the dots to create a discrete and identifiable geometric *shape*; they have used the dots to construct an infi-
nite *line* or *plane* of undifferentiated "liberty." That is, they have
tried to extract from this set of texts and from the history of their
adoption a broadly libertarian premise that no branch or level of
government may restrict any aspect of anyone's freedom of action
without a demonstrably "good" reason rooted in the safety or welfare of others and, even then, going no further than that good reason
demands.

It's hard to say what such an approach, never taken by American
courts, would mean in practice—harder, I think, than it is to say
what a "self-government" presumption would mean. One possibility is that it would restrict government action, and thus collective
self-government by the people, far more than anyone appears to
have envisioned when voting to ratify the relevant constitutional

provisions. Another possibility is that this approach would restrict government hardly at all, which is an outcome we should expect if courts and others chose to give government an enormously wide berth in identifying impacts on the welfare of others and in accordingly defining what constitutes a "good reason" to restrict liberty.

Either possibility would yield the result—which seems hard to square with the Constitution as a whole—that our constitutional enterprise could not meaningfully differentiate between trivial and fundamental encroachments on the shape of people's lives. Requiring people to drive on the right side of the road and to slow down at yellow lights would become essentially indistinguishable from demanding that they worship only as the majority of their fellow citizens worship, that they share their homes only with blood relatives or spouses, that they have sex only in approved positions or with approved body parts, or that they bear exactly the number of children the majority deems optimal. To me, a less unidimensional reading of the "living thought" over which the Constitution's various protections are stretched is far more sensible and far more consistent with the Constitution read in light of its preamble's overriding concern to "ordain and establish this Constitution" in "Order to form a more perfect Union, establish Justice, insure domestic Tranquility, provide for the common defence, promote the general Welfare, and secure the Blessings of Liberty to ourselves and our Posterity."

Lochner's Legacy Revisited

A MUCH-LAMENTED DEPLOYMENT of geometric construction emerged in the previously discussed *Lochner* era, during which the judiciary, while taking a more limited approach to rights construction than would be suggested by libertarianism, nevertheless did not confine its understanding of the fundamental aspects of "life," "liberty," and "property" to the enumeration found in the Bill of Rights. For a considerable period, roughly the 1890s to 1937, as we have seen, courts treated the "common law" created by judges to resolve controversies over the centuries—the body of judge-made rules that singled out contract and property as especially important forms of social ordering—as though it occupied a constitutionally privileged status, and as though laws reshuffling common-law rights thereby become constitutionally suspect. The *Lochner* era thrived by using this corpus of common law as a plane on which to connect the dots of "liberty," "contract," and "property"—embodied, among other places, in Article I, section 10's prohibition against any state "Law impairing the Obligation of Contracts," in the Fifth

Amendment's ban on taking private property for public use without just compensation, and in the Fourteenth Amendment's ban on depriving anyone of liberty or property without due process of law—and then by filling out the skeleton thereby identified with the flesh of what Justice Oliver Wendell Holmes Jr., in his famous dissent in *Lochner,* called "Mr. Herbert Spencer's Social Statics."

But a number of converging forces, some socioeconomic and some philosophical and legal, combined to implode the *Lochner* doctrine in 1937, and although there remains deep disagreement over just what was wrong—or if indeed anything truly *was* wrong—with that doctrine as a way of giving substantive content to the protection of "liberty," the upshot is that "Lochnerizing" now serves more as an epithet than as an analytically specific objection to the geometric mode of constitutional construction that helped to give birth to the discredited doctrine.

If the speculations offered earlier about the central role of self-governing interpersonal relationships are nonetheless to be accepted, one would probably have to say this about what went wrong in the *Lochner* era, and about what ultimately distinguishes *Lochner* from the contemporary line of privacy decisions reaching from *Griswold* to *Lawrence* and perhaps beyond: The *Lochner* decision and its immediate progeny were insufficiently attentive to the dynamics of power that rendered ostensibly self-governing relationships of employer to employee or of producer to consumer hollow forms that concealed what were, at bottom, unilateral impositions of power. Arguments for placing particular sorts of relationships presumptively beyond the reach of governmental regulation must be formulated with careful attention to whether the enclave thereby being treated as presumptively "private" or as functionally "extra-territorial" is in fact a decently functioning context of reciprocity rather than a center of exploitation. To employ "liberty of contract" rhetoric to prevent regulation of wages and working conditions in settings where lawmakers have plausibly found that severe inequalities of bargaining power exist would be akin to employing "sexual intimacy" rhetoric and the trope of "privacy" to prevent regulation of sex harassment of employees in the workplace or rape of wives by their husbands in abusive marital relationships.

Despite the suggestion here of "self-government" as an organizing principle, the fact remains that the period following *Lochner*'s collapse has lacked a forceful and generally accepted unifying vision of what particular features of human experience the Constitution should be understood to presumptively insulate from governmental control and what features should be presumptively subject to rational regulation. Even the basic question of just how fixed and universal those presumptively protected features are has been up for grabs:

Should the Constitution be understood to single out a fixed and concrete set of human activities and relationships, invariant over time, for special protection against government interference?

Should it be understood to allocate certain kinds of decisions to the private sphere, defining those privileged realms of personal choice in ways that respond to changing social and cultural conditions and norms?

Is there a difference, for purposes of questions like these, between rights the Constitution affirms in language that looks to end-states or to conditions to be avoided—such as a fusion of church and state, a fully disarmed populace, random searches and seizures, or cruel and unusual punishments—and rights the Constitution describes in language that signals a concern with the locus of choice as between individuals and the government, such as the "free exercise" of religion, or "freedom of speech, or of the press," or the enjoyment of "liberty"?

The need to answer questions like these, combined with the silence of the text, again demonstrates the unavoidable existence of a large body of "dark matter" that constitutes the Constitution's all-important set of "invisible" structures and principles. And the geometric mode of construction represents not some magic key with which to unlock the secret of that dark matter but merely the simplest way to organize its points, lines, and planes into culturally meaningful forms—forms akin to the constellations the ancients superimposed on the starry sky.

Geodesic Construction

LET'S TURN NEXT TO AN IMAGE suggested by Buckminster Fuller's famous geodesic domes, each of them constructed by linking a multitude of triangular or other "faces"—surfaces that are joined along their edges to form protective bubbles, each of which surrounds an interior that one might imagine being defined by a core right or principle whose realization requires a kind of breathing space buffered from outside forces by a suitably designed shield.

Geodesic construction is well illustrated by the way freedom of speech has been surrounded by doctrines that are not evident from the constitutional text but are designed to preserve the essence of that freedom while accommodating various competing interests. An example is *New York Times v. Sullivan,* which in 1963 held that courts could not award damages to public officials or public figures for allegedly defamatory falsehoods published about their public activities without clear and convincing proof that the statements at issue were factually false and were disseminated with knowledge of their falsehood or with reckless disregard of their truth or falsity.

Justice Goldberg's concurrence—which advocated an "absolute, unconditional privilege to criticize official conduct"—explained the necessity of the geodesic layer of the invisible Constitution. Although the First Amendment is not designed to protect libelous speech, the speech that *is* at the core of the First Amendment would be "chilled" or "constrained" without a prophylactic rule that had the effect of safeguarding nonessential speech.

Just how essential the particular prophylactic rule formulated by the Court must be is far from clear. Alternative rules, ensuring a right to reply or limiting the elements or magnitude of a damages award, might have served as well. That the rule announced by the Court was imposed on state as well as federal courts means that it was thought to be of "constitutional" origin; the Supreme Court has no other source of authority to supervise the state judiciary—no authority analogous to its supervisory power over the lower federal courts. But it is at least conceptually possible that Congress, acting under its section 5 power to enforce the Fourteenth Amendment as the vehicle through which freedom of speech is "incorporated" against the states, could share with the Supreme Court the responsibility to shape an optimal remedial regime, with the Court testing congressionally specified alternatives for their adequacy as replacements of the judicially crafted solution. Because identifying a rule as part of the invisible Constitution carries no necessary implication for the exclusivity or finality of the Supreme Court's role in selecting and enforcing that rule, elements of the "geodesic" model are potentially subject to metamorphosis under a dynamic relationship between Congress and the Court.

Another illustration is *Miranda v. Arizona*'s requirement that suspects in police custody be given a specified set of warnings about their right to remain silent and to receive the assistance of counsel, appointed at public expense if they cannot afford a lawyer of their own, before being subjected to police interrogation about the crime they are suspected of having committed. The Supreme Court concluded in *Miranda* that custodial interrogations would *inherently* violate the underlying constitutional standard—the proscription against involuntary self-incrimination—without *some* adequate prophylactic safeguard. In *Miranda*, even more clearly than in *New York Times v. Sullivan*, the Supreme Court was consciously constructing a prophylactic set of rules whose enforcement was believed to be *one* reasonable way—not necessarily the *only* reasonable way—of implementing the core constitutional value at stake, which in *Miranda*'s case was the Fifth Amendment privilege against compelled self-incrimination. Congress in 1968 enacted a statute that replaced the *Miranda* warnings not with an alternative prophylactic regime but with the stripped-down requirement, in place long before *Miranda*, that the voluntariness of any confession obtained in custodial interrogation be determined under a "totality of the circumstances" test and that only confessions found "voluntary" under that test be admitted into evidence.

For years, attorneys general, concluding that the 1968 statute was unconstitutional, declined to enforce it. When a federal circuit court undertook on its own motion to question that conclusion, a test case ultimately reached the Supreme Court. In an opinion in *Dickerson v. United States* written in 2000 by a longtime critic of *Miranda* who had long regarded that decision as the epitome of unwarranted "judicial activism," Chief Justice Rehnquist, joined by a lopsided majority of the Court, struck down the 1968 law as unconstitutional, but did so in a decision reflecting an instinct for judicial turf protection more than a coherent theory of constitutional law.

In essence, the Court bypassed the question of *Miranda*'s constitutional necessity and reasoned simply, over the stinging dissent of Justice Scalia, that Congress had no business challenging the Supreme Court's supremacy in the exposition of the Constitution. Because the *Miranda* decision, whether or not actually required by the Constitution, was announced by the Court in its "constitutional voice"—a move without which the Court could not have imposed the decision on the states—it followed that Congress was bound to accept the ruling as such and was out of bounds in challenging the Court's ruling! Only then did the Court turn to the present-day validity of *Miranda* and, rather than revisiting and reaffirming that controversial ruling on the merits—something the Chief Justice and a number of those who joined him would have been loath to do—the Court simply concluded that sticking with precedent under the familiar doctrine of stare decisis was the proper course here, inasmuch as police no longer found it difficult to live with the decision, which had indeed become so ubiquitous a part of the "national culture"—what with television and all—that it was too late in the day to reexamine it.

This seems to me more a lesson in how *not* to fill out the facets and vertices of the geodesic constitution than of how to do so properly. Evidently unprepared to conclude in 2000 that the particular prophylactic rule it had put in place in 1966 was truly necessary to protect a textually rooted constitutional right in the absence of a meaningful congressional substitute, the Court was content to observe that because it had once upon a time reached such a conclusion, and because the country had come to terms with that conclusion in the intervening years, not even Congress's explicit 1968 disagreement should lead the Court so much as to reexamine its prior reasoning. That is hardly a respectful way for the Court to treat a coequal branch of the national government.

Miranda of course overlaps *Mapp v. Ohio* and the conclusion of the Supreme Court in that 1961 ruling that an essential method of enforcing the Fourth Amendment's ban on unreasonable searches and seizures, as applied to the states through the Due Process Clause of the Fourteenth Amendment, is to prevent the prosecution from making affirmative prosecutorial use of the fruit of an unconstitutional investigation. How long the Supreme Court will continue to enforce that "exclusionary rule" is, at the time of this writing, increasingly unclear. What remains clear, however, is that formulating and implementing rules of this sort has been a vital part of the federal judiciary's function in giving practical meaning to the otherwise abstract prohibitions of the Constitution. It seems sensible to envision such augmenting rules as part of the invisible Constitution, without some version of which the visible Constitution would cease to have much force.

When an illegal search and seizure, or some other violation of a substantively protected constitutional right, does not yield evidence whose exclusion might be used to deter the underlying violation, the need for some other way to make the Constitution's mandate real is plain. In 1971, the Supreme Court responded to that need by establishing, in the case of *Bivens v. Unknown, Unnamed Agents*, a presumptive right for the victim of a constitutional violation to sue the federal government officers who were responsible for the violation, and to recover monetary damages from those officers for the harm they caused, unless Congress has enacted some alternative preventive and remedial scheme to implement the constitutional principle at stake.

Ever since the late 1980s, however, the Court has been increasingly reluctant to apply the *Bivens* approach—even when the result of not doing so appears to be a diminishing incentive for federal officers to respect the constitutional rights of individuals, and even when Congress has said nothing to discourage the Court from stepping in and has done little or nothing itself to fill the resulting implementation gap. Whether to view this as principally a congressional failure or mostly a judicial failure is unclear. What does seem clear is that the geodesically constructed invisible Constitution cannot be expected to provide an effective shield for federal constitutional rights that are vulnerable to violation by the executive branch when each of the other two branches insists on passing the buck to the other.

The absence of anything beyond purely prospective remedies for the violation of federal constitutional rights is especially problematic when it is difficult if not impossible to say in advance, with anything like the precision that is required for the formulation of a judicial injunction against future misconduct, just what conduct government officials might attempt in the effort to discourage individuals from exercising their rights. Among the few plausibly effective shields against such rights-deterring government conduct would be the threat that those who engage in it do so at the risk of being held personally liable for the economic and other injuries they inflict. So one facet of the geodesic dome that the invisible Constitution might be understood to create as a shield for the exercise of various constitutional rights is precisely a *Bivens*-like remedy of the very sort the Supreme Court has been growing reluctant to recognize.

Setting aside the sometime availability of suits for money damages against rights-abridging government officials, the anterior question remains just when a right is to be regarded as having been abridged in the first place. The easy cases are those in which a law is affirmatively applied to an individual in circumstances that unjustifiably compromise that individual's constitutional rights—thereby presenting us with government action that cannot be judicially implemented if those rights are to mean anything at all. So, for example, a criminal conviction must be reversed rather than affirmed if it is obtained either by enforcing a facially unconstitutional law or by applying a facially valid law in an unconstitutional manner. So, too, an individual cannot be unjustifiably penalized for having exercised a constitutional right—such as the right to make an interstate journey, to change domicile from one state to another, to express a point of view, to withhold criminally incriminating testimony, to insist on a trial by jury, or to demand just compensation if his or her private property is taken for public use. In an elementary sense, this antipenalizing principle can be seen as shielding the exercise of the underlying right and thus as forming a facet of the geodesic dome surrounding that right. That said, it must be conceded that it is not always easy to decide when withholding a discretionary benefit—one the government has no affirmative constitutional duty to provide in the first instance—from those who exercise a particular constitutional right constitutes an acceptable condition on provision of the benefit, and when it instead constitutes a forbidden penalty on exercise of the right.

Of particular relevance to the problem of constructing effective geodesic shields for various rights is a point quite distinct from the problem of drawing the benefit/penalty line: Once we have decided that we are dealing with an impermissible penalty, we may need to ask whether it involves not a single, well-defined official act that can readily be enjoined or made the subject of an award of monetary damages against the offending officer but, instead, a gradual series of official acts no one of which is sufficiently predictable and definable in advance to permit prospective relief through a judicial injunction, or sufficiently serious to justify an award of retrospective monetary relief, but the *cumulative effect* of which might be devastating. In that category of cases, a Supreme Court refusal to recognize a *Bivens* remedy against those responsible for the aggregate harm may subject the victim to what the Court itself, in a case decided in 2007, called "death by a thousand cuts," in essence collapsing the geodesic dome by puncturing and perforating it without ever clearly collapsing any of its visible facets.

Another illustration of an enduring geodesically constructed norm is the "one person, one vote" formula as one of several constitutional principles dealing with districting along lines that deliberately "dilute" the votes of certain groups—principles that some have found difficult to derive from the Equal Protection Clause alone. One way to conceptualize these voting principles is to recall the Supreme Court's declaration in 1886, in *Yick Wo v. Hopkins*, that the right to vote is a "fundamental political right, because preservative of all rights." Just as Congress has at times conferred voting entitlements on particular demographic groups in order to arm them with tools they might use politically to deter and punish violations of their rights to equal protection of the laws, so Congress or the Court might plausibly put in place a web of voting rights as part of the geodesic structure surrounding the entire range of textual and nontextual substantive constitutional rights.

Some justices have opined that the Supreme Court has no business erecting barriers of constitutional magnitude where it must be conceded that the Court is making a discretionary choice among a range of possible enforcement mechanisms, particularly given the open-ended nature of the judicial power thereby conferred. Exemplifying this view was the angry dissent by Justice Scalia, joined by Justice Thomas, accusing Chief Justice Rehnquist's majority opinion in *Dickerson v. United States* of "convert[ing] *Miranda* from a milestone of judicial overreaching into the very Cheops' Pyramid…of judicial arrogance."

That rhetoric, and the view wrapped in it, seems to me entirely over the top. The premise of the Scalia dissent is that any constitutional constraint imposed on Congress or the states in a prophylactic and provisional posture—with a candid recognition that it might not be the only adequate way of policing the constitutional right involved, and that Congress might permissibly provide an alternative—is ipso facto "extraconstitutional" and is accordingly automatically unlawful. To indulge that premise, however, is to limit protective constitutional norms to those we are prepared to say a conceded constitutional right or principle could not possibly survive without. A body of fundamental law could conceivably contain an invisible limitation that inflexible, but neither considerations of history nor of structure nor of text suggest that ours does.

Thus far, at least, the view of justices like Scalia and Thomas, as expressed in their *Dickerson* dissent, has not carried the day, and the "geodesic" technique has remained a vibrant option—although the facet of that technique that depends on judicial implication of a damages remedy against officials who have violated a constitutional right does seem to be on life support at the time of this writing.

Global Construction

As its name implies, the core of what I would call the "global" mode for constructing specific constraints from the constitutional shadows revolves around the comparison of our national experience with the experiences and experiments of other nations and of international groupings, institutions, and practices. In 1993, Chief Justice William Rehnquist observed that inasmuch as "constitutional law is [now] firmly grounded in so many countries, it is time that the United States courts begin looking to the decisions of other constitutional courts to aid in their own deliberative process."

Indeed, the time had evidently already arrived: A year earlier, in a partial dissent from the Supreme Court's 1992 decision in *Planned Parenthood v. Casey*, reaffirming what the plurality in that case called the "core" of the holding in the Court's famous 1973 abortion ruling, *Roe v. Wade*—a reaffirmance that the partial dissent decried—Chief Justice Rehnquist, joined by Justices Scalia, Thomas, and White, cited a 1975 judgment of the West German Constitutional Court about the right to life. And the year after the chief justice urged "looking to the decisions of other constitutional courts" as aids in the Court's "own deliberative process," Justice Thomas, concurring in the Court's judgment in *Holder v. Hall* rejecting a vote dilution challenge under section 2 of the Voting Rights Act, compared Georgia's system of "safe minority seats" to the use in Belgium, Cyprus, Lebanon, New Zealand, West Germany, and Zimbabwe of devices other than separate racial registers that end up allocating power on a de facto racial basis.

Controversy over the practice of making such comparisons arose when Justice Stephen G. Breyer, dissenting from the Supreme Court's 1997 decision in *Printz v. United States* striking down a provision of federal law requiring chief local law enforcement officers to do background checks of would-be gun purchasers, suggested that experience abroad—in federal systems sharing our concern with undue centralization of national power—provided evidence that mandates of local cooperation could serve rather than frustrate values of decentralization by "cast[ing] an empirical light on the consequences of different solutions to a common legal problem." Writing for the Court's majority, Justice Scalia did not focus on his disagreement with Justice Breyer about the relevance of empirical consequences to the meaning of the Constitution—an entirely legitimate disagreement that would surely have been relevant. Instead, Justice Scalia focused on the much more tendentious proposition that "such comparative analysis [is] inappropriate to the task of interpreting a constitution, though it was of course quite relevant to the task of writing one."

In 2002, when the Supreme Court held in *Atkins v. Virginia* that executing mentally retarded criminal defendants violates the Constitution, the Court noted in passing that executing "mentally retarded offenders is overwhelmingly disapproved...within the world community." Justice Scalia, this time in dissent, attacked that glancing reference as "the Court's Most Feeble Effort to fabricate 'national consensus,'" mischaracterizing the limited purpose for which the majority had referenced the views of the "world community" at the same time that he raised the temperature of the rhetoric.

A year later, when the Court in *Lawrence v. Texas* held a state antisodomy law unconstitutional and overruled *Bowers v. Hardwick*, its 1986 decision to the contrary, one of the points made by Justice Kennedy, writing for the *Lawrence* majority, was that Chief Justice Burger, when concurring in *Bowers*, had mischaracterized reality in dismissing as "insubstantial in our Western civilization" the foundations of the privacy claim against the law upheld in *Bowers*. To rebut that characterization, Justice Kennedy pointed to legislative activity in the United Kingdom and to a 1981 decision by the European Court of Human Rights. Despite the limited purpose of the majority's reference to foreign law, the antiglobalist tenor of Justice Scalia's dissent was particularly ferocious.

The anger had all but boiled over by 2005, when our Supreme Court held in *Roper v. Simmons* that the execution of individuals who were under 18 when they committed their capital crimes is prohibited by a combination of the Eighth Amendment's ban on "cruel and unusual punishments" and the Fourteenth Amendment's ban on deprivation of life "without due process of law." In the course of setting forth the reasons for its conclusion, the majority opinion by Justice Kennedy observed that the "opinion of the world community, while not controlling our outcome, does provide respected and significant confirmation for our own conclusions." And even in dissent, Justice Sandra Day O'Connor agreed that our nation's "evolving understanding of human dignity…is neither wholly isolated from, nor inherently at odds with, the values prevailing in other countries." Those were, of course, fighting words from the perspective of the other dissenters.

Trying as best we can to separate the heat from the light, most of us would probably acknowledge that there is much to be said for learning from other nations and from the world community as we seek to flesh out the skeleton of basic human rights that has always undergirded our own Constitution's protections for life and liberty, particularly given the strong evidence that the framers of the 1787 Constitution read widely and borrowed freely from the ideas of international law treatise–writers, and that they thought of themselves, as did those who drafted the Fourteenth Amendment nearly a century later, as protecting basic rights common to all humankind and not some peculiarly American set of rights and privileges. Drawing on foreign and international law and experience as though these materials could authoritatively resolve puzzles about our own Constitution—something nobody has proposed doing—would, of course, be deeply problematic if not per se illegitimate. But seeking to learn from foreign aspirations, experiences, successes, and missteps ought to be fairly uncontroversial.

Yet some people well to the right of center in the United States have made something of a cause célèbre out of their opposition to virtually any use of nondomestic legal sources in construing the United States Constitution, at least when the construction is one with which they disagree, suggesting that our national sovereignty is put at risk by any such use and even going so far as purporting to outlaw consultation or citation of foreign sources. Indeed, the two most recent appointees to the Supreme Court—Chief Justice John Roberts and Justice Samuel Alito—virtually pledged during their Senate confirmation hearings that they agreed with and would happily abide by such a prohibition.

The position they took has a distinguished if historically shallow pedigree. No less a conservative icon than Robert Bork, at one time a federal circuit court judge whom President Ronald Reagan sought to elevate to the Supreme Court, wrote in his 2003 book *Coercing Virtue: The Worldwide Rule of Judges* that judges across the world are being brainwashed by a "New Class" of militantly secular, eclectically socialist "faux intellectuals" who identify with "self-proclaimed victim groups [who] clamor for relief from majority rule," whose international "agenda contains a toxic measure of anti-Americanism," and whose roots in "multiculturalism, affirmative action, radical feminism, and the conflicting imperatives of the race/class/gender schema" lead them to engineer "the loss of democratic government, the incursion of politics into law, and the coerced movement of cultures to the left" through an "international culture war" that has led judges here and abroad, in national and international tribunals alike, to bring about "a coup d'etat—slow-moving and genteel, but a coup d'etat nonetheless," through which "the New Class hopes to outflank American legislatures and courts by having liberal views adopted abroad and then imposed on the United States." A mouthful, certainly, but one without any evidentiary basis of which I am aware.

As early as 1814, in a decision called *The Rapid*, the Supreme Court had openly looked for guidance from the "universal sense of nations" and the "practice[s] of the most enlightened (perhaps we may say all) commercial nations." The practice of looking abroad for whatever relevant insight one might glean, without of course allowing the sources of such insight to serve as binding authority, did not engender particular controversy in the nearly two centuries since that time—until quite recently.

Thus, nobody seems to have objected when Chief Justice Rehnquist, writing for the Supreme Court in *Washington v. Glucksberg*, or Justice David H. Souter, concurring in that case, looked to the Netherlands to cite instances of alleged abuse by family members and others who were purporting to effectuate the right to physician-assisted suicide as recognized in Dutch law, and when the chief justice made the further point that "in almost every western democracy…it is a crime to assist a suicide," plainly implying that the considered judgment of nations we should trust bore on whether the claimed right ought to be recognized as especially protected by our Constitution. Of course, those foreign law references were in service of a decision by our Supreme Court *rejecting* the liberty claim accepted by the lower court in the decision there under review. And the contemporary leader in objecting to such foreign law references of late, Justice Scalia, seemingly lost no sleep over referring to the laws and legal experiences of England, Canada, and Australia in his dissent from the Supreme Court's 1995 invalidation of state laws requiring identification of a source on every piece of political campaign literature. Nor was Justice Scalia merely looking at foreign legal regimes simply to extract factual information about the operational effects of anonymous versus identified campaign literature. His dissenting opinion cited no evidence of effects as such. He seemed content to articulate a presumption that, if the other nations he cited had managed to maintain vibrant democracies while requiring sources to be identified on the face of all campaign literature, then it was hard to dismiss as deeply wrongheaded, much less irrational, the belief of a number of American legislatures that such identification would promote rather than defeat the flourishing of democratic institutions run on behalf of an informed citizenry.

Especially when one considers that the judicious use of global sources of insight is not a new phenomenon in our constitutional discourse, one should find this recently formulated antiglobalism at least presumptively puzzling—particularly in an era when law and culture, as well as economic life and sources of environmental concern, so thoroughly cross and transcend national boundaries. In a 2005 keynote address to the American Constitution Society, I suggested that there may be deep connections between this emergent antiglobalism and the evidently rising national anxiety about immigration, the outsourcing of important economic activities to businesses and employees overseas, and the decline of American prestige abroad in the wake of the Iraq war. And Mark Tushnet likewise pointed more recently to what he called "a substratum of xenophobia" as a possible explanation, suggesting, more broadly, that we may be witnessing a "larger issue in the culture wars...a dispute over what it means to be an American patriot."

To make the point plain, one need only note a proposed 2004 measure, House Resolution 568 in the 108th Congress, "reaffirming" American independence from "judgments, laws, or pronouncements of foreign institutions" except when shown to "inform an understanding of the original meaning of the laws of the United States." That resolution, cosponsored by 60 Republican members of the House, targeted various Supreme Court decisions by name and warned that "inappropriate judicial reliance on foreign judgments, laws, or pronouncements threatens the sovereignty of the United States, the separation of powers and the President's and the Senate's treaty-making authority," singling out Justices Stevens, Kennedy, Breyer, and Ruth Bader Ginsburg for special condemnation, citing chapter and verse from speeches and Supreme Court opinions by case name, volume, and page number, and pointing with disapproval to a series of opinions rendered from 1999 to 2003. One supporter of Resolution 568, Professor John McGinnis of Northwestern Law School, testified in Congress in 2004 that the "cognoscenti" might think it "chic" to cite foreign cases but such a "cosmopolitan style" can "alienate our citizens from their own Constitution" and thereby undermine national stability.

Modestly suggesting that the critics might have a point as a psychological matter, Professor Tushnet has raised the question whether, as a matter of tactics, our Supreme Court justices should perhaps refrain from using foreign sources to put icing on cakes that they insist have already been baked. But I think the long-run costs of wearing global blinders—and even of pretending to wear them while in fact peeking across the seas when foreign experience seems potentially relevant—would outweigh the short-term tactical gains of mollifying those who fear that such glances at other lands are but the harbingers of an abandonment of our sovereignty and of our exceptionalism. In any event, it is hard to imagine that the attempt to isolate American constitutional thought from events elsewhere in the world will last very long or get very far. On that premise, I would conclude that the "global" mode of construction deserves a continuing place in the panoply of tools for making more concrete the norms that define the "invisible" Constitution.

Geological Construction

THE FIRST OF WHAT I have termed the "deconstructive" methods is "geological" in character, by which I mean that courts and others charged with obeying or enforcing constitutional commands have long engaged in a kind of analytical excavation beneath the surface of textually identified rights in order to unearth what seem to be their roots or their underlying presuppositions and premises. Thus Justice Harlan, for example, in his opinion in the first of the Court's two Connecticut birth control rulings (*Poe v. Ullman*), asked himself what could possibly be the point of the Fourth Amendment's protections of the "right of the people to be secure in their persons, houses, papers, and effects, against unreasonable searches and seizures" if there were not some substantive limit on the degree to which government agencies and legislatures could micromanage the details of personal life behind the shield thereby created. For him, at least some "right of privacy" for consensual activities undertaken among adults out of public view was a necessary presupposition of such protections as those of the Fourth Amendment.

It is in this vein that I considered the argument earlier that at least some "rights of autonomy" for choices made by a state regarding its internal governance are necessary presuppositions of the elaborate textual apparatus for dealing with the several states and for guaranteeing their equal representation in the U.S. Senate. Indeed, as I have suggested previously, *rights of self-governance*, whether on the part of individuals or on the part of states or their subdivisions, might best be understood as the most plausible, if nonetheless invisible, presuppositions of any number of the textual rights the Constitution expressly accords to individuals or to institutional collectivities—textual rights it would make relatively little sense to protect unless those in whom such rights are recognized are, first and foremost, understood to have the even more fundamental rights to govern their "internal" affairs free of all but the most compellingly justified and narrowly tailored external intrusions.

The Fourth Amendment's protections against "unreasonable searches and seizures" of "persons, houses, papers, and effects" would be difficult to comprehend in a system that did not deem what goes on within the home an important facet of the people's ability to govern themselves and their families, raising their children with the values that seem to them worth transmitting to the next generation, and shaping their own views and aspirations in accord with their own life plans. So, too, the Third Amendment's much less frequently invoked guarantee that "No Soldier shall, in time of peace be quartered in any house"—a protection against the forcible quartering of the government's military regiments within people's homes—would make little sense in a system that gave the government carte blanche to regiment every last detail of what people did in the privacy of their homes.

Probably the most influential, and certainly the most elegant, effort to find a unitary purpose beneath virtually the entire Constitution—at least insofar as its understanding and enforcement by courts is concerned—was John Hart Ely's seminal 1980 work *Democracy and Distrust*. Ely, who had served as law clerk to Chief Justice Earl Warren, dedicated his book to Warren with the words "You don't need many heroes if you choose carefully." Professor Ely took as his central challenge the justification, in terms of the written Constitution whose legitimacy Ely traced to "the People," of an active judicial role in imposing on the states and on the other federal branches constitutional principles not themselves manifest in the text the people had approved. It was a challenge Ely's mentor, Professor Alexander Bickel, had famously described as "the counter-majoritarian difficulty."

Ely drew considerable inspiration from what may be the best-known footnote in any Supreme Court opinion: footnote 4 of an otherwise eminently forgettable case, *United States v. Carolene Products Co.*, decided in 1938, shortly after the *Lochner* era had come to an abrupt end. The Court in that footnote undertook to explain the circumstances in which—having decisively abandoned close judicial scrutiny of the work of lawmakers in the socioeconomic realm—the Court could nonetheless refuse to defer to legislative choices and could engage instead in searching judicial scrutiny. This explanation spoke both of "legislation which restricts those political processes which can ordinarily be expected to bring about repeal of undesirable legislation" and of "statutes directed at particular religious...or national...or racial minorities," seemingly driven by "prejudice against [such] discrete and insular minorities" and thus perhaps reflecting "a special condition, which tends seriously to curtail the operation of those political processes ordinarily to be relied upon to protect minorities."

Viewing the Warren Court's pioneering decisions in *Baker v. Carr*, paving the way for the "one person, one vote" principle, and in *Brown v. Board of Education*, condemning racial segregation by law, as that Court's great legacy, Ely undertook to ground both lines of judicial precedent in a theory he described as "representation-reinforcement," by which he meant to signify active judicial intervention not to override the substantive preferences and conclusions of a well-functioning system of interest-representation by popularly elected lawmakers but simply to ensure that the system was indeed functioning well, and to compensate for its systemic failure when it wasn't. Building on the insights he saw reflected in that celebrated footnote, Ely argued that most other rights in whose protection the Warren Court had played an especially active role—such as freedom of speech, to which that Court had importantly added "breathing space" by limiting the reach of the libel laws against public officials and public figures—represented surface manifestations of an underlying constitutional commitment to a well-functioning representative democracy.

Ely's claim to have grounded judicial activism in a method that would enable judges to avoid having to identify "fundamental values" outside the Constitution's commitment to democracy was easy to confuse with a broader claim Ely probably had no intention to advance: a claim to have discovered a "value-free" or "value-neutral" understanding of the Constitution as a whole and of its philosophical underpinnings. A 1980 article, "The Puzzling Persistence of Process-Based Constitutional Theories," took Ely to task for overlooking the necessarily value-laden vision that would have to underlie any commitment to democracy, or to full and fair representation of minorities, or to self-government. What made one group, for example, gays or lesbians, an unfairly marginalized minority while making another, say, child predators, a justifiably disadvantaged group, that article argued, had to be an underlying substantive theory of human rights and wrongs.

The article in question was mine and, in retrospect, I think it overstated the case. For Ely was concerned less with finding a "value-neutral" understanding of the Constitution itself than with minimizing the judiciary's search for extraconstitutional values. Still, I do think Ely had given unduly short shrift to what I have come to call the invisible Constitution, insofar as that Constitution itself includes crucial elements of respect for personal dignity and autonomy. I believe Ely underestimated, for example, the way respect for the premises of self-government might entail embrace of substantive liberties such as reproductive freedom. Ely's view that the Supreme Court's abortion jurisprudence, beginning with *Roe v. Wade* in 1973, bore no connection with any value the Constitution marked as special but represented simply the Court's free-floating imposition of a judicial value choice seems myopic. As the Supreme Court described the *core* of the *Roe v. Wade* holding nearly two decades later, in *Planned Parenthood of Pennsylvania v. Casey*, it was the proposition that the Constitution must at the very least treat with special concern a woman's liberty and equality interest in determining for herself whether to carry a pregnancy to term or to end it without giving birth to a child— whatever the countervailing interests in unborn life and whatever the authority of states to accommodate those interests. That proposition, the Court argued in 1992, is difficult if not impossible to reject without repudiating virtually every dimension of substantive liberty in the realm of bodily integrity—and without ignoring the link between reproductive freedom and the ability of women to participate on an equal footing with men as full citizens in the life of society.

The great problem the Court purported to confront but never satisfactorily resolved in *Roe* and its progeny was not the magnitude and grounding in the Constitution of the interest on the *woman's* side of the equation—which seems to me to have been all but self-evident—but, rather, the distinct question of how to factor into the constitutional equation the "rights" of the human fetus (even if not yet a "person" within the meaning of the Fourteenth Amendment) and the undoubtedly great and surely legitimate interest of society in its protection. Indeed, as the Court in *Casey* pointedly noted, if one takes the position that the woman's liberty and equality interests in determining her own reproductive destiny are of no special constitutional moment when the woman's choice is to *end* her pregnancy and the state's preference is for her to continue it to term, then one must live with the corollary that those interests are of no special constitutional moment when her choice is to *continue* that pregnancy and the state's preference is for her to end it without giving birth. In either event, all the state would need to adduce would be the usual "rational basis" for imposing its preference on the resisting woman, just as in the case of other socioeconomic regulations in the post-*Lochner* era.

This is not to argue that the interests on the *state's* side of the equation would be identical in the two situations; it remains entirely possible to argue that the state's interest in preserving a new life trumps the woman's interest in ending her pregnancy under some heightened standard of review while the state's interest in avoiding or ending that new life might *not* suffice to trump the interests of the fetus under that same heightened level of review. But, as the Supreme Court noted in *Casey*, if *Roe v. Wade* erred at the threshold in treating the woman's liberty of choice as grounded in the Constitution when the state's claim is that it wishes to *save* an unborn life, then a court confronted by a state opting to *terminate* a woman's pregnancy because she would be an unfit mother or because she already has too many children would confront no countervailing *constitutional* argument based on the woman's liberty of reproductive choice. And the interests of the unborn, while offsetting the state's interests in avoiding its birth, would not be rooted in any existing *person's* rights under the Constitution and would certainly not suffice to render the state's choice irrational—as it would have to be to flunk post-*Lochner* review.

Thus, a rejection of *Roe v. Wade* predicated on a denial that the woman's liberty has constitutional grounding (rather than on an argument that her liberty is rooted in the Constitution but trumped by the interest in fetal life) would weaken the shield against state-mandated abortion. But the reason this is the case is *not* that all constitutional rights are symmetrical. They are not. For example, the right to bear arms, however one reads the Second Amendment, generates no mirror-image right to resist military conscription. And the right not to be subjected to an unreasonable search and seizure generates no mirror-image right to be arbitrarily arrested—in order, for example, to enhance one's ability to dramatize one's protest to the operation of an abortion clinic. But rights whose structure is grounded in freedom to *choose* rather than in the avoidance of some constitutionally prohibited end-state do, it seems, come in equal and opposite pairs. Witness, for instance, the right to express one's opinions, which is plainly paired with the right not to be compelled to express opinions that one does not hold.

So Ely's purely representation-reinforcing thesis that such liberties as a woman's control over her body and over her reproductive destiny fail even to get to first base in a constitutional analysis simply because they find no visible roots in the Constitution's text means not just that state rules of a "prolife" variety would be routinely upheld as consistent with the Constitution but also that state measures with an "antilife" cast would readily pass muster under the Constitution's lens as well. This consequence might not be an unthinkable one to some, but to others it would presumably lead, at the very least, to a rethinking of the "no invisible Constitution" premise.

Parts of Ely's method might best be described as "geodesic": I have in mind the way he tended to explain much of the constitutional doctrine of the First Amendment in terms of shielding the underlying democratic aims both of various constitutional clauses and of the Constitution's structure as a whole. But Ely's larger enterprise was quintessentially "geological," in that he dug beneath the Constitution's visible surface to bring to light its unifying commitment to self-government. In an article entitled "Structural Due Process" that I published a few years before the publication of Ely's book, I had explored a number of constitutional doctrines that the Court both under Chief Justice Earl Warren and under his successor as Chief, Warren Earl Burger, had developed, and I had sought—in an effort that now feels to me "geological" in character—to explain and even justify those doctrines in terms of a demand that the processes of government, and of the value-formation that underlay them, be not just formally accessible and open but porous to unconventional as well as conventional, and in any event ever-changing, visions of how people might shape their lives.

That article focused on Supreme Court decisions as disparate as the insistence that women whose pregnancies had become conspicuous to observers not be irrebuttably presumed incapable of teaching young public school children, the demand that unwed fathers not be automatically presumed unfit as parents on the untimely death of their offsprings' mothers, the insistence that governmental respect for unborn life be reflected in measures that do not compel women to nurture that life involuntarily by remaining pregnant if they have chosen to avoid motherhood, and the demand that juries entrusted to determine which capital defendants should be put to death not systematically exclude people who, while willing to enforce the capital punishment laws, had come to have moral misgivings about the acceptability of doing so. In all of these decisions, the article argued, the Court could best be understood as designing a process through which moral ambivalence could be incorporated into processes of self-government rather than stifled by majoritarian fiat. And I formulated the doctrines that emerged as concerned with something neither purely substantive nor purely procedural but "structural," describing the resulting precedents as instances of "structural due process."

Carrying that idea forward—and linking it to the thesis that a commitment to structural justice and to self-government writ small helps explain and defend decisions as obviously substantive as the Supreme Court's 2003 invalidation of laws criminalizing consensual oral and anal sex on the ground that such laws violate the respect and dignity due to all our people in their intimate personal relationships—remains among my aspirations. But what is important here is that such efforts exemplify what I am here calling the "geological" method of construction.

Gravitational Construction

THAT BRINGS US TO the fifth mode of construction, the "gravitational." I confess again to being drawn to alliteration in my selection of labels for the methods under consideration; this one in particular might have gone under any of a variety of headings, including an ungainly one that might have more quickly conveyed the idea I have in mind: We could have called it the "anti-slippery-slope" mode. As many readers will recognize, this refers to a frequently voiced type of argument: that one should reject some contested claim or proposition because accepting it would risk putting one on a dangerously "slippery slope"—a slope along which no foothold can easily be secured, and down which one is likely to plunge into a pit of terrible consequences.

The smoker who has tried mightily to quit the habit and who is offered "just this one puff" knows the feeling. Having taken "just one," the inveterate smoker (or drinker, gambler, or whatever) will be in grave danger of taking a second, and then a third—until once again completely hooked. In the world of legal and political argument, a similar concern is often voiced: Once we accept as lawful a particular technique of "enhanced interrogation" (for instance, simulated drowning, euphemistically called "waterboarding"), the stage has been set for something that is even worse—but that is not really distinguishable in principle. Or if we say it is permissible to imprison flag burners, we may be unable to define a principle that does not also condone imprisoning people who burn our elected leaders in cardboard mock-up effigy, and eventually punishing all unruly critics of those in power.

Nor is this form of argument uniquely available to the Left: If we say the death penalty is unconstitutional because it cannot be shown to be both necessary and sufficient to deter capital crimes, we might find it impossible to defend even life imprisonment. Or if we say Congress has the authority to criminalize all racially motivated or gender-motivated violence simply because such violence renders its victims less economically productive and thus affects interstate commerce, thereby triggering Congress's power to regulate commerce among the states, we might be unable to treat even a complete federal takeover of criminal law—and then a federal takeover of just about every other area of law—as beyond Congress's authority, cutting the heart out of state power and leaving the states essentially hollow shells.

To many, the image of the "slippery slope" translates examples like these into crudely physical pictures, inviting unproductive debate over possible methods to grab hold of various proposed distinctions as ways of gaining foothold on the slope in order to prevent uncontrolled slippage. Partly for this reason, I have invoked a different image—one that draws on contemporary physics. Well over a half century ago, Albert Einstein's general theory of relativity decisively demonstrated the advantages of depicting and analyzing gravity not in terms of some mysterious physical force paradoxically acting at a distance to pull objects toward one another across expanses of empty space, but in terms of the way in which any massive object curves and warps the space (actually, the space-time continuum) in which that mass is located. A planet circling a star like our sun is prevented from spinning out of its orbit not by an invisible rope of gravitational power but by the way the star alters the very geometry of the space around it, making an elliptical trajectory the shortest distance between the points it connects within that space.

Pursuing that image, legal principles can be conceptualized as inhabiting, and ultimately reshaping, the social space they help to define. Those principles deflect and redirect the paths that individuals and groups follow in society. An article I wrote in 1989 entitled "The Curvature of Constitutional Space" explored what lawyers might learn from such post-Newtonian physics. I tried to show that significantly different (and, in my view, sounder) legal conclusions could follow if we were to ask not simply who had applied physical force to whom but how a challenged system of laws and government regulations had structured behavioral incentives so as to make certain injurious outcomes more likely. Discussing a famous Supreme Court decision that involved a state's social service bureaucracy that had kept meticulous records documenting an infant's grievous injury at the hands of his abusive father but had done nothing to prevent the abuse from continuing, I argued that the right question to ask, from a "curved-space" perspective, was *not* the question the Court asked—namely, whether it was the father's arm rather than an arm of the state that had wielded the physical force leaving the child unconscious, thus rendering the federally enacted remedy against certain state-caused constitutional deprivations unavailable—but, rather, whether the state's web of rules and practices had predictably deflected the paths of the private actors who might otherwise have come to the injured child's rescue.

For my work on that article, I was fortunate enough to have the research assistance of a remarkable young man who was then my student but who has since gone on to astonishing and inspiring achievements in his own right, Barack Obama. In an insight that now-Senator Obama helped me formulate, I acknowledged that any legal principle that would automatically hold the state or its agents accountable for every intrafamily abuse that government could theoretically have prevented would run the risk of too actively and intrusively injecting the state into every detail of family life. A bare majority of the Supreme Court in that child abuse decision, *DeShaney v. Winnebago County,* invoked that risk as one of its reasons for treating none of the state bureaucrats involved in the case as legally responsible for the injuries the battered child, poor Joshua DeShaney, had suffered.

I argued in my article that the Court's majority had correctly spotted, but had unfortunately overreacted to, an entirely legitimate concern in that regard. Thinking in the Newtonian frame of reference well captured by the image of a one-way slippery slope, the Court had failed to recognize the possible existence of a gray area within which the state, conceived to include not just its physical agents but its entire system of laws and rules, might enjoy considerable wiggle room over whether and to what degree to intrude on intrafamily conduct—a zone of discretion bounded on one side by a realm of privacy within which the state was *obligated* as a constitutional matter to *withdraw* from the structuring of private family life and on the other by a realm of protection within which the state was constitutionally *required to intervene* in order to protect individuals for whose vulnerability to the predations of other private individuals it bore some significant responsibility.

Exactly how the boundaries of these three regions are to be established is a matter of no small importance in the construction of the invisible Constitution, but it raises questions more detailed than this book can hope to canvass. What seems crucial here is that we conceptualize the boundary-drawing enterprise not in the one-dimensional terms suggested by a "slippery slope avoidance" mode of analysis but in the multidimensional terms suggested by a "gravitational" one, always asking how social life, as shaped by rules regarding who is to be held responsible for what consequences, would be likely to unfold—and to gravitate toward one or another extreme—in a legal "space" whose geometry is structured according to one set of boundaries or another.

It seems useful in this connection to think of the extremes—the points at which the entire system seems to collapse on itself, either by assigning or by abdicating too much responsibility to some set of constitutionally relevant actors—as analogous to astronomical "black holes" defining the regions that constitutional rules must keep off-limits to actors operating within the constitutional system. Black holes, after all, engender all-engulfing distortions of the surrounding space, pulling into their depths everything that crosses what physicists call their "event horizons," never to be seen or heard from again. Formulating legal principles with a view to the black holes into which they might threaten to plunge all who come too close exemplifies the "gravitational" method of analysis. In essence, it is a method that insists on taking proposed rules and principles to their logical conclusions—on asking where following them would risk leading the surrounding society.

Consider, for instance, the contested proposition that the national government possesses a particular power—say, the power to ban the possession of guns near schools—simply because such possession might lower the quality of education that students receive, which in turn could yield a less-productive graduating class, which in turn would hurt the economy and thereby dampen the flow of interstate commerce, over which Congress admittedly exercises regulatory power under Article I, section 8, of the Constitution. How is one to decide whether that proposition squares with the overall plan of the Constitution?

One way is to ask: How would *accepting* that contested proposition shape, or warp, the "space" occupied by the Constitution? A plausible answer in this instance is that the resulting space would collapse into the black hole of illimitable national authority over all of American society. The reason is that a similar chain of reasoning—one indistinguishable in principle from the one being made with respect to guns near schools—would be available in literally every case, given the obvious interdependence of our political and social economies. No activity of any consequence fails to have ripple effects ultimately perceivable in economic terms and thus in terms of interstate commerce. When the Supreme Court in *Lopez v. United States* asked the defenders of the contested congressional power—a power to criminalize the possession of firearms within a stated radius of any school—to explain why their argument about indirect impact on interstate commerce would not be available in literally every case, those defenders offered no response and proposed no limiting principle. The Court's conclusion was that upholding the power in question would entail accepting a Constitution whose architecture rejected any real limits on national legislative authority. Given the general agreement on all sides that our Constitution would never have been ratified absent some such limits, and given the fact that the black hole represented by such illimitable national power would indeed have swallowed up the Constitution as a whole, the Court's holding invalidating the Gun-Free School Zones Act as an instance of unconstitutional overreaching by Congress seemed to me an entirely plausible, if not fully articulated, application of the "gravitational" method for stitching lines of limitation into an otherwise invisible constitutional tapestry.

Put otherwise, receiving basically no answer to its question about limiting principles, the *Lopez* majority reasoned that it had only two choices: either to strike down the challenged act of Congress as reaching beyond Congress's affirmative authority or to uphold the act and conclude that the principle of limited national authority—universally accepted at least in theory by every member of the Supreme Court and by every court and scholar to address the matter since the landmark decision in *McCulloch v. Maryland* in 1819—had ceased to be meaningful. Confronted with that stark pair of alternatives, a closely divided Supreme Court understandably held the congressional measure unconstitutional, over the emphatic dissent of the four liberal-leaning justices.

Conservatives might rejoice when they see this method successfully employed in the service of limiting congressional power and protecting the rights and prerogatives of the states, but they should keep this in mind: A virtually identical, and certainly no less legitimate, mode of analysis would apply were *any* level of government—federal, state, or local—to argue in favor of regulating the sexual or otherwise intimate details of someone's personal life on a basis that, if accepted, would generate a regime of unbounded power in government over the lives of all its citizens.

If, for example, government were deemed to have constitutional authority to dictate which forms of sexual gratification are lawful between consenting adults in the privacy of their homes without having to offer any reason beyond its religious convictions or its moral views, a gravitational analysis would necessarily ask: Would there remain *any limits at all* on how closely government could regiment every last detail of personal life? If government may constitutionally criminalize oral sex between consenting adults in private, why may it not similarly criminalize deep kissing or mutual masturbation or even tender consolation in identical circumstances? If only the fickle realities of politics are available to prevent such totalitarian intrusions, little is left of the Constitution's premise that, as Justice Robert H. Jackson so eloquently observed in *West*

Virginia Board of Education v. Barnette, the "very purpose of a Bill of Rights was to withdraw certain subjects from the vicissitudes of political controversy, to place them beyond the reach of majorities and officials and to establish them as legal principles to be applied by the courts." It was for this reason, Jackson concluded for the Court, that "one's right to life, liberty, and property, to free speech, a free press, freedom of worship and assembly, and other fundamental rights may not be submitted to vote; they depend on the outcome of no elections."

So it follows that the method of tracing where the acceptance of a particular intrusion into liberty might lead cannot be overcome by the response that although logic might point to such disaster, majoritarian politics will probably hold the line. Nor may "freedom to differ [be] limited to things that do not matter much. That," Justice Jackson wisely said, "would be a mere shadow of freedom. The test of its substance is the right to differ as to things that touch the heart of the existing order." So if the "existing order" commits itself to the proposition that some variant of interpersonal intimacy is to be stamped out, we must always ask: Where will that assertion of authority end? Justice Jackson's enduring warning captured what I see as the essence of the gravitational method: The Constitution "was designed to avoid these ends by avoiding these beginnings." He was speaking of the First Amendment, but his words apply with equal force to every major facet of individual liberty. If a governmental claim of authority over personal life seems in principle illimitable, then we must ask: Does not the Constitution's overarching commitment to limited government spell doom for the governmental claim of authority in the case at hand? That, at any rate, would be the line of argument the "gravitational" mode of construction would counsel.

The availability of gravitational argument to support some of the modern privacy decisions makes an important point: Those decisions, as I have shown, flow also from the geometric and geological modes of construction. We might have added that they are reinforced by the global mode, given the trend in the European Union, South Africa, and elsewhere toward the invalidation of the most intrusive government controls of intimate sexual choices—a trend the dissenters in the Supreme Court's *Lawrence* opinion noted with some resulting consternation. And some of the rights in question also operate as shields for other rights, thus bringing the geodesic mode into play as well. The lesson is that these modes are mutually reinforcing rather than competitive or mutually exclusive. When several of them converge on a particular claim of right, we have a sign that the right in question is more likely to be securely rooted in the invisible Constitution than if it is derivable in only one way.

Gyroscopic Construction

WE COME, THEN, TO the final mode of construction, the "gyroscopic." By this point, it will of course be clear that I am stretching a bit for titles, but it's not the name that counts here, it's the idea. And the idea is that just as a spinning gyroscope or a spinning Hanukah dreidel is governed by vectors of force that give it stability and enable it to resist gravitational pulls that would otherwise knock it off its axis of spin, so the Constitution embodies vector forces both centripetal (pulling toward the center) and centrifugal (pulling outward) that ensure a measure of stability.

For example, the principle that no state, once admitted, may either secede or be forcibly expelled from the Union is understandable as an indispensable centripetal device for rendering the Union a stable whole that is more than the aggregate of its separate parts. That this principle was forged in the fire of war and not in the halls of legislative assemblies or constitutional conventions does not make it any less central to our Constitution's survival and continuity. And the "dormant commerce clause," whose legitimacy some jurists question, may be almost as central although far less dramatic both in its origins and in its form. Offsetting this centripetal pull is, of course, the centrifugal pull of the federalism-based principles that prevent the collapse of the parts into the whole by preserving a degree of state sovereignty and correspondingly limiting the reach of the center's power.

Going further, I might suggest that a principle that pushes toward stability over time—the principle that carefully considered constitutional interpretations issued by the organs of government should not be revisited absent circumstances more compelling than a mere change in the identity of the individuals who authored the interpretations in question—deserves to be included in this final, gyroscopic, ensemble. It is true, as we saw earlier, that the deliberate difficulty of formally amending the Constitution through Article V argues in favor of a substantially greater judicial willingness to reconsider constitutional interpretations than statutory interpretations. But that vector, whose axis points in the direction of the future and whose rationale is the necessity of adaptation to new circumstances and improved understandings, is valuably offset by the stability-inducing vector of respect for precedent and of stare decisis, the inclination to stand by rulings once deliberately made. Note that this stare decisis vector represents not principally a stubborn inclination to stand by prior rulings while feeling confident that they are surely wrong but not worth undoing. It represents instead a resolution to stand by such rulings, at least presumptively, in the face of one's belief that one probably would have decided differently but that, not being the repository of all wisdom, one's views just might be mistaken.

The central difficulty of treating this vector as part of the invisible Constitution is that it obviously operates to cement in place—or at least to render "sticky" and resistant to corrective change—interpretations of the Constitution that one believes, on balance and however humbly, to be mistaken. How the Constitution can be said to encompass a principle whose thrust is to perpetuate probable constitutional error seems paradoxical—but only if a bright line is drawn between "the Constitution" and "constitutional law," and if one gives categorical priority to one's constitutional convictions over the collective wisdom of the past. One corollary of this book's lessons about the invisible Constitution, however, is that any such line is more blurry than bright—and that the past, although no longer clearly visible, makes claims on truth we ignore at our peril. And to the degree that a discrepancy remains, the ultimate answer may be Walt Whitman's retort to the charge of contradiction: "I am large; I contain multitudes."

Coda: Concluding
Observations

SO MUCH OF WHAT nearly everyone understands to be part of our
Constitution is nowhere to be found in its text that it's a wonder
anyone still doubts the importance, the propriety, and, indeed, the
necessity of arguing seriously and respectfully over the contents
of the Constitution's "dark matter"—the invisible portion of the
Constitution writ large. Even so basic an axiom as the impermissi-
bility of secession from the Union—an axiom written in blood rather
than ink—is invisible to the reader of the bare text. Invoking the
tacit postulates of the constitutional plan—neither a technique of
the Left nor a technique of the Right—is an enterprise that should
unite all who accept the Constitution as their lodestar.

I hope I'm not dreaming when I imagine that one consequence
of this book might be to hasten, if just by a little, the day when the
argument over whether there *is* an invisible, unwritten Constitution
gives way to the far more productive argument over what that
invisible Constitution *contains*. Certainly the enormous difficulties
attending any effort to reach consensus in that argument—indeed,

the impossibility of attaining consensus except at levels of abstraction and generality so high as to be relatively unhelpful to the resolution of most real-life controversies—must not be permitted to deflect or deflate our efforts to engage one another in the attempt. After all, the absence of consensus about the contents and application of constitutional norms hardly differentiates the invisible Constitution from the one we can all see and read. Whether and under what circumstances and standards the text of the First Amendment protects flag burning, cross burning, or the public display of religious symbols—to suggest just a handful of typical puzzles—are questions no less generative of divergent answers than are the invisible Constitution's intractable questions about rights of privacy and claims of equal dignity, or its disputes over federal-state relations and the limits of executive power in wartime.

It is not the visible or invisible character of our constitutional commitments but their irreducible ambiguity and multidimensionality that ensures our continuing struggle over their meaning. In the end, it is the struggle itself—not any of the interim destinations to which it might lead—that the constitutional quest is all about. And the quest for the invisible Constitution is surely central to any study of the Constitution we are able to see and to read. A friend recently shared with me the message from a fortune cookie he had just opened. In its contemporary reprise of the parable of Plato's cave it seems unusually apposite to this book's inquiry into that part of our Constitution that remains invisible, so I reproduce it here: "Everything that we see is a shadow cast by that which we do not see."

Sources

PART I: BEYOND THE VISIBLE

IDENTIFYING "THE CONSTITUTION"

p. 2: Justice Jackson's famous utterance about the source of the Court's authority may be found in Brown v. Allen, 344 U.S. 443, 540 (1953).

p. 3: On the history of the Twenty-seventh Amendment, see Akhil Reed Amar, AMERICA'S CONSTITUTION: A BIOGRAPHY (RANDOM HOUSE, 2005), 453–57.

p. 4: The argument that the Twenty-seventh Amendment is a valid part of the Constitution is made in Laurence H. Tribe, *The 27th Amendment Joins the Constitution*, WALL STREET JOURNAL, May 13, 1992, A15.

p. 6: The best known and most ambitious discussion of "constitutional moments" is that of Bruce Ackerman, WE THE PEOPLE: FOUNDATIONS (HARVARD UNIVERSITY PRESS, 1991), and WE THE PEOPLE: TRANSFORMATIONS (HARVARD UNIVERSITY PRESS, 1998). See also Cass Sunstein, *Constitutionalism after the New Deal*, 101 HARV. L. REV. 421 (1987). Two Supreme Court decisions are largely responsible for the association of 1937 with the idea of a constitutional shift: NLRB v. Jones & Laughlin Steel Co., 301 U.S.

1 (1937); West Coast Hotel Co. v. Parrish, 300 U.S. 379 (1937). For discussion of some antecedents, see G. Edward White, THE CONSTITUTION AND THE NEW DEAL (HARVARD UNIVERSITY PRESS, 2000).

DISTINGUISHING "THE CONSTITUTION" FROM "CONSTITUTIONAL LAW"

pp. 9–10: Early modern discussions of the "unwritten Constitution" may be found in William Bennett Munro, THE MAKERS OF THE UNWRITTEN CONSTITUTION (MACMILLAN, 1930); Christopher G. Tiedeman, THE UNWRITTEN CONSTITUTION OF THE UNITED STATES (PUTNAM'S, 1890). See also Karl N. Llewellyn, *The Constitution as an Institution*, 34 COLUM. L. REV. 1 (1934).

p. 10: The resurrection of "unwritten Constitution" scholarship was inaugurated by Thomas C. Grey, *Origins of the Unwritten Constitution: Fundamental Law in American Revolutionary Thought*, 30 STAN. L. REV. 843 (1978); William E. Nelson, *The Impact of the Antislavery Movement upon Styles of Judicial Reasoning in Nineteenth-Century America*, 87 HARV. L. REV. 722 (1974). A thoughtful recent instance of this scholarship is Benjamin L. Berger, *White Fire: Structural Indeterminacy, Constitutional Design, and the Constitution Behind the Text*, J. COMP. L. (forthcoming).

p. 10: The status of Supreme Court opinions as the "law" of the Constitution is best explored in Charles Fried, SAYING WHAT THE LAW IS (HARVARD UNIVERSITY PRESS, 2004); Richard H. Fallon Jr., IMPLEMENTING THE CONSTITUTION (HARVARD UNIVERSITY PRESS, 2001); David A. Strauss, *Common Law Constitutional Interpretation*, 63 U. CHI. L. REV. 877 (1996).

pp. 10–11: For a provocative consideration of whether executive branch interpretations of the Constitution ought to be understood as having a significance comparable to judicial—including Supreme Court—interpretations, see Michael Stokes Paulsen, *The Most Dangerous Branch: Executive Power to Say What the Law Is*, 83 GEO. L. J. 217 (1994).

p. 11: Justice Holmes famously characterized common law as a "brooding omnipresence in the sky" in Southern Pac. Co. v. Jensen, 244 U.S. 205, 222 (1917).

p. 11: The leading exploration of the "constitutional culture" is Robert C. Post, *Fashioning the Legal Constitution: Culture, Courts, and Law*, 117 HARV. L. REV. 4 (2003). The best recent elaboration is Robert C. Post & Reva Siegel, *Roe Rage: Democratic Constitutionalism and Backlash*, 42 HARV. C. R.–C. L. L.

Rev. 373 (2007). The most important scholarly work linking distinct domains of the constitutional culture to particular clusters of constitutional doctrines is Robert C. Post, CONSTITUTIONAL DOMAINS: DEMOCRACY, COMMUNITY, MANAGEMENT (HARVARD UNIVERSITY PRESS, 1995). A particularly perceptive historically focused exploration is H. Jefferson Powell, A COMMUNITY BUILT ON WORDS: THE CONSTITUTION IN HISTORY AND POLITICS (UNIVERSITY OF CHICAGO PRESS, 2002). The inquiry into the invisible Constitution, whether rooted in law or in the "legal culture," is distinguishable from the investigation of extraconstitutional features of our law that some argue function much the same way the Constitution does. See Ernest A. Young, *The Constitution outside the Constitution*, 117 YALE L. J. 408 (2007).

REMEMBERING OURS IS A "WRITTEN" CONSTITUTION

pp. 13–14: The complex relationship between parliamentary supremacy and the United Kingdom's unwritten constitution is explored ably by Pavlos Eleftheriadis, "The Constitution as Higher Law," UNIVERSITY OF OXFORD FACULTY OF LAW, LEGAL STUDIES RESEARCH PAPER SERIES (Jan. 2008), Working Paper No. 04/2008. Israel's former chief justice, Aharon Barak, explores the possibility of developing "constitutional law" without any written constitution in THE ROLE OF COURTS IN SOCIETY 448 (Shimon Shetreed ed., MARTINUS NIJHOFF PUBLISHERS, 1988).

THE VARIABLE ROLE OF INTERPRETIVE JUDICIAL PRECEDENT

p. 15: The constitutional amendments countermanding specific Supreme Court decisions are the Eleventh, Fourteenth, Sixteenth, and Twenty-sixth.

p. 16: The classic exploration of why workplace sexual harassment constitutes a form of sex discrimination that violates federal statutes (and sometimes the U.S. Constitution) is Catharine A. MacKinnon, SEXUAL HARASSMENT OF WORKING WOMEN (YALE UNIVERSITY PRESS, 1979).

pp. 17–18: The Supreme Court's declaration that its decisions must be considered—sometimes, at least—as themselves the "supreme law of the land" came in Cooper v. Aaron, 358 U.S. 1, 18 (1958).

p. 18: The sharply divided Supreme Court decision invalidating use of race, in the cases at hand, as one of several factors to assign students to schools is Parents Involved in Community Schools v. Seattle School Dist. No. 1, 127 S. Ct. 2738 (2007).

p. 18: Justice Kennedy's concurring opinion in the Seattle School District case is examined through the distinct lens of community self-definition, viewed as an expressive act, in a remarkably insightful article by Heather K. Gerken, *Justice Kennedy and the Domains of Equal Protection*, 121 HARV. L. REV. 104 (2007).

p. 19: The landmark Supreme Court decision credited with (or blamed for) establishing the power of judicial review is Marbury v. Madison, 5 U.S. 137 (1803).

p. 19: The *Miranda* warnings were held to be required in custodial police interrogation of criminal suspects in Miranda v. Arizona, 384 U.S. 436 (1966).

p. 20: For discussion of the "mirror image" parade of horribles, centering on Dred Scott v. Sandford, 60 U.S. 393 (1856), Plessy v. Ferguson, 163 U.S. 537 (1896), Lochner v. New York, 198 U.S. 45 (1905), and Korematsu v. United States, 323 U.S. 214 (1944), see William N. Eskridge Jr. & Sanford Levinson (eds.), CONSTITUTIONAL STUPIDITIES, CONSTITUTIONAL TRAGEDIES (NEW YORK UNIVERSITY PRESS, 1998).

PART II: DEFINING THE TERRAIN

INVISIBILITY DEFINED

p. 26: The Supreme Court decision extending the reach of the Fourth Amendment to include wiretapping and electronic eavesdropping was Katz v. United States, 389 U.S. 347 (1967).

p. 27: The Supreme Court decisions overturning the convictions of flag burners were Texas v. Johnson, 491 U.S. 397 (1989); United States v. Eichman, 496 U.S. 310 (1990).

pp. 27–28: On the relationships among "standard" legal argument, the Constitution's text, and the "unenumerated rights" controversy as distinct from the role of courts in enforcing the Constitution, see Frank I. Michelman, *Unenumerated Rights under Popular Constitutionalism*, 9 UNIVERSITY OF PA. J. CONST'L. LAW 121 (2006).

pp. 29–30: The discussion of Tiedeman and "natural law" draws on Christopher G. Tiedeman, THE UNWRITTEN CONSTITUTION OF THE UNITED STATES (PUTNAM'S, 1890). For a sophisticated recent effort to return natural law reasoning to constitutional law, see Randy E. Barnett, Restoring the Lost Constitution: The Presumption of Liberty (Princeton University Press, 2004).

pp. 30–31: "Energetic scholars" advocating limits on judicial review include Jeremy Waldron, *The Core of the Case against Judicial Review*, 115 Yale L. J. 1346 (2006); Mark Tushnet, Taking the Constitution Away from the Courts (Princeton University Press, 1999); Richard Parker, "Here, the People Rule": A Constitutional Populist Manifesto (Harvard University Press, 1994); Larry D. Kramer, The People Themselves: Popular Constitutionalism and Judicial Review (Oxford University Press, 2004); Adrian Vermeule, *Common Law Constitutionalism and the Limits of Reason*, 107 Colum. L. Rev. 1482 (2007). A leading rejoinder, arguing that courts are peculiarly well suited to pursue and enforce as definitive the basic requirements of political justice as expressed in constitutional terms, is Lawrence G. Sager, Justice in Plainclothes: A Theory of American Constitutional Practice (Yale University Press, 2004).

p. 31: Scholars countering the case for limiting the role of judicial review by invoking the "need for stability and the dangers of social chaos" if each government department feels free to pursue its own reading of the Constitution include Larry Alexander & Frederick Schauer, *On Extrajudicial Constitutional Interpretation*, 110 Harv. L. Rev. 1359 (1997).

p. 33: On the role of constitutional "boundaries," sometimes "shifting," in the constitutional protection of "intimate private life," see Louis Michael Seidman, Our Unsettled Constitution (Yale University Press, 2001), 61–85; *Public Principle and Private Choices: The Uneasy Case for a Boundary Maintenance Theory of Constitutional Law*, 96 Yale L. J. 558 (1987).

Not Necessarily an Ideal Constitution

p. 36: The "influential law review article" accusing "liberal" legal scholars of "smuggling" their personal and political preferences into their interpretations of the Constitution is Henry P. Monaghan, *Our Perfect Constitution*, 56 N.Y.U. L. Rev. 353 (1981).

The Politics of Constitutional Invisibility

p. 41: On the variable political valence of "unenumerated rights," see Mark Tushnet, *Can You Watch Unenumerated Rights Drift?* 9 University of Pa. J. Const'l Law 209 (2006).

THIS BOOK'S MISSION: MAKING INVISIBILITY VISIBLE

p. 44: The landmark Supreme Court decision (in)famously constraining the interpretation of the Privileges or Immunities Clause of the Fourteenth Amendment was the Slaughterhouse Cases, 83 U.S. 36 (1873).

SUPREME LAW, NOT THE SUPREME COURT

p. 47: Chief Justice John Marshall's pronouncements about judicial review came in Marbury v. Madison, 5 U.S. 137, 163, 177, 180 (1803).

pp. 49–50: The point involving consequentialist arguments, "high-level claims," and "the best effect over all" is developed in Adrian Vermeule, JUDGING UNDER UNCERTAINTY: AN INSTITUTIONAL THEORY OF LEGAL INTERPRETATION (HARVARD UNIVERSITY PRESS, 2006).

p. 50: Thayer's famous thesis originated in James Bradley Thayer, *The Origin and Scope of the American Doctrine of Constitutional Law*, 7 HARV. L. REV. 129 (1893).

THE CONSTITUTION'S ARCHITECTURE, NOT ITS "CONSTRUCTION"

p. 52: The idea of transformative "constitutional moments" was first developed comprehensively by Bruce Ackerman, WE THE PEOPLE: FOUNDATIONS (HARVARD UNIVERSITY PRESS, 1991); WE THE PEOPLE: TRANSFORMATIONS (HARVARD UNIVERSITY PRESS, 1998).

pp. 52–53: The concept of intertemporally reverberating constitutional amendments is most thoughtfully explored by Akhil Reed Amar, AMERICA'S CONSTITUTION: A BIOGRAPHY (RANDOM HOUSE, 2005), 405–30.

p. 53: For models of gradual constitutional change, see David Strauss, *Common Law Constitutional Interpretation*, 63 U. CHI. L. REV. 877 (1996); Jed Rubenfeld, *The Paradigm-Case Method*, 115 YALE L. J. 1977 (2006). For the most important elaboration of the overarching theme that the Constitution is best understood in terms of a continuous, intergenerational commitment to a self-governing polity's set of core principles, see Jed Rubenfeld, FREEDOM AND TIME (YALE UNIVERSITY PRESS, 2001).

p. 55: The cases best illustrating Warren Court and Rehnquist Court congruences are Miranda v. Arizona, 383 U.S. 436 (1966); Katz v. United States, 389 U.S. 347 (1967); City of Boerne v. Flores, 521 U.S. 507 (1997); Seminole Tribe of Florida v. Florida, 517 U.S. 44 (1996).

p. 56: On the structural theory of presidential leadership, see Stephen Skowronek, THE POLITICS PRESIDENTS MAKE (HARVARD UNIVERSITY PRESS, 1993).

PART III: EXPLORATIONS BEYOND THE TEXT

INVISIBILITY EXEMPLIFIED: THE MOVING FINGER WRITES

p. 60: "The moving finger" language is from Omar Khayyam, THE RUBAIYAT, stanza 71.

pp. 61–63: On the "dormant" commerce clause and its interactions with the Twenty-first Amendment, see Gibbons v. Ogden, 22 U.S. 1, 71 (1824); Tyler Pipe Industries v. Department of Revenue, 483 U.S. 232, 259–60 (1987); Granholm v. Heald, 544 U.S. 460, 486 (2005).

CLEO'S CLAIMS

pp. 67–68: For Justice Scalia's conclusion that the Fourteenth Amendment proscribes *any* classification based on race, see Oral Argument in Parents Involved in Community Schools v. Seattle School District (Dec. 4, 2006), 49–50. Justice Scalia has asserted this view repeatedly. See, e.g., City of Richmond v. J. A. Croson Co., 488 U.S. 469, 520–28 (1989) (Scalia, J., concurring).

p. 68: Judge McConnell's argument that *Brown* is consistent with the original understanding of the Fourteenth Amendment appeared in Michael W. McConnell, *Originalism and the Desegregation Decisions*, 81 VA. L. REV. 947 (1995).

p. 68: That the "relevant inquiry" is an inquiry into what the text was *intended to mean*, as distinct from what its authors *expected* the text would be used to uphold or invalidate, is argued best in Ronald Dworkin, FREEDOM'S LAW (HARVARD UNIVERSITY PRESS, 1996), 7–12.

p. 69: For Charles Black's defense of *Brown*, see Charles L. Black, *The Lawfulness of the Segregation Decisions*, 69 YALE L. J. 421 (1960).

p. 72: "Fixed stars in our constitutional constellation": West Virginia State Board of Education v. Barnette, 319 U.S. 624, 642 (1943).

TWO TYPES OF EXTRATEXTUAL NORMS

p. 80: The view of the Ninth Amendment as an "inkblot" is stated in Robert H. Bork, THE TEMPTING OF AMERICA: THE POLITICAL SEDUCTION OF THE LAW (FREE PRESS, 1990), 166.

INVISIBILITY ILLUMINATED: A GOVERNMENT OF LAWS

p. 83: The "government of laws, not men" language appears in Cooper v. Aaron, 358 U.S. 1, 23 (1958) (Frankfurter, J., concurring); MASS. CONST. of 1780, pt. 1, art. XXX; Marbury v. Madison, 5 U.S. (1 Cranch) 137, 163 (1803).

INVISIBILITY ELABORATED: GOVERNMENT OF THE PEOPLE, BY THE PEOPLE, FOR THE PEOPLE

p. 86: For the classic invocation of "the better angels of our nature," see Abraham Lincoln, First Inaugural Address (Mar. 4, 1861), in ABRAHAM LINCOLN, SPEECHES AND WRITINGS 1859–1865, at 224 (Don E. Fehrenbacher ed., LIBRARY OF AMERICA, 1989).

p. 86: "No taxation without representation": THE DECLARATION OF INDEPENDENCE, para. 19 (U.S. 1776). The Supreme Court decision invalidating Maryland's tax on the Bank of the United States and reasoning that its fundamental flaw was that it selectively imposed a financial burden on out-of-staters who lacked the power to hold state lawmakers accountable was McCulloch v. Maryland, 17 U.S. (4 Wheat.) 316, 427–32 (1819).

p. 90: On John Adams's admission that he "never understood" the republican form clause, and his belief that no one ever did or will, see John Adams to Mercy Warren (July 20, 1807), in CORRESPONDENCE BETWEEN JOHN ADAMS AND MERCY WARREN 353 (Charles F. Adams ed., ARNO PRESS, 1972).

p. 91: The principal Supreme Court rulings striking down as unconstitutional the congressional commandeering of state executive and legislative officials and agendas, and emphasizing that such commandeering systematically frustrates political accountability and denies the respect owed by the national government to state governments and their sovereign responsibilities, are Printz v. United States, 521 U.S. 898, 920–21 (1997); New York v. United States, 505 U.S. 144, 175–76, 182–83 (1992).

p. 93: For the full text of the Military Commissions Act of 2006, see Pub. L. No. 109–366, 120 Stat. 2600 (to be codified in scattered sections of 10, 18, 28, and 42 U.S.C.).

p. 94: On the significance of the writ of habeas corpus as a long-established means for judges to examine the legality of the grounds asserted to justify an individual's executive detention, see Richard H. Fallon Jr. & Daniel J. Meltzer, *Habeas Corpus Jurisdiction, Substantive Rights, and the War on Terror*, 120 Harv. L. Rev. 2029, 2032–40 (2007).

p. 94: On the Civil War habeas corpus controversy, see Daniel Farber, Lincoln's Constitution (University of Chicago Press, 2003), 157–63.

pp. 94–95: In Boumediene v. Bush, decided June 12, 2008, as this book went to press, the Court struck down Congress's 2006 Act suspending access to habeas corpus for aliens detained as enemy combatants in Guantanamo, a military base entirely under American control in Cuba, holding that Article I's conditions for suspending the writ had not been met and that the tribunals Congress created to decide which aliens were enemy combatants and whether they were being held lawfully were constitutionally inadequate. Although neither the Constitution's text nor its history firmly established a right to habeas corpus for aliens outside our sovereign territory, the majority opinion by Justice Kennedy (joined by Justices Stevens, Souter, Ginsburg, and Breyer) argued that our "[s]ecurity depends [not only] upon . . . the ability of our armed forces to act" but also upon "fidelity to freedom's first principles," including "freedom from arbitrary and unlawful restraint." To the dissenting accusation of Chief Justice Roberts and Justices Scalia, Thomas, and Alito that the Court lacked authority to undermine the nation's war on terrorism in this way, the majority responded that our laws and Constitution "are designed to survive, and remain in force, in extraordinary times. Liberty and security can be reconciled; and in our system they are reconciled within the framework of the law."

p. 96: The challenge to prevalent lethal injection protocols for capital punishment, alleging that those protocols inflict needless pain and paralyze the prisoner so that neither movement nor screams of pain are possible, failed in Baze v. Rees, 128 S. Ct. 1520 (2008).

p. 97: Concerning the unreliability of information extracted through torture, see Harold Hongju Koh, *A World without Torture*, 43 COLUM. J. TRANSNAT'L L. 653 & n. 48 (2005).

FEDERALISM—AND "THE RIGHT OF THE PEOPLE TO KEEP AND BEAR ARMS"

p. 99: For Justice Scalia's marijuana argument, see his concurrence in Gonzales v. Raich, 545 U.S. 1, 33–42 (2005).

p. 100: In District of Columbia v. Heller, decided June 26, 2008, as this book went to press, the Court struck down the D.C. statute banning handguns and requiring all other guns to be kept "unloaded and disassembled or bound by a trigger lock." The majority opinion by Justice Scalia (joined by Chief Justice Roberts and Justices Kennedy, Thomas, and Alito) construed the Second Amendment to guarantee an individual's right to possess firearms, unconnected with service in the militia, for such traditionally lawful purposes as self-defense within the home. Justices Breyer, Stevens, Souter, and Ginsburg dissented. The Court drew no distinction between the D.C. ban and a federal ban elsewhere and left open the right's applicability to state laws as well as the range of permissible firearms regulations. See Mark Tushnet, OUT OF RANGE: WHY THE CONSTITUTION CAN'T END THE BATTLE OVER GUNS (OXFORD UNIVERSITY PRESS, 2007).

STATES AS SOVEREIGNS?

pp. 101–2: The Supreme Court "anticommandeering" decisions are New York v. United States, 505 U.S. 144, 177 (1992); Printz v. United States, 521 U.S. 898, 920–21, 935 (1997).

p. 102: The "tacit postulates" of the constitutional plan "are as much engrained in the fabric of the document as its express provisions": Nevada v. Hall, 440 U.S. 410, 433 (1979) (Rehnquist, J., dissenting).

pp. 102–3: For the dissenting justices' arguments in the commandeering cases, see Printz v. United States, 521 U.S. 898, 939–48, 957–62 (1997) (Stevens, J., dissenting); New York v. United States, 505 U.S. 144, 196–199 (1992) (White, J., dissenting).

p. 103: That the dissenting justices' constitutional jurisprudence has likewise often relied on nontextual constraints—including, for example, the "right to privacy"—is demonstrated by, e.g., Planned Parenthood of Se. Pa. v. Casey, 505 U.S. 833, 912 (1992) (Stevens, J., concurring in part, citing, e.g., Griswold v. Connecticut, 381 U.S. 479 (1965)).

pp. 104–5: "The state does not act by its people in their collective capacity, but through such political agencies as are duly constituted and established. The legislative power is the supreme authority, except as limited by the constitution of the state, and the sovereignty of the people is exercised through their representatives in the legislature, unless by the fundamental law power is elsewhere reposed." McPherson v. Blacker, 146 U.S. 1, 25 (1892).

PART IV: THE CONTENT OF LIBERTY AND EQUALITY AND THE BOUNDARIES OF GOVERNMENT POWER

THE "SUBSTANTIVE DUE PROCESS" CONUNDRUM

p. 109: The seminal Supreme Court decision adopting a narrow (and increasingly doubted) interpretation of the phrase "privileges or immunities" is the Slaughterhouse Cases, 83 U.S. 36, 74–83 (1872).

pp. 110–11: The earliest Supreme Court decision substantively "incorporating" freedom of speech into the Fourteenth Amendment's ban on state deprivations of "liberty" "without due process of law" is Gitlow v. New York, 268 U.S. 652, 666 (1925).

pp. 111–12: *Dred Scott* treated the Fifth Amendment Due Process Clause as encompassing a set of substantive limitations on the permissible content of government's commands or penalties, a view that was independent of the Court's far more widely noted (and justly condemned) assertion that persons of African descent who were either slaves or the descendants of slaves could not be citizens of any state and had "no rights which the white man was bound to respect." Dred Scott v. Sandford, 60 U.S. (19 How.) 393, 407, 450 (1857). It is the latter assertion, and not the former view, that accounts for the occasional invocation of *Dred Scott* as demonstrating the folly of "substantive due process" in the right to reproductive freedom context. See, e.g., Planned Parenthood of Se. Pa. v. Casey, 505 U.S. 833, 998 (1992) (Scalia, J., dissenting).

pp. 113–14: That Congress deprives public schoolchildren of their "liberty" without "due process of law" when it forces racial minorities to attend schools of their own and forbids racial mixing in the public schools of the nation's capital is the holding of Bolling v. Sharpe, 347 U.S. 497, 499–500 (1954).

pp. 113–14: Virginia's statute forbidding white/black intermarriage was held unconstitutional both as a denial of the equal protection of the laws and as an unconstitutional deprivation of liberty without due process of law in the aptly named case of Loving v. Virginia, 388 U.S. 1 (1967).

p. 114: For the emergence of "entitlement" analysis in connection with "new property" created by government programs, see Goldberg v. Kelly, 397 U.S. 254 (1970): Board of Regents v. Roth, 408 U.S. 564, 576–578 (1972).

THE JAGGED ROAD TO EQUALITY

pp. 116–17: The Massachusetts Supreme Judicial Court ruling that racial segregation imposed by law in public schools did not violate the state constitution's declaration that all men are "born free and equal" is Roberts v. City of Boston, 59 Mass. 198 (1849).

p. 117: The Supreme Court decision upholding the constitutionality of racial segregation in public transportation (and expressing the view that such segregation would certainly be permissible in "separate but equal" public school facilities) is Plessy v. Ferguson, 163 U.S. 537 (1896).

p. 117: On the inconclusive evidence bearing on whether the drafters and ratifiers of the Fourteenth Amendment understood the Amendment's Equal Protection Clause to bar racial segregation of the sort upheld in *Plessy* and struck down in *Brown v. Board of Education* (and strongly suggesting that they probably did not), see Alexander M. Bickel, *The Original Understanding and the Segregation Decision*, 69 HARV. L. REV. 1, 47, 58 (1955).

pp. 117–18: The Supreme Court declared unconstitutional state laws establishing racial segregation in public schools, even if the racially separate schools were in some sense "equal," in the landmark case of Brown v. Board of Educ., 347 U.S. 483 (1954).

THE REAPPORTIONMENT REVOLUTION

p. 119: On the "reapportionment revolution," see Gordon E. Baker, THE REAPPORTIONMENT REVOLUTION: REPRESENTATION, POLITICAL POWER, AND THE SUPREME COURT (RANDOM HOUSE, 1966).

p. 119: For Ronald Dworkin's division of equality claims into two categories— claims to be "treated as an equal" and claims to "equal treatment," see Ronald Dworkin, SOVEREIGN VIRTUE: THE THEORY AND PRACTICE OF EQUALITY (HARVARD UNIVERSITY PRESS, 2000), 11.

pp. 120–21: The "one person, one vote" principle: Reynolds v. Sims, 377 U.S. 533 (1964); Gray v. Sanders, 372 U.S. 368 (1963). Justice Douglas: "The conception of political equality from the Declaration of Independence, to Lincoln's Gettysburg Address, to the Fifteenth, Seventeenth, and Nineteenth Amendments can mean only one thing—one person, one vote." Gray v. Sanders, 372 U.S. 368, 381 (1963). Chief Justice Warren: the "one person, one vote" principle is "the clear and strong command of our Constitution's Equal Protection Clause. [It] is an essential part of the concept of a government of laws and not men. [It] is at the heart of Lincoln's vision of 'government of the people, by the people, (and) for the people.'" Reynolds v. Sims, 377 U.S. 533, 567 (1964).

pp. 121–22: The "one person, one vote" principle was applied to state congressional districting plans under Article I, section 2 of the Constitution, providing that members of the House of Representatives shall be chosen "by the People." Wesberry v. Sanders, 376 U.S. 1, 7–8 (1964).

LOCHNER *AND SELECTIVE "INCORPORATION"*

p. 124: For the argument that the entire Bill of Rights is incorporated against the states through the Fourteenth Amendment, see Betts v. Brady, 316 U.S. 455, 474–75 & n. 1 (1942) (Black, J., dissenting).

pp. 124–25: The Supreme Court decision holding that a New York law setting maximum hours for bakers could not be justified out of a concern for either the public's or the bakers' health and thus was an infringement of due process "liberty" is Lochner v. New York, 198 U.S. 45, 56–65 (1905). Similarly reasoned is Coppage v. Kansas, 236 U.S. 1 (1915). Supreme Court decisions of the period illustrating cases in which labor regulations and other socioeconomic measures were challenged on *Lochner*-like grounds but were deemed constitutional prominently include Muller v. Oregon, 208 U.S. 412 (1908) (upholding maximum hours law for women); Holden v. Hardy, 168 U.S. 366 (1898) (upholding maximum hours law for miners).

p. 126: The landmark 1937 decision in which a "switch in view" by Justice Owen Roberts marked the end of the *Lochner*-era jurisprudence is West Coast Hotel Co. v. Parrish, 300 U.S. 379 (1937).

p. 127: Justice Holmes's famous *Lochner* dissent may be found in Lochner v. New York, 198 U.S. 45, 75–76 (1905) (Holmes, J., dissenting).

FROM LIBERTY OF CONTRACT TO FORMS OF SELF-GOVERNMENT

p. 129: The Supreme Court decision holding that the Impairment of Contract Clause restricted only retroactive legislative impairments of contractual obligation is Ogden v. Saunders, 25 U.S. 213, 264 (1827). Chief Justice Marshall's dissent in that case—his only published dissent in over 34 years from a ruling based on the Constitution—argued that the clause included a substantive command to respect the autonomy of bargaining parties and left the state legislatures with strictly limited power to police the boundaries of contractual arrangements: Ogden, 25 U.S. at 369 (Marshall, C.J., dissenting).

pp. 129–30: The Supreme Court decision holding that every contract implicitly incorporates certain basic presuppositions of the legal order is Home Bldg. & Loan Ass'n v. Blaisdell, 290 U.S. 398, 434–35 (1934).

INTIMATE ASSOCIATION AND PRIVATE SELF-GOVERNMENT

pp. 132–33: The classic early decisions dealing with the authority of parents to "govern" their families, regarded as a facet of Fifth and Fourteenth Amendment "liberty," are Pierce v. Soc'y of Sisters, 268 U.S. 510, 534–35 (1925); Meyer v. Nebraska, 262 U.S. 390, 399–401 (1923). The contemporary pertinence of these decisions, notwithstanding the eclipse of the *Lochner* era in which they arose, is illustrated, e.g., by Winkelman v. Parma City Sch. Dist., 127 S. Ct. 1994, 2003 (2007).

p. 133: The Supreme Court decision holding that a state may not criminalize medical provision of contraceptives for use by married couples is Griswold v. Connecticut, 381 U.S. 479, 482–86 (1965). For a self-government-focused perspective on the rights recognized in such cases, treating the autonomy they protect as indispensable to democracy itself, see James E. Fleming, SECURING CONSTITUTIONAL RIGHTS: THE CASE OF AUTONOMY (UNIVERSITY OF CHICAGO PRESS, 2006).

pp. 133–34: The decision extending *Griswold* to unmarried couples is Eisenstadt v. Baird, 405 U.S. 438, 454–55 (1972). The decision striking down a municipal zoning ordinance restricting residence to essentially nuclear families is Moore v. East Cleveland, 431 U.S. 494, 506 (1977). The abortion decision is Roe v. Wade, 410 U.S. 113, 164–65 (1973).

pp. 134–36: The decision rejecting a claim to constitutional autonomy for intimate sexual relations is Bowers v. Hardwick, 478 U.S. 186, 193–94 (1986).

pp. 135–37: The decision declaring that *Bowers* had been wrong since "the day it was decided" is Lawrence v. Texas, 539 U.S. 558, 578 (2003).

MAINTAINING BOUNDARIES: FROM TERRITORIALITY TO PRIVACY

p. 139: Justice Thomas (joined by Justice Scalia) argued that the dormant commerce clause has no basis in the text of the Constitution and thus should be eliminated from the Court's jurisprudence in Camps Newfound/Owatonna v. Town of Harrison, 520 U.S. 564, 610 (1997) (Thomas, J., dissenting).

p. 140: On the presumption against extraterritorial application of law, see Foley Bros. v. Filardo, 336 U.S. 281, 285 (1949).

PART V: VISUALIZING THE INVISIBLE

ONCE AGAIN: THE NINTH AMENDMENT'S RULE OF CONSTRUCTION

p. 145: For the Ninth Amendment's invocation in *Griswold*, see Griswold v. Connecticut, 381 U.S. 479, 484 (1965) (majority opinion by Douglas, J.); 381 U.S. at 479, 487–96 (Goldberg, J., concurring).

p. 146: For the Supreme Court's post-*Griswold* references to the Ninth Amendment, see Planned Parenthood of Se. Pa v. Casey, 505 U.S. 833, 848 (1992) (plurality opinion of O'Connor, Kennedy, and Souter, JJ.); Richmond Newspapers, Inc. v. Virginia, 448 U.S. 555, 579 n. 15 (1980) (Burger, C.J., plurality opinion); see also Richmond Newspapers, 448 U.S. at 603 (Blackmun, J., concurring). For a general discussion, see Daniel A. Farber, RETAINED BY THE PEOPLE: THE "SILENT" NINTH AMENDMENT AND THE CONSTITUTIONAL RIGHTS AMERICANS DON'T KNOW THEY HAVE (BASIC BOOKS, 2007).

p. 147: See Charles L. Black Jr., A NEW BIRTH OF FREEDOM: HUMAN RIGHTS, NAMED AND UNNAMED (PUTNAM, 1997); Charles L. Black Jr., STRUCTURE AND RELATIONSHIP IN CONSTITUTIONAL LAW (LOUISIANA STATE UNIVERSITY PRESS, 1969); Charles L. Black Jr., *Further Reflections on the Constitutional Justice of Livelihood*, 86 COLUM. L. REV. 1103 (1986).

p. 147: On how one might read "a clause proclaiming the existence of ghosts," see John Hart Ely, DEMOCRACY AND DISTRUST: A THEORY OF JUDICIAL REVIEW (HARVARD UNIVERSITY PRESS, 1980), 39.

THE INESCAPABLE ROLE OF CONSTITUTIONAL "DARK MATTER"

p. 149: Jonathan Safran Foer, EVERYTHING IS ILLUMINATED (HOUGHTON MIFFLIN, 2002).

p. 150: Amending the Articles of Confederation: ARTICLES OF CONFEDERATION, art. xiii (U.S. 1977) ("And the Articles of this Confederation shall be inviolably observed by every State, and the Union shall be perpetual; nor shall any alteration at any time hereafter be made in any of them; unless such alteration be agreed to in a Congress of the United States, and be afterwards confirmed by the legislatures of every State").

p. 151: On baselines, see Cass R. Sunstein, THE PARTIAL CONSTITUTION (HARVARD UNIVERSITY PRESS, 1993), 3–7, 45–62, 347–53.

THE ANALOGY TO GÖDEL'S INCOMPLETENESS THEOREM

p. 153: Janna Levin, A MADMAN DREAMS OF TURING MACHINES (KNOPF, 2006).

GEOMETRIC CONSTRUCTION

pp. 158–60: Justice Jackson, "laws, not men," King James: Youngstown Sheet & Tube Co. v. Sawyer, 343 U.S. 579, 654–55, 655 n. 27 (1952) (Jackson, J., concurring). Justice Black, "faithfully executed": Youngstown Sheet & Tube Co. v. Sawyer, 343 U.S. 579, 587, 589 (1952). Justice Jackson, Louisiana Purchase, steel seizure: Youngstown Sheet & Tube Co. v. Sawyer, 343 U.S. 579, 638 n. 5 (1952) (Jackson, J., concurring). Jackson's endorsement of "implied powers": Youngstown Sheet & Tube Co. v. Sawyer, 343 U.S. 579, 640 (1952) (Jackson, J., concurring). Jackson, "Pharaoh": Youngstown Sheet & Tube Co. v. Sawyer, 343 U.S. 579, 634 (1952) (Jackson, J., concurring).

p. 160: The language about a word as but "the skin of a living thought" is that of Justice Holmes in Towne v. Eisner, 245 U.S. 418, 425 (1918).

pp. 161–62: Justice Harlan's characterization of liberty as constituting a continuum comes from his much-quoted dissent in Poe v. Ullman, 367 U.S. 497, 543 (1961) (Harlan, J., dissenting).

p. 163: "Had those who drew...freedom": Lawrence v. Texas, 539 U.S. 558, 578–79 (2003).

TIME'S GEOMETRY

p. 165: On the influence of both world wars in shifting the meaning and import of the Equal Protection Clause, see generally Michael J. Klarman, FROM JIM CROW TO CIVIL RIGHTS: THE SUPREME COURT AND THE STRUGGLE FOR RACIAL EQUALITY (OXFORD UNIVERSITY PRESS, 2004), 310; William E. Nelson, *The Changing Meaning of Equality in Twentieth-Century Constitutional Law*, 52 WASH. & LEE L. REV. 3, 100 (1995). See also Mary Dudziak, *Desegregation as a Cold War Imperative*, 41 STAN. L. REV. 61 (1988). For Justice Murphy's declaration, see Hirabayashi v. United States, 320 U.S. 81, 110 (1943) (Murphy, J., concurring).

p. 165: On Cold War politics and "one person, one vote," see Mary L. Dudziak, COLD WAR CIVIL RIGHTS (PRINCETON UNIVERSITY PRESS, 2000), 231–38.

A LIBERTARIAN PRESUMPTION?

p. 166: Defending an attribution of broadly libertarian premises to the Constitution is Richard A. Epstein, TAKINGS (HARVARD UNIVERSITY PRESS, 1985); see also Randy E. Barnett, RESTORING THE LOST CONSTITUTION: THE PRESUMPTION OF LIBERTY (PRINCETON UNIVERSITY PRESS, 2004).

LOCHNER'S *LEGACY REVISITED*

p. 169: "Mr. Herbert Spencer's Social Statics": Lochner v. New York, 198 U.S. 45, 75 (1905) (Holmes, J., dissenting).

GEODESIC CONSTRUCTION

pp. 172–73: New York Times Co. v. Sullivan, 376 U.S. 254 (1964). For Justice Goldberg's concurrence, see 376 U.S. at 298 (1964) (Goldberg, J., concurring).

pp. 173–75: On the required warnings, see Miranda v. Arizona, 384 U.S. 436, 457–58 (1966). The act of Congress replacing those warnings with a test of "voluntariness" is 18 U.S.C.A. § 3501 (1968). The Supreme Court decision holding that statute unconstitutional is Dickerson v. United States, 530 U.S. 428 (2000).

pp. 175–76: The exclusionary rule decision is Mapp v. Ohio, 367 U.S. 643 (1961). That the victims of a constitutional violation by federal officials have a presumptive right to bring federal suit to recover monetary damages against those officials was the teaching of Bivens v. Unknown, Unnamed Agents of Fed. Bureau of Narcotics, 403 U.S. 388 (1971).

p. 178: "Death by a thousand cuts": Wilkie v. Robbins, 127 S.Ct. 2588, 2600 (2007); see also 2608 (Ginsburg, J., concurring in part and dissenting in part). I should disclose that I argued unsuccessfully for a *Bivens* remedy in *Robbins* and wrote a no-holds-barred critique of the Court's majority opinion in Laurence H. Tribe, *Death by a Thousand Cuts: Constitutional Wrongs without Remedies after Wilkie v. Robbins*, CATO SUP. CT. REV. 2006–7 (2007), 23.

pp. 178–79: The 1886 decision proclaiming the right to vote to be a "fundamental political right," Yick Wo v. Hopkins, 118 U.S. 356, 370 (1886), did not itself involve the right to vote but involved the application of the Equal Protection Clause to strike down a pattern of law enforcement that demonstrably discriminated against the Chinese in San Francisco.

p. 179: The colorful "Cheops' Pyramid" language is from Dickerson v. United States, 530 U.S. 428, 465 (2000) (Scalia, J., dissenting).

GLOBAL CONSTRUCTION

p. 181: "So many countries": William H. Rehnquist, *Constitutional Courts— Comparative Remarks*, in GERMANY AND ITS BASIC LAW: PAST, PRESENT, AND FUTURE 411, 412 (Paul Kirchhof & Donald P. Kommers eds., NOMOS, 1993).

pp. 182–83: Citation of a judgment of the West German Constitutional Court regarding the right to life: Planned Parenthood of Se. Pa v. Casey, 505 U.S.833, 945 n. 1 (1992) (Rehnquist, C.J., dissenting). Justice Thomas's citation of international sources in vote dilution challenge case: Holder v. Hall, 512 U.S. 874, 906 n. 14 (1994) (Thomas, J., dissenting). Justice Breyer's dissenting opinion in Printz citing international sources: Printz v. United States, 521 U.S. 898, 976–77 (1997) (Breyer, J., dissenting). Justice Scalia's response: Printz v. United States, 521 U.S. at 921 n. 11 (1997). Supreme Court's reference to international community regarding execution of mentally retarded criminal defendants: Atkins v. Virginia, 536 U.S. 304, 316 n. 21 (2002). Justice Scalia's dissent: Atkins v. Virginia, 536 U.S. at 347–48 (Scalia, J., dissenting). Justice Kennedy, Bowers v. Hardwick, and international reality: Lawrence v. Texas, 539 U.S. 558, 572–73 (2003). Justice Scalia's antiglobalist dissent: Lawrence v. Texas, 539 U.S. at 598 (Scalia, J., dissenting). For Justice Kennedy's reference to international opinion regarding execution of individuals under the age of 18, see Roper v. Simmons, 543 U.S. 551, 578 (2005). Justice O'Connor's dissenting opinion noting that the country's "evolving understanding of human dignity" is not at odds with international values: Roper v. Simmons, 543 U.S. 551, 605 (2005) (O'Connor, J., dissenting).

pp. 184–85: Confirmation statements of Chief Justice Roberts and Justice Alito: *Confirmation Hearing of the Nomination of John G. Roberts, Jr. to Be Chief Justice of the United States: Hearing before the Senate Committee on the Judiciary,* 109th Cong. 200–201 (2005) (statement of Judge John G. Roberts Jr.); *Confirmation Hearing on the Nomination of Samuel Alito to Be Associate Justice of the United States Supreme Court: Hearing before the Senate Committee on the Judiciary,* 109th Cong. 370–71 (2006) (Statement of Judge Samuel A. Alito). Robert Bork's view: Robert Bork, COERCING VIRTUE: THE WORLDWIDE RULE OF JUDGES (AEI PRESS, 2003), 2, 10, 12, 13, 16.

p. 185: The "universal sense of nations": The Rapid, 8 Cranch 155, 161–62 (1814).

pp. 185–86: Netherlands and physician-assisted suicide: Washington v. Glucksberg, 521 U.S. 702, 710, 710 n. 8, 730, 734 (1997); 785–86 (1997) (Souter, J., concurring). Justice Scalia's reference to international sources: McIntyre v. Ohio Elections Comm'n, 514 U.S. 334, 381–82 (1995) (Scalia, J., dissenting).

pp. 186–87: Laurence H. Tribe, keynote address at the 2005 American Constitution Society National Convention (July 30, 2005), www.acslaw.org/node/506. Professor Tushnet's discussion of possible explanations for recent antiglobal tenor of judicial review: Mark Tushnet, *Referring to Foreign Law in Constitutional Interpretation: An Episode in the Culture Wars,* 35 U. BALT. L. REV. 299, 310–11 (2006).

p. 187: House Resolution 568 in the 108th Congress. See H.R.J. Res. 568, 108th Cong. (2004). For the hearings on the resolution, see *Appropriate Role of Foreign Judgments in the Interpretation of American Law: Hearing on H.R. Res. 568 before the Subcommittee on the Constitution of the House Committee on the Judiciary,* 108th Congress (2004).

p. 187: For the testimony of Professor McGinnis before Congress regarding Resolution 568, s*ee Appropriate Role of Foreign Judgments in the Interpretation of American Law: Hearing before the Subcommittee on the Constitution of the House Committee on the Judiciary,* 108th Congress 60–61 (2004).

GEOLOGICAL CONSTRUCTION

p. 189: On Justice Harlan's derivation of certain Fourth Amendment presuppositions, see Poe v. Ullman, 367 U.S. 497, 551 (1961) (Harlan, J., dissenting).

pp. 191–92: Ely's theory: John Hart Ely, DEMOCRACY AND DISTRUST: A THEORY OF JUDICIAL REVIEW (HARVARD UNIVERSITY PRESS, 1980). Bickel's "countermajoritarian difficulty": Alexander M. Bickel, THE LEAST DANGEROUS BRANCH: THE SUPREME COURT AT THE BAR OF POLITICS 16 (1962). Footnote 4: United States v. Carolene Prods. Co., 304 U.S. 144, 152 n. 4 (1938). Ely's Warren Court legacies: Baker v. Carr, 369 U.S. 186 (1962); Brown v. Board. of Educ. of Topeka, 347 U.S. 483 (1954).

pp. 192–93: Criticism: Laurence H. Tribe, *The Puzzling Persistence of Process-Based Constitutional Theories*, 89 YALE L. J. 1063 (1980). Ely's discussion of *Roe v. Wade*: DEMOCRACY AND DISTRUST, 2.

pp. 193–94: For the Supreme Court's characterization of the core holding of *Roe v. Wade*, see Planned Parenthood of Se. Pa v. Casey, 505 U.S. 833 (1992). The *Casey* plurality's argument that if a woman's liberty interests were of no special constitutional moment when her choice was to end her pregnancy (and the state's preference was to continue it) then her interests would likewise be of no special constitutional moment in the converse situation when her choice was to continue her pregnancy (and the state's preference was to end it) may be found in *Casey*, 505 U.S. at 852.

p. 196: Laurence H. Tribe, *Structural Due Process*, 10 HARV. C. R.–C. L. L. REV. 269 (1975).

GRAVITATIONAL CONSTRUCTION

pp. 200–201: Laurence H. Tribe, *The Curvature of Constitutional Space: What Lawyers Can Learn from Modern Physics*, 103 HARV. L. REV. 1 (1989). "Poor Joshua": DeShaney v. Winnebago County Dep't of Soc. Servs., 489 U.S. 189 (1989).

pp. 203–4: For the Supreme Court decision holding that Congress overreached its affirmative power under the Commerce Clause when it enacted the Gun-Free Zones Act, see Lopez v. United States, 514 U.S. 549 (1995).

SOURCES

p. 204: Although upholding Congress's creation of the Bank of the United States as a constitutionally permissible exercise of power reasonably ancillary to its enumerated sources of law-making authority, the Supreme Court in McCulloch v. Maryland, 17 U.S. 316 (1819), treated as axiomatic the proposition that congressional action falling outside those sources and not ancillary to their exercise would be unconstitutional.

pp. 204–5: The language quoted from Justice Jackson is from West Virginia State Board of Education v. Barnette, 319 U.S. 624, 638, 641, 642 (1943).

Gyroscopic Construction

p. 209: "Multitudes": see Walt Whitman, *Song of Myself*, in LEAVES OF GRASS 1, 43 (BOOK JUNGLE, 2007) (1892).

The Visible Constitution:
Its Text and Accompanying
Resolutions

WE THE PEOPLE OF THE United States, in Order to form a more perfect Union, establish Justice, insure domestic Tranquility, provide for the common defence, promote the general Welfare, and secure the Blessings of Liberty to ourselves and our Posterity, do ordain and establish this Constitution for the United States of America.

Article I.

Section 1. All legislative Powers herein granted shall be vested in a Congress of the United States, which shall consist of a Senate and House of Representatives.

Section 2. The House of Representatives shall be composed of Members chosen every second Year by the People of the several States, and the Electors in each State shall have the Qualifications requisite for Electors of the most numerous Branch of the State Legislature.

No Person shall be a Representative who shall not have attained to the Age of twenty five Years, and been seven Years a Citizen of the

United States, and who shall not, when elected, be an Inhabitant of that State in which he shall be chosen.

Representatives and direct Taxes shall be apportioned among the several States which may be included within this Union, according to their respective Numbers, which shall be determined by adding to the whole Number of free Persons, including those bound to Service for a Term of Years, and excluding Indians not taxed, three fifths of all other Persons.

The actual Enumeration shall be made within three Years after the first Meeting of the Congress of the United States, and within every subsequent Term of ten Years, in such Manner as they shall by Law direct. The Number of Representatives shall not exceed one for every thirty Thousand, but each State shall have at Least one Representative; and until such enumeration shall be made, the State of New Hampshire shall be entitled to choose three, Massachusetts eight, Rhode Island and Providence Plantations one, Connecticut five, New York six, New Jersey four, Pennsylvania eight, Delaware one, Maryland six, Virginia ten, North Carolina five, South Carolina five and Georgia three.

When vacancies happen in the Representation from any State, the Executive Authority thereof shall issue Writs of Election to fill such Vacancies.

The House of Representatives shall choose their Speaker and other Officers; and shall have the sole Power of Impeachment.

Section 3. The Senate of the United States shall be composed of two Senators from each State, chosen by the Legislature thereof, for six Years; and each Senator shall have one Vote.

Immediately after they shall be assembled in Consequence of the first Election, they shall be divided as equally as may be into three Classes. The Seats of the Senators of the first Class shall be vacated at the Expiration of the second Year, of the second

Class at the Expiration of the fourth Year, and of the third Class at the Expiration of the sixth Year, so that one third may be chosen every second Year; and if Vacancies happen by Resignation, or otherwise, during the Recess of the Legislature of any State, the Executive thereof may make temporary Appointments until the next Meeting of the Legislature, which shall then fill such Vacancies.

No person shall be a Senator who shall not have attained to the Age of thirty Years, and been nine Years a Citizen of the United States, and who shall not, when elected, be an Inhabitant of that State for which he shall be chosen.

The Vice President of the United States shall be President of the Senate, but shall have no Vote, unless they be equally divided.

The Senate shall choose their other Officers, and also a President pro tempore, in the absence of the Vice President, or when he shall exercise the Office of President of the United States.

The Senate shall have the sole Power to try all Impeachments. When sitting for that Purpose, they shall be on Oath or Affirmation. When the President of the United States is tried, the Chief Justice shall preside: And no Person shall be convicted without the Concurrence of two thirds of the Members present.

Judgment in Cases of Impeachment shall not extend further than to removal from Office, and disqualification to hold and enjoy any Office of honor, Trust or Profit under the United States: but the Party convicted shall nevertheless be liable and subject to Indictment, Trial, Judgment and Punishment, according to Law.

Section 4. The Times, Places and Manner of holding Elections for Senators and Representatives, shall be prescribed in each State by the Legislature thereof; but the Congress may at any time by Law make or alter such Regulations, except as to the Place of Choosing Senators.

The Congress shall assemble at least once in every Year, and such Meeting shall be on the first Monday in December, unless they shall by Law appoint a different Day.

Section 5. Each House shall be the Judge of the Elections, Returns and Qualifications of its own Members, and a Majority of each shall constitute a Quorum to do Business; but a smaller number may adjourn from day to day, and may be authorized to compel the Attendance of absent Members, in such Manner, and under such Penalties as each House may provide.

Each House may determine the Rules of its Proceedings, punish its Members for disorderly Behavior, and, with the Concurrence of two-thirds, expel a Member.

Each House shall keep a Journal of its Proceedings, and from time to time publish the same, excepting such Parts as may in their Judgment require Secrecy; and the Yeas and Nays of the Members of either House on any question shall, at the Desire of one fifth of those Present, be entered on the Journal.

Neither House, during the Session of Congress, shall, without the Consent of the other, adjourn for more than three days, nor to any other Place than that in which the two Houses shall be sitting.

Section 6. The Senators and Representatives shall receive a Compensation for their Services, to be ascertained by Law, and paid out of the Treasury of the United States. They shall in all Cases, except Treason, Felony and Breach of the Peace, be privileged from Arrest during their Attendance at the Session of their respective Houses, and in going to and returning from the same; and for any Speech or Debate in either House, they shall not be questioned in any other Place.

No Senator or Representative shall, during the Time for which he was elected, be appointed to any civil Office under the Authority of the United States which shall have been created, or the Emoluments whereof shall have been increased during such time; and no Person holding any Office under the United States, shall be a Member of either House during his Continuance in Office.

Section 7. All bills for raising Revenue shall originate in the House of Representatives; but the Senate may propose or concur with Amendments as on other Bills.

Every Bill which shall have passed the House of Representatives and the Senate, shall, before it become a Law, be presented to the President of the United States; If he approve he shall sign it, but if not he shall return it, with his Objections to that House in which it shall have originated, who shall enter the Objections at large on their Journal, and proceed to reconsider it. If after such Reconsideration two thirds of that House shall agree to pass the Bill, it shall be sent, together with the Objections, to the other House, by which it shall likewise be reconsidered, and if approved by two thirds of that House, it shall become a Law. But in all such Cases the Votes of both Houses shall be determined by Yeas and Nays, and the Names of the Persons voting for and against the Bill shall be entered on the Journal of each House respectively. If any Bill shall not be returned by the President within ten Days (Sundays excepted) after it shall have been presented to him, the Same shall be a Law, in like Manner as if he had signed it, unless the Congress by their Adjournment prevent its Return, in which Case it shall not be a Law.

Every Order, Resolution, or Vote to which the Concurrence of the Senate and House of Representatives may be necessary (except on a question of Adjournment) shall be presented to the President of the United States; and before the Same shall take Effect, shall be approved by him, or being disapproved by him, shall be repassed by two thirds of the Senate and House of Representatives, according to the Rules and Limitations prescribed in the Case of a Bill.

Section 8. The Congress shall have Power To lay and collect Taxes, Duties, Imposts and Excises, to pay the Debts and provide for the common Defence and general Welfare of the United States; but all Duties, Imposts and Excises shall be uniform throughout the United States;

To borrow money on the credit of the United States;

To regulate Commerce with foreign Nations, and among the several States, and with the Indian Tribes;

To establish an uniform Rule of Naturalization, and uniform Laws on the subject of Bankruptcies throughout the United States;

To coin Money, regulate the Value thereof, and of foreign Coin, and fix the Standard of Weights and Measures;

To provide for the Punishment of counterfeiting the Securities and current Coin of the United States;

To establish Post Offices and Post Roads;

To promote the Progress of Science and useful Arts, by securing for limited Times to Authors and Inventors the exclusive Right to their respective Writings and Discoveries;

To constitute Tribunals inferior to the supreme Court;

To define and punish Piracies and Felonies committed on the high Seas, and Offenses against the Law of Nations;

To declare War, grant Letters of Marque and Reprisal, and make Rules concerning Captures on Land and Water;

To raise and support Armies, but no Appropriation of Money to that Use shall be for a longer Term than two Years;

To provide and maintain a Navy;

To make Rules for the Government and Regulation of the land and naval Forces;

To provide for calling forth the Militia to execute the Laws of the Union, suppress Insurrections and repel Invasions;

To provide for organizing, arming, and disciplining the Militia, and for governing such Part of them as may be employed in the Service of the United States, reserving to the States respectively, the Appointment of the Officers, and the Authority of training the Militia according to the discipline prescribed by Congress;

To exercise exclusive Legislation in all Cases whatsoever, over such District (not exceeding ten Miles square) as may, by Cession of particular States, and the acceptance of Congress, become the Seat of the Government of the United States, and to exercise like Authority over all Places purchased by the Consent of the Legislature of the State in which the Same shall be, for the Erection of Forts, Magazines, Arsenals, dock-Yards, and other needful Buildings; And

To make all Laws which shall be necessary and proper for carrying into Execution the foregoing Powers, and all other Powers vested by this Constitution in the Government of the United States, or in any Department or Officer thereof.

Section 9. The Migration or Importation of such Persons as any of the States now existing shall think proper to admit, shall not be prohibited by the Congress prior to the Year one thousand eight hundred and eight, but a tax or duty may be imposed on such Importation, not exceeding ten dollars for each Person.

The privilege of the Writ of Habeas Corpus shall not be suspended, unless when in Cases of Rebellion or Invasion the public Safety may require it.

No Bill of Attainder or ex post facto Law shall be passed.

No capitation, or other direct, Tax shall be laid, unless in Proportion to the Census or Enumeration herein before directed to be taken.

No Tax or Duty shall be laid on Articles exported from any State.

No Preference shall be given by any Regulation of Commerce or Revenue to the Ports of one State over those of another: nor shall

Vessels bound to, or from, one State, be obliged to enter, clear, or pay Duties in another.

No Money shall be drawn from the Treasury, but in Consequence of Appropriations made by Law; and a regular Statement and Account of the Receipts and Expenditures of all public Money shall be published from time to time.

No Title of Nobility shall be granted by the United States: And no Person holding any Office of Profit or Trust under them, shall, without the Consent of the Congress, accept of any present, Emolument, Office, or Title, of any kind whatever, from any King, Prince or foreign State.

Section 10. No State shall enter into any Treaty, Alliance, or Confederation; grant Letters of Marque and Reprisal; coin Money; emit Bills of Credit; make any Thing but gold and silver Coin a Tender in Payment of Debts; pass any Bill of Attainder, ex post facto Law, or Law impairing the Obligation of Contracts, or grant any Title of Nobility.

No State shall, without the Consent of the Congress, lay any Imposts or Duties on Imports or Exports, except what may be absolutely necessary for executing its inspection Laws: and the net Produce of all Duties and Imposts, laid by any State on Imports or Exports, shall be for the Use of the Treasury of the United States; and all such Laws shall be subject to the Revision and Control of the Congress.

No State shall, without the Consent of Congress, lay any duty of Tonnage, keep Troops, or Ships of War in time of Peace, enter into any Agreement or Compact with another State, or with a foreign Power, or engage in War, unless actually invaded, or in such imminent Danger as will not admit of delay.

Article II.

Section 1. The executive Power shall be vested in a President of the United States of America. He shall hold his Office during the Term of four Years, and, together with the Vice-President chosen for the same Term, be elected, as follows:

Each State shall appoint, in such Manner as the Legislature thereof may direct, a Number of Electors, equal to the whole Number of Senators and Representatives to which the State may be entitled in the Congress: but no Senator or Representative, or Person holding an Office of Trust or Profit under the United States, shall be appointed an Elector.

The Electors shall meet in their respective States, and vote by Ballot for two persons, of whom one at least shall not lie an Inhabitant of the same State with themselves. And they shall make a List of all the Persons voted for, and of the Number of Votes for each; which List they shall sign and certify, and transmit sealed to the Seat of the Government of the United States, directed to the President of the Senate. The President of the Senate shall, in the Presence of the Senate and House of Representatives, open all the Certificates, and the Votes shall then be counted. The Person having the greatest Number of Votes shall be the President, if such Number be a Majority of the whole Number of Electors appointed; and if there be more than one who have such Majority, and have an equal Number of Votes, then the House of Representatives shall immediately choose by Ballot one of them for President; and if no Person have a Majority, then from the five highest on the List the said House shall in like Manner choose the President. But in choosing the President, the Votes shall be taken by States, the Representation from each State having one Vote; a quorum for this Purpose shall consist of a Member or Members from two-thirds of the States, and a Majority of all the States shall be necessary to a Choice. In every Case, after the Choice of the President, the Person having the greatest Number of Votes of the Electors shall be the Vice President. But if there should remain two or more who have equal Votes, the Senate shall choose from them by Ballot the Vice-President.

The Congress may determine the Time of choosing the Electors, and the Day on which they shall give their Votes; which Day shall be the same throughout the United States.

No person except a natural born Citizen, or a Citizen of the United States, at the time of the Adoption of this Constitution, shall be eligible to the Office of President; neither shall any Person be eligible to that Office who shall not have attained to the Age of thirty-five Years, and been fourteen Years a Resident within the United States.

In Case of the Removal of the President from Office, or of his Death, Resignation, or Inability to discharge the Powers and Duties of the said Office, the same shall devolve on the Vice President, and the Congress may by Law provide for the Case of Removal, Death, Resignation or Inability, both of the President and Vice President, declaring what Officer shall then act as President, and such Officer shall act accordingly, until the Disability be removed, or a President shall be elected.

The President shall, at stated Times, receive for his Services, a Compensation, which shall neither be increased nor diminished during the Period for which he shall have been elected, and he shall not receive within that Period any other Emolument from the United States, or any of them.

Before he enters on the Execution of his Office, he shall take the following Oath or Affirmation:

"I do solemnly swear (or affirm) that I will faithfully execute the Office of President of the United States, and will to the best of my Ability, preserve, protect and defend the Constitution of the United States."

Section 2. The President shall be Commander in Chief of the Army and Navy of the United States, and of the Militia of the several States, when called into the actual Service of the United States;

he may require the Opinion, in writing, of the principal Officer in each of the executive Departments, upon any subject relating to the Duties of their respective Offices, and he shall have Power to Grant Reprieves and Pardons for Offenses against the United States, except in Cases of Impeachment.

He shall have Power, by and with the Advice and Consent of the Senate, to make Treaties, provided two thirds of the Senators present concur; and he shall nominate, and by and with the Advice and Consent of the Senate, shall appoint Ambassadors, other public Ministers and Consuls, Judges of the supreme Court, and all other Officers of the United States, whose Appointments are not herein otherwise provided for, and which shall be established by Law: but the Congress may by Law vest the Appointment of such inferior Officers, as they think proper, in the President alone, in the Courts of Law, or in the Heads of Departments.

The President shall have Power to fill up all Vacancies that may happen during the Recess of the Senate, by granting Commissions which shall expire at the End of their next Session.

Section 3. He shall from time to time give to the Congress Information of the State of the Union, and recommend to their Consideration such Measures as he shall judge necessary and expedient; he may, on extraordinary Occasions, convene both Houses, or either of them, and in Case of Disagreement between them, with Respect to the Time of Adjournment, he may adjourn them to such Time as he shall think proper; he shall receive Ambassadors and other public Ministers; he shall take Care that the Laws be faithfully executed, and shall Commission all the Officers of the United States.

Section 4. The President, Vice President and all civil Officers of the United States, shall be removed from Office on Impeachment for, and Conviction of, Treason, Bribery, or other high Crimes and Misdemeanors.

Article III.

Section 1. The judicial Power of the United States, shall be vested in one supreme Court, and in such inferior Courts as the Congress may from time to time ordain and establish. The Judges, both of the supreme and inferior Courts, shall hold their Offices during good Behavior, and shall, at stated Times, receive for their Services a Compensation which shall not be diminished during their Continuance in Office.

Section 2. The judicial Power shall extend to all Cases, in Law and Equity, arising under this Constitution, the Laws of the United States, and Treaties made, or which shall be made, under their Authority; to all Cases affecting Ambassadors, other public Ministers and Consuls; to all Cases of admiralty and maritime Jurisdiction; to Controversies to which the United States shall be a Party; to Controversies between two or more States; between a State and Citizens of another State; between Citizens of different States; between Citizens of the same State claiming Lands under Grants of different States, and between a State, or the Citizens thereof, and foreign States, Citizens or Subjects.

In all Cases affecting Ambassadors, other public Ministers and Consuls, and those in which a State shall be Party, the supreme Court shall have original Jurisdiction. In all the other Cases before mentioned, the supreme Court shall have appellate Jurisdiction, both as to Law and Fact, with such Exceptions, and under such Regulations as the Congress shall make.

The Trial of all Crimes, except in Cases of Impeachment, shall be by Jury; and such Trial shall be held in the State where the said Crimes shall have been committed; but when not committed within any State, the Trial shall be at such Place or Places as the Congress may by Law have directed.

Section 3. Treason against the United States, shall consist only in levying War against them, or in adhering to their Enemies, giving them Aid and Comfort. No Person shall be convicted of Treason unless on the Testimony of two Witnesses to the same overt Act, or on Confession in open Court.

The Congress shall have power to declare the Punishment of Treason, but no Attainder of Treason shall work Corruption of Blood, or Forfeiture except during the Life of the Person attainted.

Article IV.

Section 1. Full Faith and Credit shall be given in each State to the public Acts, Records, and judicial Proceedings of every other State. And the Congress may by general Laws prescribe the Manner in which such Acts, Records and Proceedings shall be proved, and the Effect thereof.

Section 2. The Citizens of each State shall be entitled to all Privileges and Immunities of Citizens in the several States.

A Person charged in any State with Treason, Felony, or other Crime, who shall flee from Justice, and be found in another State, shall on demand of the executive Authority of the State from which he fled, be delivered up, to be removed to the State having Jurisdiction of the Crime.

No Person held to Service or Labour in one State, under the Laws thereof, escaping into another, shall, in Consequence of any Law or Regulation therein, be discharged from such Service or Labour, But shall be delivered up on Claim of the Party to whom such Service or Labour may be due.

Section 3. New States may be admitted by the Congress into this Union; but no new States shall be formed or erected within the Jurisdiction of any other State; nor any State be formed by the Junction of two or more States, or parts of States, without the Consent of the Legislatures of the States concerned as well as of the Congress.

The Congress shall have Power to dispose of and make all needful Rules and Regulations respecting the Territory or other Property belonging to the United States; and nothing in this Constitution shall be so construed as to Prejudice any Claims of the United States, or of any particular State.

Section 4. The United States shall guarantee to every State in this Union a Republican Form of Government, and shall protect each of them against Invasion; and on Application of the Legislature, or of the Executive (when the Legislature cannot be convened) against domestic Violence.

Article V.

The Congress, whenever two thirds of both Houses shall deem it necessary, shall propose Amendments to this Constitution, or, on the Application of the Legislatures of two thirds of the several States, shall call a Convention for proposing Amendments, which, in either Case, shall be valid to all Intents and Purposes, as part of this Constitution, when ratified by the Legislatures of three fourths of the several States, or by Conventions in three fourths thereof, as the one or the other Mode of Ratification may be proposed by the Congress; Provided that no Amendment which may be made prior to the Year One thousand eight hundred and eight shall in any Manner affect the first and fourth Clauses in the Ninth Section of the first Article; and that no State, without its Consent, shall be deprived of its equal Suffrage in the Senate.

Article VI.

All Debts contracted and Engagements entered into, before the Adoption of this Constitution, shall be as valid against the United States under this Constitution, as under the Confederation.

This Constitution, and the Laws of the United States which shall be made in Pursuance thereof; and all Treaties made, or which shall be made, under the Authority of the United States, shall be the supreme Law of the Land; and the Judges in every State shall be bound thereby, any Thing in the Constitution or Laws of any State to the Contrary notwithstanding.

The Senators and Representatives before mentioned, and the Members of the several State Legislatures, and all executive and judicial Officers, both of the United States and of the several States, shall be bound by Oath or Affirmation, to support this Constitution; but no religious Test shall ever be required as a Qualification to any Office or public Trust under the United States.

Article VII.

The Ratification of the Conventions of nine States, shall be sufficient for the Establishment of this Constitution between the States so ratifying the Same.

Done in Convention by the Unanimous Consent of the States present the Seventeenth Day of September in the Year of our Lord one thousand seven hundred and Eighty seven and of the Independence of the United States of America the Twelfth. In Witness whereof We have hereunto subscribed our Names.

Resolution 1

In Convention, Monday, Sept. 17th, 1787

Present

The States of

New Hampshire, Massachusetts, Connecticut, Mr. Hamilton from New York, New Jersey, Pennsylvania, Delaware, Maryland, Virginia, North Carolina, South Carolina and Georgia.

Resolved,

That the preceding Constitution be laid before the united States in Congress assembled, and that it is the Opinion of this Convention, that it should afterwards be submitted to a Convention of Delegates, chosen in each State by the People thereof, under the Recommendation of its Legislature, for their Assent and Ratification; and that each Convention assenting to, and ratifying the Same, should give Notice thereof, to the United States in Congress assembled. Resolved, That it is the Opinion of this Convention, that as soon as the Conventions of nine States shall have ratified this Constitution, the United States in Congress assembled should fix a Day on which Electors shall be appointed by the States which shall have ratified the same, and a day on which the Electors should assemble to vote for the President, and the Time and Place for commencing Proceedings under this Constitution.

That after such Publication the Electors should be appointed, and the Senators and Representatives elected: That the Electors should meet on the Day fixed for the Election of the President, and should transmit these Votes, certified, signed, sealed and directed, as the Constitution requires, to the Secretary of the United States in Congress assembled, that the Senators and Representatives should convene at the Time and Place assigned; that the Senators should appoint a President of the Senate, for the sole Purpose of receiving, opening and counting the Votes for President; and, that after he shall be chosen, the Congress, together with the President, should, without Delay, proceed to execute this Constitution.

By the unanimous Order of the Convention

G. WASHINGTON—President

Resolution 2

Sept 25th, 1789

Congress of the United States begun and held at the City of New-York, on Wednesday the fourth of March, one thousand seven hundred and eighty nine.

THE Conventions of a number of the States, having at the time of their adopting the Constitution, expressed a desire, in order to prevent miscon-struction or abuse of its powers, that further declaratory and restrictive clauses should be added: And as extending the ground of public confidence in the Government, will best ensure the beneficent ends of its institution:

RESOLVED by the Senate and House of Representatives of the United States of America, in Congress assembled, two thirds of both Houses concurring, that the following Articles be proposed to the Legislatures of the several States, as Amendments to the Constitution of the United States, all, or any of which Articles, when ratified by three fourths of the said Legislatures, to be valid to all intents and purposes, as part of the said Constitution; viz.

ARTICLES in addition to, and Amendment of the Constitution of the United States of America, proposed by Congress, and ratified by the Legislatures of the several States, pursuant to the fifth Article of the original Constitution.

Amendment I (1791)

Congress shall make no law respecting an establishment of religion, or prohibiting the free exercise thereof; or abridging the freedom of speech, or of the press; or the right of the people peaceably to assemble, and to petition the Government for a redress of grievances.

Amendment II (1791)

A well regulated Militia, being necessary to the security of a free State, the right of the people to keep and bear Arms, shall not be infringed.

Amendment III (1791)

No Soldier shall, in time of peace be quartered in any house, without the consent of the Owner, nor in time of war, but in a manner to be prescribed by law.

Amendment IV (1791)

The right of the people to be secure in their persons, houses, papers, and effects, against unreasonable searches and seizures, shall not be violated, and no Warrants shall issue, but upon probable cause, supported by Oath or affirmation, and particularly describing the place to be searched, and the persons or things to be seized.

AMENDMENT V (1791)

No person shall be held to answer for a capital, or otherwise infamous crime, unless on a presentment or indictment of a Grand Jury, except in cases arising in the land or naval forces, or in the Militia, when in actual service in time of War or public danger; nor shall any person be subject for the same offense to be twice put in jeopardy of life or limb; nor shall be compelled in any criminal case to be a witness against himself, nor be deprived of life, liberty, or property, without due process of law; nor shall private property be taken for public use, without just compensation.

AMENDMENT VI (1791)

In all criminal prosecutions, the accused shall enjoy the right to a speedy and public trial, by an impartial jury of the State and district wherein the crime shall have been committed, which district shall have been previously ascertained by law, and to be informed of the nature and cause of the accusation; to be confronted with the witnesses against him; to have compulsory process for obtaining witnesses in his favor, and to have the Assistance of Counsel for his defence.

AMENDMENT VII (1791)

In Suits at common law, where the value in controversy shall exceed twenty dollars, the right of trial by jury shall be preserved, and no fact tried by a jury, shall be otherwise re-examined in any Court of the United States, than according to the rules of the common law.

Amendment VIII (1791)

Excessive bail shall not be required, nor excessive fines imposed, nor cruel and unusual punishments inflicted.

Amendment IX (1791)

The enumeration in the Constitution, of certain rights, shall not be construed to deny or disparage others retained by the people.

Amendment X (1791)*

The powers not delegated to the United States by the Constitution, nor prohibited by it to the States, are reserved to the States respectively, or to the people.

["The first ten amendments (the "Bill of Rights") were transmitted to the state legislatures by Congress on September 25, 1789, as part of a set of 12, one of which (dealing with congressional representation) was never adopted and the other of which (the Twenty-seventh) was adopted (some argue) on ratification by the thirty-eighth state on May 7, 1992.]

Amendment XI (1795)

The Judicial power of the United States shall not be construed to extend to any suit in law or equity, commenced or prosecuted against one of the United States by Citizens of another State, or by Citizens or Subjects of any Foreign State.

Amendment XII (1804)

The Electors shall meet in their respective states, and vote by ballot for President and Vice-President, one of whom, at least, shall not be an inhabitant of the same state with themselves; they shall name in their ballots the person voted for as President, and in distinct ballots the person voted for as Vice-President, and they shall make distinct lists of all persons voted for as President, and of all persons voted for as Vice-President and of the number of votes for each, which lists they shall sign and certify, and transmit sealed to the seat of the government of the United States, directed to the President of the Senate;

The President of the Senate shall, in the presence of the Senate and House of Representatives, open all the certificates and the votes shall then be counted;

The person having the greatest Number of votes for President, shall be the President, if such number be a majority of the whole number of Electors appointed; and if no person have such majority, then from the persons having the highest numbers not exceeding three on the list of those voted for as President, the House of Representatives shall choose immediately, by ballot, the President. But in choosing the President, the votes shall be taken by states, the representation from each state having one vote; a quorum for this purpose shall consist of a member or members from two-thirds of the states, and a majority of all the states shall be necessary to a choice. And if the House of Representatives shall not choose a President whenever the right of choice shall devolve upon them, before the fourth day of March next following, then the Vice-President shall act as President, as in the case of the death or other constitutional disability of the President.

The person having the greatest number of votes as Vice-President, shall be the Vice-President, if such number be a majority of the whole number of Electors appointed, and if no person have a majority, then from the two highest numbers on the list, the Senate shall choose the Vice-President; a quorum for the purpose shall consist of two-thirds of the whole number of Senators, and a majority of the whole number shall be necessary to a choice. But no person constitutionally ineligible to the office of President shall be eligible to that of Vice-President of the United States.

Amendment XIII (1865)

Section 1. Neither slavery nor involuntary servitude, except as a punishment for crime whereof the party shall have been duly convicted, shall exist within the United States, or any place subject to their jurisdiction.

Section 2. Congress shall have power to enforce this article by appropriate legislation.

Amendment XIV (1868)

Section 1. All persons born or naturalized in the United States and subject to the jurisdiction thereof, are citizens of the United States and of the State wherein they reside. No State shall make or enforce any law which shall abridge the privileges or immunities of citizens of the United States; nor shall any State deprive any person of life, liberty, or property, without due process of law; nor deny to any person within its jurisdiction the equal protection of the laws.

Section 2. Representatives shall be apportioned among the several States according to their respective numbers, counting the whole number of persons in each State, excluding Indians not taxed. But when the right to vote at any election for the choice of electors for President and Vice-President of the United States, Representatives in Congress, the Executive and Judicial officers of a State, or the members of the Legislature thereof, is denied to any of the male inhabitants of such State, being twenty-one years of age, and citizens of the United States, or in any way abridged, except for participation in rebellion, or other crime, the basis of representation therein shall be reduced in the proportion which the number of such male citizens shall bear to the whole number of male citizens twenty-one years of age in such State.

Section 3. No person shall be a Senator or Representative in Congress, or elector of President and Vice-President, or hold any office, civil or military, under the United States, or under any State, who, having previously taken an oath, as a member of Congress, or as an officer of the United States, or as a member of any State legislature, or as an executive or judicial officer of any State, to support the Constitution of the United States, shall have engaged in insurrection or rebellion against the same, or given aid or comfort to the enemies thereof. But Congress may by a vote of two-thirds of each House, remove such disability.

Section 4. The validity of the public debt of the United States, authorized by law, including debts incurred for payment of pensions and bounties for services in suppressing insurrection or rebellion, shall not be questioned. But neither the United States nor any State shall assume or pay any debt or obligation incurred in aid of insurrection or rebellion against the United States, or any claim for the loss or emancipation of any slave; but all such debts, obligations and claims shall be held illegal and void.

Section 5. The Congress shall have power to enforce, by appropriate legislation, the provisions of this article.

AMENDMENT XV (1870)

Section 1. The right of citizens of the United States to vote shall not be denied or abridged by the United States or by any State on account of race, color, or previous condition of servitude.

Section 2. The Congress shall have power to enforce this article by appropriate legislation.

AMENDMENT XVI (1913)

The Congress shall have power to lay and collect taxes on incomes, from whatever source derived, without apportionment among the several States, and without regard to any census or enumeration.

AMENDMENT XVII (1913)

The Senate of the United States shall be composed of two Senators from each State, elected by the people thereof, for six years; and each Senator shall have one vote. The electors in each State shall have the qualifications requisite for electors of the most numerous branch of the State legislatures.

When vacancies happen in the representation of any State in the Senate, the executive authority of such State shall issue writs of election to fill such vacancies: Provided, That the legislature of any State may empower the executive thereof to make temporary appointments until the people fill the vacancies by election as the legislature may direct.

This amendment shall not be so construed as to affect the election or term of any Senator chosen before it becomes valid as part of the Constitution.

AMENDMENT XVIII (1919)

Section 1. After one year from the ratification of this article the manufacture, sale, or transportation of intoxicating liquors within, the importation thereof into, or the exportation thereof from the United States and all territory subject to the jurisdiction thereof for beverage purposes is hereby prohibited.

Section 2. The Congress and the several States shall have concurrent power to enforce this article by appropriate legislation.

Section 3. This article shall be inoperative unless it shall have been ratified as an amendment to the Constitution by the legislatures of the several States, as provided in the Constitution, within seven years from the date of the submission hereof to the States by the Congress.

AMENDMENT XIX (1920)

The right of citizens of the United States to vote shall not be denied or abridged by the United States or by any State on account of sex.

Congress shall have power to enforce this article by appropriate legislation.

Amendment XX (1933)

Section 1. The terms of the President and Vice President shall end at noon on the 20th day of January, and the terms of Senators and Representatives at noon on the 3d day of January, of the years in which such terms would have ended if this article had not been ratified; and the terms of their successors shall then begin.

Section 2. The Congress shall assemble at least once in every year, and such meeting shall begin at noon on the 3d day of January, unless they shall by law appoint a different day.

Section 3. If, at the time fixed for the beginning of the term of the President, the President elect shall have died, the Vice President elect shall become President. If a President shall not have been chosen before the time fixed for the beginning of his term, or if the President elect shall have failed to qualify, then the Vice President elect shall act as President until a President shall have qualified; and the Congress may by law provide for the case wherein neither a President elect nor a Vice President elect shall have qualified, declaring who shall then act as President, or the manner in which one who is to act shall be selected, and such person shall act accordingly until a President or Vice President shall have qualified.

Section 4. The Congress may by law provide for the case of the death of any of the persons from whom the House of Representatives may choose a President whenever the right of choice shall have devolved upon them, and for the case of the death of any of the persons from whom the Senate may choose a Vice President whenever the right of choice shall have devolved upon them.

Section 5. Sections 1 and 2 shall take effect on the 15th day of October following the ratification of this article.

Section 6. This article shall be inoperative unless it shall have been ratified as an amendment to the Constitution by the legislatures of three-fourths of the several States within seven years from the date of its submission.

AMENDMENT XXI (1933)

Section 1. The eighteenth article of amendment to the Constitution of the United States is hereby repealed.

Section 2. The transportation or importation into any State, Territory, or possession of the United States for delivery or use therein of intoxicating liquors, in violation of the laws thereof, is hereby prohibited.

Section 3. The article shall be inoperative unless it shall have been ratified as an amendment to the Constitution by conventions in the several States, as provided in the Constitution, within seven years from the date of the submission hereof to the States by the Congress.

AMENDMENT XXII (1951)

Section 1. No person shall be elected to the office of the President more than twice, and no person who has held the office of President, or acted as President, for more than two years of a term to which some other person was elected President shall be elected to the office of the President more than once. But this Article shall not apply to any person holding the office of President, when this Article was proposed by the Congress, and shall not prevent any person who may be holding the office of President, or acting as President, during the term within which this Article becomes operative from holding the office of President or acting as President during the remainder of such term.

Section 2. This article shall be inoperative unless it shall have been ratified as an amendment to the Constitution by the legislatures of three-fourths of the several States within seven years from the date of its submission to the States by the Congress.

Amendment XXIII (1961)

Section 1. The District constituting the seat of Government of the United States shall appoint in such manner as the Congress may direct: A number of electors of President and Vice President equal to the whole number of Senators and Representatives in Congress to which the District would be entitled if it were a State, but in no event more than the least populous State; they shall be in addition to those appointed by the States, but they shall be considered, for the purposes of the election of President and Vice President, to be electors appointed by a State; and they shall meet in the District and perform such duties as provided by the twelfth article of amendment.

Section 2. The Congress shall have power to enforce this article by appropriate legislation.

Amendment XXIV (1964)

Section 1. The right of citizens of the United States to vote in any primary or other election for President or Vice President, for electors for President or Vice President, or for Senator or Representative in Congress, shall not be denied or abridged by the United States or any State by reason of failure to pay any poll tax or other tax.

Section 2. The Congress shall have power to enforce this article by appropriate legislation.

Amendment XXV (1967)

Section 1. In case of the removal of the President from office or of his death or resignation, the Vice President shall become President.

Section 2. Whenever there is a vacancy in the office of the Vice President, the President shall nominate a Vice President who shall take office upon confirmation by a majority vote of both Houses of Congress.

Section 3. Whenever the President transmits to the President pro tempore of the Senate and the Speaker of the House of Representatives his written declaration that he is unable to discharge the powers and duties of his office, and until he transmits to them a written declaration to the contrary, such powers and duties shall be discharged by the Vice President as Acting President.

Section 4. Whenever the Vice President and a majority of either the principal officers of the executive departments or of such other body as Congress may by law provide, transmit to the President pro tempore of the Senate and the Speaker of the House of Representatives their written declaration that the President is unable to discharge the powers and duties of his office, the Vice President shall immediately assume the powers and duties of the office as Acting President.

Thereafter, when the President transmits to the President pro tempore of the Senate and the Speaker of the House of Representatives his written declaration that no inability exists, he shall resume the powers and duties of his office unless the Vice President and a majority of either the principal officers of the executive department or of such other body as Congress may by law provide, transmit within four days to the President pro tempore of the Senate and the Speaker of the House of Representatives their written declaration that the President is unable to discharge the powers and duties of his office. Thereupon Congress shall decide the issue, assembling within forty eight hours for that purpose if not in session. If the Congress, within twenty one days after receipt of the latter written declaration, or, if Congress is not in session, within twenty one days after Congress is required to assemble, determines by two thirds vote of both Houses that the President is unable to discharge the powers and duties of his office, the Vice President shall continue to discharge the same as Acting President; otherwise, the President shall resume the powers and duties of his office.

Amendment XXVI (1971)

Section 1. The right of citizens of the United States, who are eighteen years of age or older, to vote shall not be denied or abridged by the United States or by any State on account of age.

Section 2. The Congress shall have power to enforce this article by appropriate legislation.

Amendment XXVII (1992)

No law, varying the compensation for the services of the Senators and Representatives, shall take effect, until an election of Representatives shall have intervened.

The Declaration
of Independence

IN CONGRESS, July 4, 1776.

The unanimous Declaration of the thirteen united States of America,

When in the Course of human events, it becomes necessary for one people to dissolve the political bands which have connected them with another, and to assume among the powers of the earth, the separate and equal station to which the Laws of Nature and of Nature's God entitle them, a decent respect to the opinions of mankind requires that they should declare the causes which impel them to the separation.

We hold these truths to be self-evident, that all men are created equal, that they are endowed by their Creator with certain unalienable Rights, that among these are Life, Liberty and the pursuit of Happiness.—That to secure these rights, Governments are instituted among Men, deriving their just powers from the consent of the governed,—That whenever any Form of Government becomes destructive of these ends, it is the Right of the People to alter or to abolish it, and to institute new Government, laying its foundation on such principles and organizing its powers in such form, as to them shall seem most likely to effect their Safety and Happiness. Prudence, indeed, will dictate that Governments long established should not be changed for light and transient causes; and accordingly all experience hath shewn, that mankind are more disposed to suffer, while evils are sufferable, than to right themselves by abolishing the forms to which they are accustomed. But when a long train of abuses and usurpations, pursuing invariably the same Object evinces a design to reduce them under absolute Despotism, it is their right, it is their duty, to throw off such Government, and to provide new Guards for their future security. —Such has been the patient sufferance of these Colonies; and such is now the necessity which constrains them to alter their former Systems of Government. The history of the present King of Great Britain is a history of repeated injuries and usurpations, all having in direct object the establishment of an absolute Tyranny over these States. To prove this, let Facts be submitted to a candid world.

He has refused his Assent to Laws, the most wholesome and necessary for the public good.

He has forbidden his Governors to pass Laws of immediate and pressing importance, unless suspended in their operation till his Assent should be obtained; and when so suspended, he has utterly neglected to attend to them.

He has refused to pass other Laws for the accommodation of large districts of people, unless those people would relinquish the right of Representation in the Legislature, a right inestimable to them and formidable to tyrants only.

He has called together legislative bodies at places unusual, uncomfortable, and distant from the depository of their public Records, for the sole purpose of fatiguing them into compliance with his measures.

He has dissolved Representative Houses repeatedly, for opposing with manly firmness his invasions on the rights of the people.

He has refused for a long time, after such dissolutions, to cause others to be elected; whereby the Legislative powers, incapable of Annihilation, have returned to the People at large for their exercise; the State remaining in the mean time exposed to all the dangers of invasion from without, and convulsions within.

He has endeavoured to prevent the population of these States; for that purpose obstructing the Laws for Naturalization of Foreigners; refusing to pass others to encourage their migrations hither, and raising the conditions of new Appropriations of Lands.

He has obstructed the Administration of Justice, by refusing his Assent to Laws for establishing Judiciary powers.

He has made Judges dependent on his Will alone, for the tenure of their offices, and the amount and payment of their salaries.

He has erected a multitude of New Offices, and sent hither swarms of Officers to harrass our people, and eat out their substance.

He has kept among us, in times of peace, Standing Armies without the Consent of our legislatures.

He has affected to render the Military independent of and superior to the Civil power.

He has combined with others to subject us to a jurisdiction foreign to our constitution, and unacknowledged by our laws; giving his Assent to their Acts of pretended Legislation:

For Quartering large bodies of armed troops among us:

For protecting them, by a mock Trial, from punishment for any Murders which they should commit on the Inhabitants of these States:

For cutting off our Trade with all parts of the world:

For imposing Taxes on us without our Consent:

For depriving us in many cases, of the benefits of Trial by Jury:

For transporting us beyond Seas to be tried for pretended offences:

For abolishing the free System of English Laws in a neighbouring Province, establishing therein an Arbitrary government, and enlarging its Boundaries so as to render it at once an example and fit instrument for introducing the same absolute rule into these Colonies:

For taking away our Charters, abolishing our most valuable Laws, and altering fundamentally the Forms of our Governments:

For suspending our own Legislatures, and declaring themselves invested with power to legislate for us in all cases whatsoever.

He has abdicated Government here, by declaring us out of his Protection and waging War against us.

He has plundered our seas, ravaged our Coasts, burnt our towns, and destroyed the lives of our people.

He is at this time transporting large Armies of foreign Mercenaries to compleat the works of death, desolation and tyranny, already begun with circumstances of Cruelty & perfidy scarcely paralleled in the most barbarous ages, and totally unworthy the Head of a civilized nation.

He has constrained our fellow Citizens taken Captive on the high Seas to bear Arms against their Country, to become the executioners of their friends and Brethren, or to fall themselves by their Hands.

He has excited domestic insurrections amongst us, and has endeavoured to bring on the inhabitants of our frontiers, the merciless Indian Savages, whose known rule of warfare, is an undistinguished destruction of all ages, sexes and conditions.

In every stage of these Oppressions We have Petitioned for Redress in the most humble terms: Our repeated Petitions have been answered only by repeated injury. A Prince whose character is thus marked by every act which may define a Tyrant, is unfit to be the ruler of a free people.

Nor have We been wanting in attentions to our Brittish brethren. We have warned them from time to time of attempts by their legislature to extend an unwarrant-able jurisdiction over us. We have reminded them of the circumstances of our emigration and settlement here. We have appealed to their native justice and magnanimity, and we have conjured them by the ties of our common kindred to disavow these usurpations, which, would inevitably interrupt our connections and correspondence. They too have been deaf to the voice of justice and of con-sanguinity. We must, therefore, acquiesce in the necessity, which denounces our Separation, and hold them, as we hold the rest of mankind, Enemies in War, in Peace Friends.

We, therefore, the Representatives of the united States of America, in General Congress, Assembled, appealing to the Supreme Judge of the world for the rectitude of our intentions, do, in the Name, and by Authority of the good People of these Colonies, solemnly publish and declare, That these United Colonies are, and of Right ought to be Free and Independent States; that they are Absolved from all Allegiance to the British Crown, and that all political connection between them and the State of Great Britain, is and ought to be totally dissolved; and that as Free and Independent States, they have full Power to levy War, conclude Peace, contract Alliances, establish Commerce, and to do all other Acts and Things which Independent States may of right do. And for the support of this Declaration, with a firm reliance on the protection of divine Providence, we mutually pledge to each other our Lives, our Fortunes and our sacred Honor.

Index